Blues Harmonica

by Winslow Yerxa

for dummies®

A Wiley Brand

Blues Harmonica For Dummies®

Published by **John Wiley & Sons, Inc.**111 River St. Hoboken, NJ 07030-5774 www.wiley.com

Copyright © 2020 by John Wiley & Sons, Inc., Hoboken, New Jersey

Published by John Wiley & Sons, Inc., Hoboken, New Jersey

Published simultaneously in Canada

For general information on our other products and services, please contact our Customer Care Department within the U.S. at 877-762-2974, outside the U.S. at 317-572-3993, or fax 317-572-4002.

For technical support, please visit www.wiley.com/techsupport.

Library of Congress Control Number: 2020931540

ISBN 978-1-119-69451-9 (pbk); ISBN 978-1-119-69453-3 (ebk); ISBN 978-1-119-69455-7 (ebk)

Manufactured in the United States of America

V10017992_031720

Contents at a Glance

Table of Contents

Introduction

The harmonica is a mysterious instrument — you can't tell much about how to play it from looking. It has no keys or strings so you won't see any hands or fingers moving around on them. All you see is someone's hands pressed to his face and maybe cheeks puffing in and out. Yet the harmonica exerts a fascination for everyone who hears it. It's tiny but can make a big sound, and it makes such a pretty yet plaintive, voice-like sound.

When you try to play the harmonica, though, you can get frustrated easily. Harmonicas come in a dizzying array of sizes and types, and if you get one and just try breathing through it, you'll get musical sounds but not like what you hear from the players whose expressive sounds you find so compelling.

Fortunately, you have *Blues Harmonica For Dummies* in your hands. Whether you're just beginning to act on your curiosity or you're a seasoned player looking for the next stage in your musical growth, this book offers solid information and advice.

About This Book

Blues Harmonica For Dummies gives you all the information you need to get started playing the blues on the harmonica. But you don't need to sneak down a dark alley and give a secret password to get at this stash of essential knowledge. All that treasure is in broad daylight, with plenty of easy ways to help yourself to whatever you need, including

>> **Step-by-step descriptions:** I break every action and task into a series of numbered steps that you can master one at a time.

>> **Pictures and diagrams:** I illustrate the internal actions that you perform with your tongue and throat and the external actions of using your hands and lips on the harmonica.

>> **Tablature:** I include tab that shows the actions you use to play each note of a song or segment of music.

>> **A Companion Website:** You can visit the website at www.dummies.com/go/bluesharmonicafd.

Conventions Used in This Book

Throughout the book, I use the following conventions consistently to make the text easy to understand:

>> *Italics* mark a new term, and I follow with a simple explanation and then use the term again in context.

>> I highlight in **bold** the keywords in bulleted lists and the action parts of numbered steps.

>> All web addresses appear in `mono font`.

I use the terms *harmonica* and *harp* interchangeably. These are only two of the many colorful monikers the harmonica enjoys, including *French harp*, *Mississippi saxophone*, *mouth organ*, and several others. I managed to limit myself to only the two most common names.

What You're Not to Read

Ultimately, you become a blues harmonica player by listening, imitating, and then letting your own imagination come up with ways to express yourself. This book is here to help you through that process, and you can skip anything that doesn't seem to help you right now. Later on you may come back and look for something when you feel that it will help you.

You can ignore the written music, though you may find the arrow-and-number tablature helpful because it tells you what holes, breaths, and bends to play.

You can skip paragraphs that have a Technical Stuff icon attached to them, though I've tried to keep those to a minimum.

Harmonica lore is one of the great pleasures of knowing about the instrument and its traditions, but you don't need it to get down to the nuts and bolts of playing, so you can skip any sidebars, those gray boxes sprinkled throughout the book.

Foolish Assumptions

I assume that you've never played music before and don't know a beat from a B♭ or an octave from an ocarina. That's okay. What's important is that you have the desire, the curiosity, and the motivation to express yourself by playing blues on the harmonica.

Still, I know that you may already play the harmonica and are looking to sharpen your skills. If so, I include enough information to take you to the next stage in your playing.

I also assume that you're interested in playing the most popular type of harmonica, the 10-hole diatonic harmonica (often called the *blues harp*) — the same type of harmonica that's used by every blues player, in addition to rock and country musicians. You can play almost everything in this book on a single diatonic harmonica tuned to the key of C. As you develop your playing skills, you'll want to get harmonicas in other keys, but to get started, and for easy reference, a *C-harp* (harmonica in C) is all you need.

However, I also assume that you'll get curious about the chromatic harmonica, a larger type of harmonica that's designed to play in every key. The chromatic has a unique sound and is an important part of the modern blues harmonica player's *kit*, or set of harmonicas, so I cover the basics of blues chromatic as well.

How This Book Is Organized

Blues Harmonica For Dummies is organized to give you easy, direct access to the information you're looking for. You can read the book from beginning to end or you can browse and skip around to find the most interesting topics or helpful information. The chapters are clustered in six parts, each focusing on a different stage of your growth as a player, and I also include two appendixes with handy information you'll need.

Part 1: So You Wanna Play Blues Harmonica?

In this part, you find out what you need to prepare for your adventure. You get some background on the blues, not only as a musical style, but also as an attitude for communicating and sharing with others. Just as important, you discover how the harmonica contributes and fits into the music. Then you survey the types of harmonicas available — which ones to start with, which are the best values, where to shop, and how to add to your collection as you advance. You also get an orientation on some music fundamentals, including how to read the harmonica *tab* — the symbols that tell you what actions to perform to play melodies and rhythms on the harmonica.

Part 2: Doin' the Crawl: Your First Harmonica Moves

This is the part where you start to play the harmonica. You pick it up and hold it, breathe through it, and make rhythmic sounds. Then you start to move around and play melodies along with *licks* and *riffs*, those nuggets of bluesy melody that make up the building blocks of blues harmonica playing. Finally, you start using those licks and riffs to fill up the container of the blues song — the 12-bar blues.

Part 3: Beyond the Basics: Getting Bluesy

Part 3 takes you into the territory where you find the real gold of harmonica expressiveness. You start ranging all over the harmonica and discovering how to get around its entire range. You start making the harmonica sound more like a human voice by using your hands, lips, tongue, throat, and lungs to shape your sound and create sonic texture. Finally — the pièce de résistance — you start bending notes to make that classic wailing, slithering sound of blues harmonica.

Part 4: Developing Your Style

Blues harmonica is surprisingly versatile, and in this part you start to explore how to play in different keys, play dark-sounding minor blues, use the chromatic harmonica, and play blues songs that have unusual formats.

Part 5: Taking It to the Streets: Sharing Your Music

When you express yourself, you probably want to start sharing your passion at some point. When you're ready (or just eager — sometimes doing it is more important than being ready), you can use this part of the book to help you put together a repertoire of tunes to play, to amplify your playing with electronic equipment to sound even cooler and to be heard in a noisy world, and to connect with the larger world in two important ways: by finding other musicians to collaborate with and by playing for audiences other than your dog and the goldfish in your aquarium.

Part 6: The Part of Tens

Would you eat a hot dog without mustard? (Hey, even a tofu dog needs the proper presentation!) Would a *For Dummies* book be complete without its Part of Tens? I think you know the answer to both questions. In this part I share ten important points about blues harmonica history.

Part 7: Appendixes

At some point you may want to know what notes are in what holes in every key of harmonica. You may need this as much as you need the handshake protocols for communications satellites (apologies to any telecom geeks out there!), but this information may just come in handy, so I include it in Appendix A. Appendix B gives you the complete list of tracks on the website including where you can find and hear the tabs, or musical examples, that are scattered throughout the book.

Icons Used in This Book

The icons in the margins of this book may look like whimsical decorations, but they're more than eye candy. Each icon is a signpost that tips you off to something that's either important enough to read carefully or dull enough to skip if you're not interested in too much detail.

REMEMBER

This icon highlights information that you want to keep in mind to help you as you acquire a skill or understanding.

TIP

Every now and then, I can offer a little insight or useful bit of information that makes an idea easier to understand or a task easier to accomplish. This icon helps you spot those little nuggets.

TECHNICAL STUFF

Sometimes you want to skip the why and just get to the how. Technical talk can be helpful to your understanding, but if you just want to cut to the chase, you can safely skip the text near this icon without compromising your understanding of the subject at hand.

WARNING

The Warning icon alerts you to things that you shouldn't touch, swallow, or even think about trying if you value life, limb, and the continued ability to pursue happiness (or maybe if you just want to avoid bruising your ego).

PLAY THIS

When you see this icon, you know that you can go to a specific track on the website to hear and play along with the musical examples and songs in the book. If you are reading this text in an electronic format, The website where you will find the audio tracks is www.dummies.com/go/bluesharmonicafd.

Where to Go from Here

You can dive into this book at any point, but you may want to target a specific area to suit your interest and your level of experience. Here are a few possibilities:

» If you're at the beginning of your journey and still don't have a harmonica or know much except that you like the blues, check out Chapters 1 and 2. After you get a harmonica, Chapters 2 through 7 get you up and running.

» If you just want to learn how to bend notes, you can jump directly to Chapter 11, though you may benefit from first spending some time with Chapter 9.

» If you can play already but want to get more expression into your playing, flip to Chapters 9 and 10.

» If you're finding that the covers of the harp are turning blue on the left side while the right side stays gleaming and pristine, turn to Chapter 8 to get you playing through the entire range of the harmonica.

» If you want to try new approaches to get more variety out of your playing, have a look at Chapters 12, 13, and 14 to start playing in different keys, or *positions*, on the harmonica. You can also check out Chapter 15 to get acquainted with adding chromatic harmonica to your bag of tricks for a whole new sound or Chapter 16 to start playing in minor keys.

» If you want to sound loud and proud and start getting that distorted, amplified blues sound, see Chapter 19, which covers using microphones, amplifiers, and effects to beef up your sound and broadcast it to the world.

» If you want to develop your blues repertoire, flip to Chapter 18, which has lists of important harmonica recordings in a broad range of historical periods and blues styles.

If none of these suggestions are quite what you have in mind, take a look at the index or table of contents to find what you're looking for — or just open the book and see what you stumble across.

1

So You Wanna Play Blues Harmonica?

IN THIS PART . . .

You discover the strong bond between blues and the harmonica, find out which harmonicas to get and how to care for them, pick up on some essential musician's lingo, and then get started with the basics of playing blues on the harmonica.

Chapter **1**

Connecting with the Blues

The blues is a uniquely American art form that got its start from the collision of African and European cultures in the American South. First documented around the beginning of the 20th century, blues has continued to expand in popularity ever since. Blues began with its original base of African Americans in the rural South and then migrated — first to regional population centers, then to the industrial North, then to the West Coast, and finally to Great Britain and Europe during the 1960s.

At the same time, as African Americans moved on to newer musical styles, middle-class Caucasian Americans took up the blues, both as listeners and players, making the blues a truly integrated style. But even before this passing of the cultural torch, blues exerted a profound influence on other American music styles, including jazz, country, and rock. And blues isn't done extending its reach. I've heard musicians from Brazil creating new flavors of the blues by infusing it with their own traditions. I wouldn't be surprised if a fur-clad Inuit in an igloo somewhere in the Canadian Arctic is whiling away the long winter nights by singing the blues in the Inuktitut language by the light of a whale oil lantern.

The harmonica has been an integral part of the blues odyssey from the beginning. During the golden age of Chicago blues, pianist Otis Spann once remarked, "Harmonica is the mother of the band." (See Chapters 18 and 21 for more on the history and great players of blues harmonica.) Spann's piano playing was beautiful, but that statement has also been sweet music to the ears of harmonica players ever since.

What the Blues Is All About

Blues seems to defy the standards of how notes fit together — a legacy of that cultural collision of African and European musical ideas. Wherever a clear, straight path leads to certainty about how the elements of music combine in a systematic way, blues finds a way around it or simply veers off on a tangent. If you try to relate the blues to that straight path, you can do it, but you have to come up with some sophisticated theories to make it all fit together. Jazz musicians do that, and they do it in a convincing way.

When they feel the need to do so, blues musicians can also come up with sophisticated explanations of how the blues works. But they seldom focus on such explanations because, ultimately, blues is about expressing yourself in a direct (though often sly and humorous) way by using the expressive tools of the blues. Who cares how your cellphone works? You can use it to communicate, and the same goes for the blues.

In Chapter 3 I discuss the basics of how notes fit together, and in Chapter 7 I relate some of the classic methods that blues harmonica players use to adapt the harmonica's notes to the musical forms used in the blues.

Blues is about natural expression

Blues musicians often adapt their song lyrics to the immediate circumstance, commenting on current events or to people in the room by name. At the same time, blues is full of clichés. By having the clichés to fall back on, blues singers can feel free to add or change those clichés in a way that feels comfortable. They don't have to stick to the program, but at the same time, they don't have to come up with something totally original and new. They can change a few words or notes or phrase the rhythm differently and thereby express themselves more vitally in that moment than if they had to perform something locked down on a page. Audience members familiar with the clichés that blues singers draw on appreciate the singers' skills in using the materials.

Playing blues harmonica also uses many clichés that you can alter at will. Short sequences of notes called *licks* are like little sayings that you can drop into a conversation wherever they seem to fit. Blues harmonica players often string together clichés that they may have heard and played many times, but they string them together in a new sequence, maybe change some notes, or alter the rhythm to make it fresh, just as singers do.

Blues gives you a safe kind of musical freedom

Like any art form, blues requires you to hone your craft in order to perform it well. But blues also offers you a lot of flexibility to express yourself without worrying whether you'll fall off the tightrope or commit some terrible faux pas. If you're a beginner, you can get started without fearing that glowering critics will be staring down their noses at you for transgressing some esoteric rule known only to the high mavens of the art. Consider some of the no-fault aspects of the blues:

>> Playing a wrong note in the blues actually takes a lot of effort and planning. Notes that shouldn't fit according to traditional rules of music theory and harmony somehow always seem to work in the blues. I cover a little bit of music theory in Chapter 3.

>> The simplicity of the blues verse makes losing your way kind of hard because you can always tell where you are. Each blues verse is short, consisting of three segments that each begin with a different background chord. You'll learn to identify those chords as you listen and play. You can even repeat the same melody fragment over all three segments of the verse if you want to. I cover this topic in Chapter 7 and extend it in Chapter 17.

>> Repetition is a big part of blues, and so is playing short sequences of as few as three notes — as long as you do so rhythmically. This book is full of these short segments, called *licks* and *riffs*. I go into detail on blues harmonica licks and riffs in Chapters 6, 13, 14, 15, and 18.

Why the Harmonica Is Cool All on Its Own

The harmonica has been a part of the blues pretty much since the beginning. One reason for this is that the harmonica has always been inexpensive; another is that, no matter where you lived, you could buy harmonicas by mail order. But price and availability aren't the only reasons the harmonica is attractive. The harmonica has a natural genius for the blues, which is remarkable when you consider that the people in Germany who designed the harmonica in the early 19th century were interested in playing cheerful, sprightly, German folk melodies. They never envisioned the moaning, wailing sounds that people now associate with the harmonica. (For more on blues harmonica history, have a look at Chapter 21.)

The sound of the blues, built right in

Two things about the blues immediately strike the ear of anyone whose main musical experience has been with the piano's precise sound and European music's do-re-mi scale:

>> **Some of the notes sound flat compared to the do-re-mi scale.** If a blues singer sang a song like "Do-Re-Mi" from *The Sound of Music,* the first thing you'd notice is that some of the notes sound different because they're sung at a lower pitch. The lowered notes are called *blue notes.* Blue notes can sound dark, mean, and hard. They also conflict with the musical background, which breaks rules but is part of the characteristic sound of blues. To help create this effect, blues musicians often play the harmonica in the "wrong" key — a key different from the key that the harmonica is tuned to. Because the scale isn't right for the key, it includes some notes that don't belong, and they just happen to be some of the blue notes. (For more on how notes fit together, see Chapter 3.)

>> **Notes often slide from one to the other.** This slurring sound is called *bending notes.* You start playing a note and then you bend, or slide, away from it, creating a wailing, slithering sound. The harmonica bends notes in a way that creates a strong impression on listeners. (I show you how to bend notes in Chapter 11.)

A third aspect of the harmonica is also very conducive to playing the blues. Playing *chords* (several notes at once) with catchy rhythms is a big part of the blues. The harmonica is built to play chords and works really well for playing chord rhythms, which is also a lot of fun.

The harmonica goes everywhere

The harmonica is one of the most portable instruments in existence. It was the first musical instrument played in outer space, during the early days of space travel, when even an extra ounce of weight was critically important. You can carry one or more harmonicas in your car, purse, backpack, or pocket and play during those odd moments when you have an opportunity. I first started playing by noodling on a harmonica as I walked from class to class during high school. If you play whenever you have an extra few moments, you'll start to get good at it really quickly.

What It Takes to Get Started

Anytime you take up something new, you develop a feel for the style and attitude of doing it. You pick up some of the special lingo, you get acquainted with some of the history and lore, and, most important, you master the specific skills that you use to participate. This is true for golf, quilting, rock climbing, and playing blues harmonica.

Getting the blues in your ears

No one can learn to play blues solely from reading a book (even a book as well written as this one). You get to know the blues only by hearing it. Chapter 18 lists blues harmonica recordings in several styles that will get the sound and the glory of blues harmonica in your ears. Of course, the blues isn't played exclusively on the harmonica. To really broaden the base of your understanding and appreciation, listen to great singers, guitarists, saxophonists, and piano players who may not have played with harmonica players. You might start by listening to classic blues on your favorite alternative radio station or online music channel and letting the sound seep into your ears and your consciousness.

Knowing the story of the blues

The history of the blues is fascinating all by itself, starting as it does in a place and time that is deeply American and yet is almost exotic to most Americans. When you're starting to play the blues, knowing its story enriches your appreciation of the art form. I sketch out this history from a harmonica perspective in Chapter 21, but you can deepen your understanding with some good blues history books written for the general public and also by reading biographies of such blues icons as Little Walter, Muddy Waters, B. B. King, and anyone else whose story has been told in print.

Digging in on Blues Harmonica: Getting Your Playing Going

Wouldn't it be great if you could just buy a harmonica, pick it up, and instantly express your feelings with astonishing fluency, wit, and beauty? I'd love to design the harmonica that would do that. But until I do (or someone beats me to it), I can offer a few recommendations to help you develop your harmonica-playing abilities.

Taking the time to make it happen

Rome wasn't built in a day or, as it turns out, even in a thousand years. Am I trying to tell you that you'll be in a nursing home before you develop any harmonica *chops* (ability)? No, of course not. But skills don't happen by magic. If you're determined, you can become good enough to play in public as a fully fluent musician within about two years. Chapters 18 and 20 can help you develop the skills you'll need as a performing musician.

Maybe you're not looking to become a professional musician. Maybe you just want to take the trip and enjoy the ride but also want to experience a noticeable development in your abilities. The key is to find the time and opportunity to play on a regular basis. A few minutes every day does more for your progress than a marathon three-hour session once every couple of months.

TIP

If you really look at your daily activities, you may find some opportunities to play regularly. A few examples:

» Can you play in your car for a few minutes, before you start for your destination, after you arrive, or in the evening, when you don't want to disturb anyone or be heard making awful noises?

» Can you find a quiet spot to be alone and practice during your lunch hour?

» Do you sometimes just kill time channel-surfing or doing something equally fascinating? Maybe you can use that time to play your harmonica instead.

REMEMBER

Working with a teacher or coach, whether in person or online, can help you assess your progress, identify what you need to work on, and set goals. Having that person expecting work from you also motivates you to find time to practice. And if you work with a really good player, you'll also gain inspiration by hearing him or her play.

Becoming fluent in the language of blues harmonica

Ever notice how a 3-year-old boy walks almost exactly like his dad? He doesn't study this consciously; he just does it. If you listen to enough blues harmonica, you'll start to absorb and emulate the characteristic approaches to rhythm, phrasing, and many other details that you hear in the playing of others. Chapter 18 lists some great harmonica recordings that can give you a starting point for feeding your blues ear.

However, you won't pick up everything automatically. The only way to know what you're doing (as opposed to what you may think you're doing) is to record yourself and listen back. You'll experience some good surprises ("Wow, I had no idea that sounded so good!") and some not-so-good ones ("Yeesh, that sucks more than I realized!"). Armed with that feedback, you can then strengthen the good stuff, work on improving the bad stuff, and fill in the blanks — the parts of your playing that just sound sort of bland or flavorless.

After you become aware of your playing details, you'll start to develop a keener awareness of what the best players do. At first you'll just want to enjoy the greatness of these artists, but as you become aware of your own playing, you'll want to take out your pencil and clipboard, put on the white lab coat (at least virtually), knit your eyebrows together in a determined and focused way, and say, "Okay, just precisely what is he or she doing that makes that sound so good?" You'll begin to notice several of the nuances that I discuss in Part 2, such as *articulation* (how you start and end notes and sequences of notes) and sound textures that you create with your tongue and hands.

As you start playing with the techniques I describe, you'll get to know what they sound like, and you'll start noticing and identifying those techniques in the players you listen to. Instead of going, "Wow, what is that he's doing?" you'll start saying, "Wow, that's a great use of tongue slaps!" Listening and doing will chase each other in a spiral, spurring your development as a player to improve faster and faster.

Getting in the blues harmonica groove

When you're *in the groove*, you're traveling in a way that feels natural and good. Everything seems to move at exactly the right pace and rhythm and falls into place at the right time without strain or effort.

REMEMBER

To find your groove when you play the harmonica, first work on the absolute foundations, such as the ones in Part 2 of this book. No matter what your playing level is, you can always benefit by working the fundamentals, and many advanced players do this regularly. They know from experience that a tiny improvement in the basics magnifies your abilities at every level that's built on those foundations. The more mastery you have over the basics, the easier your groove is to find.

Another thing you can do to find your groove is to listen to as many players and styles as possible and find the ones that really inspire you. When you have something that moves you enough to want to do it, your motivation helps lock you into a groove.

Finally, having fun is a huge element in finding your groove. Some folks believe that the blues is all about heartbreak and misery. It's true that the blues, just like country music and the tabloids in the supermarket, tends to deal in stories of strong emotions and extreme actions and circumstances. But a central message of the blues is to rise above it all and have a good time. Listen for the relaxed humor and the catchy, bouncy grooves that inform a lot of blues tunes. When you feel that groove, hitch your wagon to a goal that inspires you, and focus on the fundamentals, you'll have a powerful combination that will pull everything you need into place as you move along.

Chapter **2**

Getting Your Harmonicas Together

You can play the blues on any musical instrument. Heck, you can even play down-home music on washtubs and other household items. But to find harmonicas that are well suited to playing blues, that deliver solid quality at a reasonable cost, and that project a cool blues image, you can benefit from a few tips from an expert who's wiser — but not always sadder. By "expert," of course, I mean someone who knows what doesn't work because he's tried it all!

Finding Good Harmonicas for Playing Blues

Some harmonicas have names like *Blues Harp* or *Blues Session* or *Bluesmaster.* But what's in a name? You could get a *Hot Pink Harp* or even a *Fluffy Bunny Harp* and still play blues, if you could keep from getting laughed out of jam sessions. The fact is, people were playing blues harmonica long before some marketing genius decided to add *Blues* to the model name.

The really important things about a harmonica are that it be airtight, in tune, and not likely to make you bleed, turn green, or otherwise endanger your health. If it also plays easily, makes a big sound, looks cool, lasts a long time, and doesn't cost an arm and a leg, then it's a winner.

But if you look at a harmonica catalog, you'll find a dizzying array of types, models, and brands that cost as little as a sandwich or as much as a car. Which types are the best for playing blues?

Blues is mostly played on two types of harmonica, and I recommend that you focus on them:

>> The *diatonic* harmonica: Most of the time you'll use this type of harmonica (often referred to simply as the *diatonic*). It has a few important characteristics, including

- **Being tuned to a single key:** The word *diatonic* is musical lingo meaning "only in one key." Each diatonic harmonica includes the notes that belong to just one key, such as the key of C, G, or B♭. So you'll eventually own several diatonics to play in several keys.

- **Having a single reed for each note:** The diatonic is a *single reed* harmonica, with only one reed to play each note. *Double reed* harmonicas, with two reeds per note, such as tremolos, are very common, but they're almost never used in blues.

- **Having 10 holes:** You can get diatonics with 4, 6, 10, 12, or 14 holes, and you can use any of them to play blues. But most of the time, you'll use the 10-hole diatonic.

>> The *chromatic* harmonica: This type of harmonica is bigger and more expensive than the diatonic, and you may use it for one song out of ten. Yet its distinctive sound is an important element in urban blues harmonica.

Other types of harmonicas — such as bass harmonicas, chord harmonicas, tremolo harmonicas, and octave harmonicas — are seldom if ever used in blues. With ingenuity you could probably coax blues out of just about any kind of harmonica. However, the core repertoire and techniques of the blues style focus mainly on the diatonic, with the chromatic running a distant second.

What harmonica you need to study this book

This book was written for a 10-hole diatonic harmonica in the key of C. That said, you can play the songs, licks, and other music on any key of harmonica. However, the note names will be different (but that won't be your focus anyway). More important, you'll be in the wrong key to work with the accompanying audio tracks. The examples will sound different when you play them, and you won't be able to play along with the recorded tracks.

If you want to develop your chromatic harmonica skills with Chapter 15, you'll need a chromatic harmonica in the key of C. I discuss this further in the section on chromatics.

Figure 2-1 shows a 10-hole diatonic, as well as two chromatics — a 12-holer and a 16-holer.

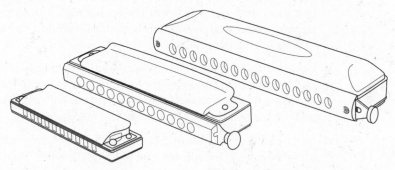

FIGURE 2-1:
Diatonic and chromatic harmonicas.

Illustration by Wiley, Composition Services Graphics

What features to look for in a harmonica for blues

Okay, so you need a 10-hole diatonic in the key of C, and maybe a 12-hole chromatic in C. What else do you need to look for — or avoid?

I'll start with price, using the price printed on the back of this book as a reference.

>> **Cheap diatonics:** Diatonic harmonicas that cost less than half the price of this book are easy on the wallet but may be leaky, out of tune, have weak sound, and break quickly (though you may get lucky and find a good one). If that's all your budget allows, go for it, but upgrade when you can.

>> **Mid-priced diatonics:** Diatonic harmonicas that cost about the same as the price of this book or a bit more (up to about double the price of the book) tend to be well made and to perform well. This is the price range you should focus on.

>> **High-end diatonics:** Diatonic harmonicas that cost more than double the price of this book may be worth it if you're already a highly skilled player who has the finesse to exploit a high performance instrument. If you're just starting out, save your money to buy more mid-priced harmonicas.

So, what should you look for in a mid-priced harmonica? I'll focus first on the *comb*, the middle part of the harmonica sandwich.

>> Wood combs are traditional but can swell with moisture and abrade your lips. Wood also can crack and warp. Many players prefer the look and feel of wood and believe that it delivers superior sound (though scientific data is lacking). But if you're just starting out, you may experience a lot of saliva production until your mouth gets used to this foreign object called a harmonica. A wood comb will respond by swelling, so you may be safer with a non-wood comb until the waterfall subsides.

>> Plastic combs don't swell or shrink with moisture conditions and tend to be durable if you don't take a hammer or a blowtorch to them. Plastic combs are also found on a wide range of both low-priced and mid-priced harmonicas, and I recommend them for beginner or intermediate players.

>> Metal combs look impressive, and some players claim that metal delivers superior sound (again, scientific data is lacking). However, metal-bodied harps are usually expensive, and you may not gain any real advantage from a metal-combed harmonica at this stage in your playing development.

How the harmonica is assembled is another key factor to consider. I recommend harmonicas that are held together with screws and bolts. Traditional wood-combed harmonicas are held together with nails and are hard to get apart and put back together. Modern construction uses screws, nuts, and bolts, even on wood-bodied harmonicas, making them much easier to reassemble properly.

REMEMBER

A mid-priced, plastic, combed, 10-hole diatonic in the key of C is what I recommend you look for. Manufacturers with good reputations for quality include Hering, Hohner, Lee Oskar, Seydel, and Suzuki.

Shopping tips

You can shop online or in your local music store. Comparing prices online is easy and you can find good bargains. On the other hand, if you need to replace a harmonica quickly or suddenly need a harp in a key that you don't have, then nothing beats your local music store. That store isn't going to stock much in the way of harmonicas unless you buy from it, so make your choices accordingly.

TIP

Never buy a used harmonica unless you know how to sterilize and repair it or are prepared to pay someone for these services.

Acquiring the Most Useful Keys and Types of Harmonica

Over time you'll start to build a collection of different harmonicas. Even if you're not a hoarder who feels driven to fill a house to the rafters with your precious obsession, you're going to need a *kit* — a collection of harmonicas that you use to cover all the musical situations you normally encounter.

The most often used harmonica keys for blues

For blues, plan to acquire harmonicas in this order of keys, more or less: C, A, D, G, F, B♭ — that's the basic set you need for most blues. This set covers most of the keys that guitarists like to play in and the keys used in Chicago blues, which go a bit beyond customary guitar keys.

So far that covers half of the 12 different keys. However, if you play with horns such as saxophone, clarinet, trumpet, and trombone, you'll also want E♭, A♭, and maybe D♭ to cover horn keys.

After you have the basic blues keys and a few horn keys, you may want to fill in the missing keys — E, B and F♯ — just in case you need them on a rainy day.

TIP

Some manufacturers offer starter sets of harmonicas in an array of popular keys, along with a carrying case or pouch — an instant harp kit. In some cases, the harmonicas are at the lower end of the quality scale to keep the cost of the kit down. However, you could get such a set and gradually replace each key with a better harmonica over time.

Smashing the limits with the low and high keys

But wait, there's more — there's always another cool type of harmonica to discover and acquire, just like in those infomercials where the incredible gizmo being offered comes with all sorts of extra stuff. In addition to different keys, you can get harmonicas in extended high and low ranges.

The lower the lowest note on a harmonica, the lower the whole harmonica sounds and feels. A low harmonica sounds deep, lush, dark, and quieter. At the same time, it doesn't respond as quickly as a higher-pitched instrument — the reeds weigh more, and they vibrate slower. A high harmonica sounds brighter than a low harmonica, and its response seems whip-fast, as the reeds weigh less, vibrate faster, and produce more volume.

The key of a harmonica is linked to its place on the low-to-high spectrum. At the low end of the spectrum is the G harmonica, then A♭, A, B♭, B, and C. C is in the middle of the spectrum, and its lowest note is Middle C, right in the middle of the piano keyboard. The higher keys go up through D♭, D, E♭, E, and F to F♯.

Harmonica players have always taken advantage of the contrasts between the tonal qualities of high, middle, and low keys. But harmonica players are always pushing the limits, and manufacturers have responded by producing some models in extended high and low keys of harmonica tuned either an octave above or an octave below the standard versions:

>> **Extended high keys:** High G and High A harmonicas are tuned an octave above the standard keys, for super-bright sounding harmonicas.

>> **Extended low keys:** Low keys extend much farther than high keys. Both players and listeners are thrilled to hear a tiny harmonica start to sound like a saxophone or even a bass, and low keys extend from Low F through Low E, Low E♭, Low D, Low C, Low B♭, Low A, Low G, and even Double Low F, two octaves below a regular F-harp (and also the quietest harp). Seydel offers several models in extended low tunings, and Hohner now offers its specially designed Thunderbird series of extended low tunings.

Adding to your kit with a chromatic harmonica

Blues played on the chromatic harmonica is an urban phenomenon that got started one day in the early 1950s when legendary player Little Walter was intrigued by a huge, gleaming, and mysterious 16-hole chromatic he saw in a Chicago music store. After a few weeks of experimenting, Walter found an intuitive way to play the chromatic and quickly adapted it to the emerging Chicago blues. Ever since then, the chromatic has been an integral part of the blues harmonica player's kit.

Here are some important things to know about chromatic harmonicas:

>> **Size:** Chromatics come in several sizes, and blues players use mostly the 12-hole and 16-hole sizes. Players often refer to the 16-hole size as a "64" because it has 64 reeds.

>> **Note layout:** On most chromatics, the notes are laid out in a pattern called *solo tuning,* which helps give blues chromatic its unique sound. Avoid chromatics that use the same note layout as the diatonic, such as the Koch 980 or the Hohner Slide Harp.

>> **Range:** The 12-hole chromatic has a three-octave range (same as a 10-hole diatonic), while the 16-hole size covers four octaves, with an extra low octave that gives the deep, growly sound that works well in blues.

>> **Keys:** Sixteen-hole chromatics come only in the key of C, but 12-hole models come in several additional keys, usually pitched lower than C. Some 12-hole models also come in a *Tenor C,* which is pitched an octave below the regular C and gives you that same growly bottom octave that you get on the 16-hole model, but without the huge size.

>> **Positions:** Chromatics are designed to play in all keys on one harmonica, but blues musicians create the classic blues chromatic by playing a C chromatic in the key of D, or *third position,* or with the button held in, in E♭, or *tenth position.* (For more on positions, check out Chapter 12.) To get the third position sound in other keys, you can get 12-hole chromatics in different keys.

When you decide to go shopping for a chromatic harmonica, keep these things in mind as you make your selection:

>> **Construction:** As with diatonics, chromatics that are constructed with screws instead of nails are easier to service, while plastic or metal combs are more stable than wood. Two other things to consider:

- **Valves:** Most (but not all) chromatic harmonicas have *valves,* flexible plastic strips mounted over the reed slots to conserve air. Valves are important because chromatics are more likely to leak than diatonics because of their larger contact surfaces and multilayer mouthpiece assemblies. If you get a valved chromatic, you won't have to gasp just to produce a tiny, weak sound.

- **Mouthpiece profile:** Look at the harmonica in profile. Do the mouthpiece and the covers form a smooth line that fits easily in your mouth or do the front edges of the covers present a sudden steep slope where they meet the mouthpiece? A smooth profile fits more easily and comfortably in your mouth.

>> **Cost:** Chromatic harmonicas cost a lot more than diatonics. Cheap chromatics may cost twice the price of this book, and some of those, even the ones from famous-name manufacturers, are extremely leaky. Count on paying anywhere from four to six times the price of this book for a good 12-hole chromatic, and maybe ten times the book price for a 16-holer.

Using harmonicas in alternate tunings

Harmonicas with an altered pattern of notes are said to be in *alternate tunings*. Alternate tunings are seldom used in blues, but every now and then you may encounter them. A famous example is Canned Heat's tune "On the Road Again," where harmonica player Alan "Blind Owl" Wilson raised the pitch of the draw reed in Hole 6 to add a missing note. One alternate tuning that may be useful in blues in minor keys is the natural minor tuning (for more on major and minor keys, see Chapter 3). In Chapter 16, I go into several strategies for playing minor blues on diatonic, including using harmonicas in natural minor tuning.

Organizing and Protecting Your Harmonicas

As you acquire harmonicas in multiple keys and ranges, one or two chromatics, and maybe some alternate tunings, you're going to have a lot of stuff to carry around, and when you sit down to play, you'll need to organize your vast array of instruments so you can find the one you want. The information in this section can help keep you sane and stylin' in your harping life.

Carrying your harmonicas around

Each harmonica comes in its own hard-shell box or pouch for protection from dirt, debris, and hard knocks. That's very helpful if you just own one or two harps, but as your collection grows, those individual boxes will add to the bulk and weight of your kit. Now, you could just toss all your harps naked into a paper bag and let them jostle and scuff against each other. I know some pros who actually do this, but most players like to find a more elegant and secure way to carry their harps.

If you just have a few harps and like to travel light, you can get soft pouches and hard cases such as the ones shown in Figure 2-2. If you get one of the multi-key kits with several keys of harmonica in a pouch, you're already in good shape.

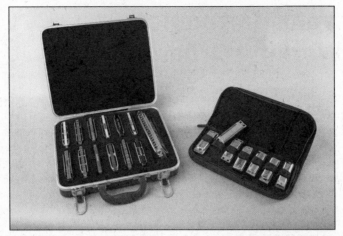

FIGURE 2-2:
Harmonica cases
and pouches.

Photograph by Anne Hamersky

However, you may also want to carry spare harmonicas in the keys that you use the most, maybe some tools, and a microphone and other bits of electronic gear. You need a way to gather all this stuff together and tote it around safely and conveniently.

Organizing your harps when you play

When you play a gig or a jam session or even when you practice, you may not have time to paw through a jumble of harmonicas to find the one you need. You may want to lay them out on top of an amplifier, speaker cabinet, or table. Or you can leave them in the opened carrying case. Either way, organize them so that you can instantly find the key you need:

>> **Make sure you can see the key markings on the harmonicas when they're stored**. Write the key on the top or end of the harp or use commercially available adhesive harmonica key labels (both Seydel and TurboHarp offer these).

>> **Arrange the harmonicas in a series of keys that makes sense, such as**

- Low to high in alphabetical order.

- In the following arrangement, known as the *circle of fifths:* G, D, A, E, B, F♯, D♭, A♭, E♭, B♭, F, C. When you start using positions, which I cover in Chapters 12, 13, 14, and 15, this arrangement can help you find the harmonica you need when you use a harmonica tuned to a key that's different from the key of the song.

>> **When you're done playing a harp, replace it in its assigned spot so you can find it again.**

Keeping Your Harmonicas in Good Working Order

Harmonicas are working machines. They have stress limits when you play them, and they're affected by being jostled around and by heat and cold, just like you are. They also get dirty, mostly from whatever you eat, drink, inhale, or cough up.

To get the most out of your harps, you can follow a few simple tips. You can get deep into cleaning and servicing them, but even the most basic harmonica care will help keep your harps in good shape.

Knowing the parts of your harmonica

Understanding how a harmonica is put together and how it works can help you appreciate how to care for it — and how to fix it when it something goes wrong. So let me take you on a quick tour.

Reeds and reedplates

The *reeds* are the heart of the harmonica. Each reed is a thin strip of metal that responds to your breath, vibrating to create one of the notes you hear when you play.

>> Reeds that vibrate slowly to produce low notes are longer and may be thicker near the tip to slow down the rate of vibration, while reeds that vibrate faster to produce high-pitched notes are shorter.

>> Harmonicas, like accordions and concertinas, use *free reeds* — reeds that are anchored at one end and are free to vibrate along their entire length without hitting anything (clarinets and saxophones use beating reeds, which beat against the edge of the mouthpiece).

>> Each reed is riveted or welded at its *reed pad*, or base, to a *reedplate*, a thin metal plate that anchors half of the reeds in the harmonica.

>> A *slot* is cut into the reedplate under the reed, allowing air to pass through and allowing the reed to swing into its slot as it vibrates.

Figure 2-3 shows a reedplate and reeds from a 10-hole diatonic harmonica.

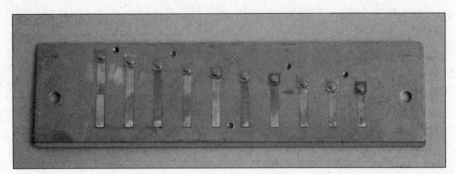

FIGURE 2-3:
Reedplate and
reeds from a
10-hole diatonic
harmonica.

Photograph by Anne Hamersky

Comb and covers

Early harmonicas were just reedplates that you could put your lips on. But the
reeds were vulnerable to damage, and naked reedplates were awkward to play. So
the harmonica evolved into a five-layer sandwich that includes a *comb* and *covers*,
as shown in Figure 2-4.

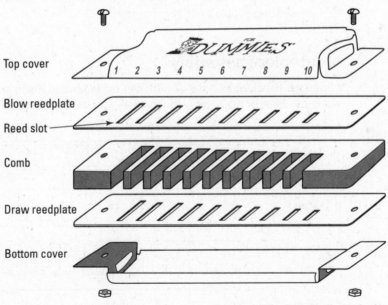

Top cover

Blow reedplate

Reed slot

Comb

Draw reedplate

Bottom cover

FIGURE 2-4:
The five layers of
a harmonica.

Illustration by Wiley, Composition Services Graphics

>> The *comb* is at the center of the harmonica sandwich and may be made of wood, plastic, or metal. In between the "teeth" of the comb are *channels,* spaces that channel air to and from the reeds. When the harmonica is assembled, each channel forms a *hole* in the front of the harmonica where you apply your mouth and breathe to sound the reeds that are located in that hole.

>> The reedplates are fastened to the top and bottom surfaces of the comb.

>> The *covers* (or cover plates) are fastened on the outsides of the reedplates. The covers give your fingers a way of holding the harmonica without touching (and blocking) the reeds, and they help project the sound outward toward the listener.

Every harmonica has two different sets of reeds:

>> *Blow reeds* are mounted inside the hole and sound when your exhaled breath pushes them into their slots.

>> *Draw reeds* are mounted on the outside of the hole and sound when your inhaled breath pulls them into their slots.

Mouthpiece assembly

Chromatic harmonicas have a multilayer *mouthpiece assembly* that runs vertically along the front of the harp. (See Figure 2-5 for an exploded view.)

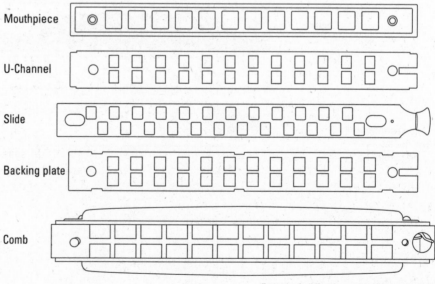

Mouthpiece

U-Channel

Slide

Backing plate

FIGURE 2-5:
Parts of a chromatic harmonica mouthpiece assembly, with the outermost part at the top.

Comb

Illustration by Wiley, Composition Services Graphics

>> **The mouthpiece:** The *mouthpiece* is mounted on the front of the harmonica over the holes. It's the main visible layer of the assembly, and it protects your lips and tongue from the moving parts below.

>> **The slide:** The *slide* (or slider) is a flat strip of metal sticking out from under the mouthpiece on the right end of the harmonica, with a metal button attached to the end.

- When you play the harmonica without pressing the slide button, you get the notes of the key of the harmonica. For instance, on a C chromatic you'll get the notes of the C major scale.

- When you press the button in toward the body of the harmonica, the slide shifts and directs your breath to a different set of reeds that sound a different scale tuned a semitone higher (see Chapter 3 for information on semitones).

- When you release pressure on the slide button, the slide springs back to its original position and you return to the first set of notes.

Some mouthpiece assemblies have two additional layers:

>> The *backing plate* provides a floor-like sliding surface for the slider so that it won't grind against the front edges of the reedplate and comb. (Some plastic chromatic combs integrate the backing plate into the front of the comb.)

>> The *U-channel* (or slide cage) locks together with the backing plate to form a ceiling and pair of side walls, giving the slide a channel to move in without grinding against the mouthpiece. (Some chromatics integrate the U-channel into the design of the mouthpiece.)

Protecting your harps from damage

In addition to protecting harmonicas from debris and hard knocks, try to keep them from getting too hot or cold — think of your harmonicas as having the same frailties and comfort levels as humans.

Don't blast hard on your harmonicas. You can get a full sound with very little breath, and forcing excessive air through the reeds at high pressure gives them more stress than they can handle, leading them to go out of tune and even fracture and break off.

Keeping your harmonicas clean

When you exhale through a harmonica, you generously share with it whatever you've been eating or drinking or your body has been secreting into your mouth, throat, and breath stream. The single thing you can do to keep your harmonicas clean is to play with a mouth free of food and drink residues. To do so, follow these practices:

>> Never eat while you play.

>> Drink only water while you play. Other beverages can gum up your harmonicas with sugars, oils, fats, and various particulate residues.

>> Rinse your mouth, at a minimum, before playing, to get rid of food matter, and drink some water to wash down anything you can't rinse away.

Inevitably, some dried saliva will collect on the holes and covers of your harmonicas. You can brush this out of the holes with a toothbrush and wipe off the covers and mouthpiece with a moist cloth.

What about the insides of your harmonica? To remove dried saliva that creeps inside the front edges of the covers, you can unscrew the covers and brush or wipe away any accumulation.

Some players completely disassemble the harmonica, soak everything in alcohol, and then brush and polish all parts to a shine. Doing this is a personal choice, and most harmonicas will work fine without such thorough cleaning.

You can immerse plastic and metal combed harmonicas in warm, soapy water to rinse them, but doing so may dislodge some dried crud that will migrate to a reed and block its free vibration in its slot.

WARNING

Never immerse or soak a wood-combed harmonica, as this can cause the comb to swell and warp.

Servicing and repairing your harmonicas

Harmonicas don't require regular maintenance aside from minimal cleaning. However, a brand-new harmonica can have manufacturing defects right out of the box. Or it can go out of tune after you play it for awhile. Even a harmonica in good condition can be souped up to play louder and more responsively. To deal with these situations, consult the manufacturer for repairs or look for an independent service technician.

IN THIS CHAPTER

» **Reading harmonica tab**

» **Talking musical time**

» **Understanding melody and harmony**

» **Exploring phrases, verses, and musical form**

» **Getting on the same page with other musicians**

Chapter **3**

Deciphering the Code: A Blues Guide to Music Symbols

Sometimes, thumping your chest and pointing just aren't enough to describe what you're thinking. So instead, over the centuries, musicians have developed concepts and language to describe music and the specifics of playing each instrument.

Tablature uses symbols to describe the physical actions that you use to play a specific instrument. Guitar *tab* (short for tablature) wouldn't work for harmonica; there's nothing for the guitar pick to pluck. So instead, in this chapter I show you harmonica tab, which works great for harmonica but not so great for guitar — blowing on the strings doesn't have a very impressive effect.

When you talk about how music fits together, you call it *music theory*. When you write down the details of a song and how it sounds, you call it *music notation*. In this chapter I give you the basics of both theory and notation. Not enough to hurt too badly (I hope) but enough so that you can understand basic concepts and terms and then use them to communicate with other musicians — even with guitar players (I know, I'm an incurable optimist).

And hey, if you play guitar, I'm *joking* — guitar and harmonica make a wonderful combination.

TIP

If you want to get started playing right away, go ahead and dive into whatever chapter you'd like. You don't have to wade all the way through this chapter or learn to play any of the figures or tabs. Use this chapter as a reference when you're puzzled by something elsewhere in the book. However, if you're really curious about how music works, go ahead and read the whole chapter.

Getting to Know the Shorthand of Harmonica Tab

Tab is a simple way to describe the actions you use when you play a musical instrument. When you want to play music on the harmonica, you need to know two things:

>> Which hole(s) to play

>> Whether to inhale or exhale

Most harmonicas have hole numbers — numbers above the holes that you use to identify the hole(s) you're going to play. Have a look at your harmonica and you'll probably see them.

After you identify the hole by its number, you need to know whether you *draw* (inhale) or *blow* (exhale) air through the hole.

I use a system of harmonica tab that shows you the hole number with an arrow above it. An arrow pointing up tells you to blow (exhale), and an arrow pointing down tells you to draw (inhale). One way to remember this is to set the book down on a table in front of you and move your air in the same direction that the arrow is pointing.

Figure 3-1 shows some basic tab with breath arrows and hole numbers.

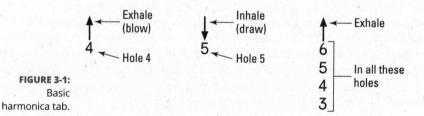

FIGURE 3-1: Basic harmonica tab.

Harmonica tab can also indicate several other actions:

>> Whether to *bend* a note (change how fast it vibrates) and by how much.

>> When and how to create special effects by

- Shaping the way you cup your hands around the harmonica

- Using your tongue on the holes of the harmonica

- Moving the harmonica in your mouth

I show you tab for special effects in Part 3, where I go into detail about those effects.

I tell you about tab for bending notes right here.

Most harmonicas don't have all the notes of the scale built in. To create the missing notes, you can use a technique called *note bending* to change the rate at which a sound vibrates. When you *bend notes down,* you slow down the vibration rate, and when you *bend notes up,* you speed up the vibration rate. (I explain bending in detail in Chapter 11.)

When you bend a note down or up, you can measure how much the vibration slows down or speeds up, and you can include that information in the tab. When you use bending to move to a missing note in the scale, you measure the change in semitones. In a standard musical scale, a *semitone* is the smallest move you can measure, like moving one fret on a guitar or moving to the neighboring key on a piano. (I go into more detail on semitones later in this chapter.) Blues never sticks with standards, though, and often uses even tinier moves called *microtones* that help give the blues its unique sound. Notating these microtonal moves can get mighty fussy, though, so at a certain point you have to rely on your ear to make the fine adjustments that help you sound bluesier.

When you bend a note down one semitone, you indicate it with one diagonal slash through the tab arrow. Bend the note down two semitones, and the tab shows two slashes. Three slashes indicate — you guessed it — a three-semitone bend.

Bending a note up is called either an *overblow* if you're exhaling or an *overdraw* if you're inhaling (or you can just call them all *overbends*). An overblow or overdraw is indicated by a circle through the arrow shaft. (In Chapter 11 I describe how to measure how many semitones a note goes up when you play an overbend.)

Figure 3-2 shows tab with bends and overblows.

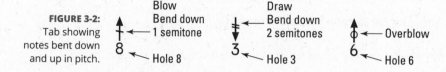

FIGURE 3-2:
Tab showing
notes bent down
and up in pitch.

Blow
Bend down
1 semitone

←— Hole 8

Draw
Bend down
2 semitones

←— Hole 3

←— Overblow

←— Hole 6

Understanding Musical Time

Blues is all about rhythm, and rhythm is just sound arranged in time. You may have heard that time is nature's way to prevent everything from happening at once. In music, especially danceable music such as blues, time is the most important element — more important than melody, harmony, or anything else.

Beats and tempo

Musical time evolved from human activities that repeat at a steady rate, such as hearts beating and legs walking. In the American South, blues was influenced by the work songs that people sang in time with repeated cycles of activity, such as plucking cotton bolls and turning to toss them in an 11-foot sack, or swinging pickaxes and scythes. In music, that steady, repeating cycle of sound is called the *beat*.

REMEMBER

Music measures time in beats. You measure the speed of musical beats the same way as your heart rate — in number of beats per minute.

The *tempo* is the speed of the beat. A crawling, slow-blues tempo might be 40 beats per minute (or *bpm*). A relaxed, medium-tempo blues might be around 92 bpm. A medium dance tempo might be 120 bpm, while a fast blues-rock tune might be 220 bpm or faster.

Before you begin to play a song, you can set the tempo by counting several beats at the desired tempo. You've probably heard a bandleader call out, "A-one, a-two, a-one, two, three, four!" at the beginning of a tune. He's *counting off the tune* — setting the tempo so that everyone plays together *in time* (in synchronization) with the beat. (The term *counting in* means the same thing.)

TIP

You can use a metronome to play the beat when you practice. Hearing the beat as you play helps you play in time with a steady tempo, without accidentally speeding up or slowing down. You set the metronome to the tempo you want and then turn it on to hear the beat played back with a clicking sound. You can buy stand-alone metronomes in music stores or get metronome apps for your mobile phone, tablet, or computer.

Time values and rhythm

You use *time values* to measure three things:

>> **The beat:** When you play a tune, the beat is constantly marking time, even when you don't hear it. Each beat has a time value.

>> **How long you play each sound:** Each sound you play is called a *note.*

>> **How long you wait between notes:** Often, one note comes right after another, but sometimes you *lay out* — you fall silent and wait awhile before starting again. Time values for silence are called *rests.*

Time values start with the largest unit, a *whole note* (or a *whole rest*), which divides into smaller units to create the other values.

>> **A whole note divides into two half notes.** A half note is half as long as a whole note.

>> **A whole note divides into four quarter notes.** A quarter note is one-fourth as long as a whole note (or half as long as a half note).

>> **A quarter note divides into two eighth notes.**

>> **An eighth note divides into two sixteenth notes.**

>> (Do you really want to keep going? Let's stop here.)

Figure 3-3 shows time values for notes and rests from whole notes to sixteenth notes.

Some time values can't be represented by the time values shown in Figure 3-3. To deal with these, you can use

>> **Ties:** A *tie* joins two or more notes into one longer note. For instance, if you need a note that's five quarters long, you can tie a whole note (which is four quarters long) to a quarter note.

>> **Dots:** A *dot* makes a note 50 percent longer. For instance, a dotted half note is three quarter notes long, and a dotted quarter note is three eighth notes long.

>> **Triplets:** Let's say you have three notes of equal length that fit in the space of a quarter note. A twelfth note would do the trick, but there's no such thing — note values always divide in two and four, not in three. But if you use *a triplet,* you can put three eighth notes in the space where two would normally go, effectively dividing the quarter note into three equal parts.

Figure 3-4 shows ties, dots, and triplets.

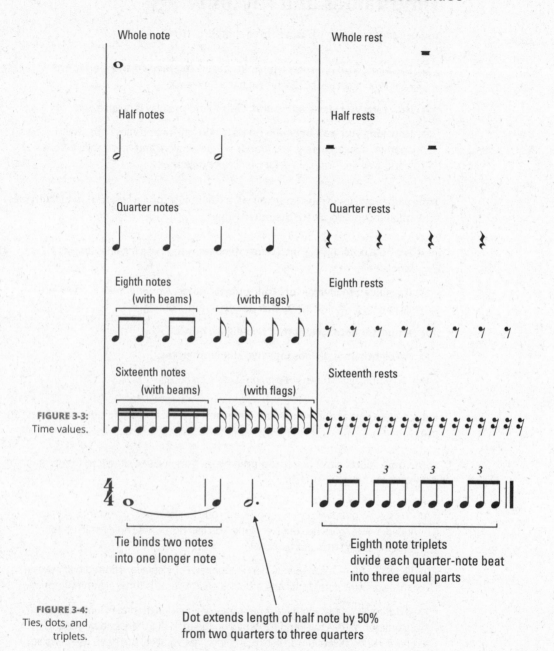

Note Values

Whole note

Half notes

Quarter notes

Eighth notes
(with beams)   (with flags)

Sixteenth notes
(with beams)   (with flags)

Rest Values

Whole rest

Half rests

Quarter rests

Eighth rests

Sixteenth rests

FIGURE 3-3:
Time values.

3   3   3   3

Tie binds two notes
into one longer note

Eighth note triplets
divide each quarter-note beat
into three equal parts

FIGURE 3-4:
Ties, dots, and
triplets.

Dot extends length of half note by 50%
from two quarters to three quarters

Bars and measures

Beats are grouped together in repeating cycles of two, three, or four. You emphasize the first beat in the group by playing it the loudest.

For instance, when you march, you alternate your right leg and your left leg in a cycle of two: "ONE, two, ONE, two." When music uses this two-beat cycle, you say that it's *in two.*

Waltzes are *in three:* "ONE, two, three, ONE, two, three." Most popular music nowadays is *in four* — "ONE, two, three, four, ONE, two, three, four."

REMEMBER

A measure is one cycle of beats.

>> When a song is in two, the measure is two beats long.

>> When a song is in three, the measure is three beats long.

>> When a song is in four, the measure is four beats long.

You measure beats by using a time value, such as a quarter note. At the beginning of a song, you can see the *time signature,* which shows you how many beats are in a measure and the time value that represents the beat.

The end of each measure is marked with a vertical line, called a *bar line,* that makes it easy for you to see where one measure ends and the next one begins. Over time, musicians started using the word *bar* to refer to the measure, so the terms *measure* and *bar* are interchangeable.

Figure 3-5 shows music in 2/4, 3/4, and 4/4.

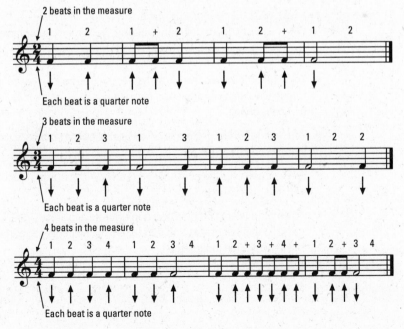

FIGURE 3-5:
Time signatures and bar lines.

PLAY THIS

You can hear examples of 2/4, 3/4, and 4/4 time on Track 1.

The ABCs of Melody and Harmony

When you sing or play instruments such as harmonica or guitar, you make sounds that create melodies and harmonies. The blues sounds called *licks* and *riffs* are a type of melody, and the chords that musicians often talk about are a type of harmony. They're all based on sounds that vibrate at a steady rate.

Vibrations and pitch

When you make sounds, you send waves through the air, similar to the waves that you'd see if you dropped a rock into a pool and watched the waves ripple out through the water in all directions.

Sound waves are called *vibrations*, and vibrations have two main characteristics, size and rate.

» The height and depth of a wave's ripples determine how loud it is. This is called *amplitude*.

- A wave with big ripples (high amplitude) makes a loud sound. When you say, "Turn up the volume," you're asking for higher amplitude.

- A wave that barely makes a ripple (low amplitude) makes a very soft sound. When you say, "Turn down the volume," you're asking for lower amplitude.

» The rate of the waves — how many come in a second — is called *frequency*.

- The faster the waves come, the higher the frequency. You hear high frequencies (fast vibrations) as high sounds, such as a mouse squeaking or a baby crying.

- You hear low frequencies (slow vibrations) as low sounds, such as a foghorn or a bass guitar.

- Some sounds vibrate at a steady frequency. These are the sounds you can sing and play as melodies.

- Other sounds are complex and don't vibrate at a steady rate. These are noises, and most drums and percussion instruments generate noises (no, that's not a value judgment).

A sound that vibrates at a steady frequency has *pitch*. You can measure pitch in *hertz* (abbreviated Hz), which just means vibrations per second. The faster the vibration, the more vibrations per second and the higher the pitch.

If you look at a table of frequencies for musical pitches, you'll see numbers that go to three or four decimal points. This information is great for making precise measurements, but you won't hear anybody in a blues club saying, "Hey, man, let's groove on a slow blues in 261.63!" Instead, you'll hear letter names, which describe a series of pitches that form a *scale*.

The notes of the scale

For thousands of years, musicians have chosen certain pitches to play or sing, and they've given each pitch a name, using special syllables — such as *do*, *re*, and *mi* — or using the letters of the alphabet.

>> The modern American system uses the first seven letters of the alphabet to name pitches: A, B, C, D, E, F, and G.

>> Each letter in the alphabet represents a higher pitch than the one that comes before it. B is higher than A, C is higher than B, and so on.

>> The collection of pitches is called a *scale*. You can play the scale in ascending order of pitch (A, B, C, D, E, F, G) or in descending order of pitch (G, F, E, D, C, B, A). Or you can move around among the notes of the scale to create melodies.

But the letter names A, B, C, D, E, F, and G only cover seven pitches. A diatonic harmonica has 19 pitches built into it, while a piano has 88! How can you use only seven letters to name all those notes?

Figure 3-6 shows part of a piano keyboard. As your gaze travels from left to right, you notice a pattern:

>> You see two black keys, then a gap, then three black keys, and then another gap. Then you see the pattern repeat several times.

>> Every time the pattern repeats, the note names also repeat.

>> If you count from a note name up or down to its repetition, the two note names are always eight notes apart. This distance of eight notes between two notes with the same name is called an *octave*.

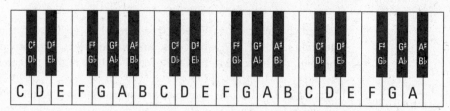

FIGURE 3-6:
Three octaves of
a piano keyboard.

Illustration by Wiley, Composition Services Graphics

So how can you get away with giving two different pitches the same name without getting confused? Because they sound like the same note, just higher or lower. Two interesting facts may help you understand this phenomenon:

>> If you check the frequency of any two notes an octave apart, one vibrates twice as fast as the other — they have a simple 2:1 ratio. For instance, if one A vibrates 440 times a second, the A an octave lower vibrates at 220 Hz (half the frequency of A440), while the A an octave higher vibrates at 880 Hz (double the frequency of A440).

>> If you ask men, women, and children to sing the same note or the same melody, the women and children will sing an octave higher than the men. People do this without even being aware of it. Humans seem to be hard-wired to let their ears do the math and use that 2:1 ratio to find a singing range that's comfortable for their voices.

Sharps and flats

Okay, so you can use just seven letters to name notes that reach all the way to the limits of human hearing (let's not get into dog hearing or bee hearing). But so far I've named only the white notes on the keyboard. What about all those black keys?

The black keys represent the notes that were left out of the naming scheme centuries ago. Musicians knew the notes were there but thought of them as sort of occasional indulgences, like sneaking an ice cream cone when you're on a diet and pretending that you didn't. So instead of giving those notes their own names, musicians considered them raised or lowered versions of the standard notes.

REMEMBER

The lowered versions are *flats* and the raised versions are *sharps*. The notes that are neither sharp nor flat are considered to be *naturals*.

You indicate that a note is flat by adding the flat symbol (♭) after the letter name. For instance, the flattened version of D is written as D♭. When you say it, you just say, "D flat." In music notation, however, the flat always comes before the note.

You indicate that a note is sharp by adding the sharp symbol (♯) after the letter name. For instance, the sharp version of D is written as D♯. When you say it, you say, "D sharp." In music notation, however, the sharp always comes before the note.

Sometimes you need to be clear that a note is a natural note, not a sharp or a flat. Then you use the natural symbol (♮). This goes after the letter name (for instance, D♮) but before a written note. You refer to it by saying "D natural."

TECHNICAL STUFF

Look at the note between C and D. You can call it C♯ (C sharp) or D♭ (D flat). When two notes produce the same pitch, they're considered to be *enharmonic.* Another way to talk about this is to note that C♯ and D♭ are two different ways of *spelling* the same pitch. Just as in writing words, rules exist for the correct spelling of notes, but I'm not going to go into the details here. You can get hip to that in a music theory book such as *Music Theory For Dummies,* by Michael Pilhofer and Holly Day (Wiley).

Semitones and whole tones

A *semitone* is the distance between any key and its immediate neighbor. For instance, from C to the black key to its immediate right (C♯ or D♭) is one semitone. From E to F, with no black key in between, is also one semitone.

If you start at C, count the semitone to C♯, then the semitone to D, and so on until you reach the next C, you'll come up with 12 semitones. So an octave contains 8 note names but 12 semitones.

The distance between C and D is two semitones, or one *whole tone* (not to be confused with a whole note, which is a unit of musical time).

Semitones and whole tones are important when you start measuring the quality of intervals, which I cover in the next section.

Intervals

Intervals describe the distance between one musical letter name and another. When I talk about an octave, I'm referring to an interval — to the relationship of two musical letter names that are eight notes apart.

Intervals have two characteristics, *size* and *quality.*

Size

You describe the size of an interval using Arabic numerals. To figure out an interval's size, follow these steps:

1. **Start at the letter name of one pitch and call that "1."**

For instance, to describe the interval between A and the E above it, you would designate A as 1.

2. **Count up from the lower note to the higher note, adding one number for each letter name in between the two notes.**

For instance, if A is 1, then B is 2, C is 3, D is 4, and E is 5.

3. **The number you get from counting up is the number that describes the interval.**

For instance, if you get the number 5 by counting from A up to E, then the interval between A and the E above it is the interval of a *fifth*. The interval from A to B is a *second,* from A to C is a *third,* and from A to D is a *fourth.*

If you count down between the same two note names, you get a different interval. Counting down from A to E (A–G–F–E) gives you the interval of a fourth instead of a fifth.

Quality

In addition to size, intervals have different qualities. *Quality* refers to the size when you count the semitones in an interval instead of the letter names. Every interval can have at least two qualities that differ by at least one semitone.

For an example of an interval with two different qualities, refer to the piano keyboard in Figure 3-6. Count the interval from C up to E and then count the interval from D up to F. Both are thirds — they're the same size of interval.

However, when you count the semitones in each of these intervals, you get different results:

>> When you count from C to E you get four semitones. This larger third is called a *major* third.

>> When you count from D to F you get only three semitones. This smaller third is called a *minor* third.

Each different quality of interval creates its own musical impression. Scales and chords both get their identities from the different qualities of intervals they contain and where those qualities are placed.

You can change the quality of an interval by using sharps and flats.

>> You can make an interval smaller by subtracting a semitone from its size.

- Raise the lower pitch of the interval by adding a sharp or removing a flat with a natural sign.

- Lower the higher pitch of the interval by adding a flat or canceling a sharp with a natural sign.

>> You can make an interval larger by adding a semitone to its size.

- Raise the higher pitch of the interval by adding a sharp or removing a flat with a natural sign.

- Lower the lower pitch of the interval by adding a flat or canceling a sharp with a natural sign.

Terms used to describe interval qualities include *major, minor, perfect, augmented,* and *diminished.*

Fourths, fifths, and octaves can be

>> Perfect (their standard size)

>> Augmented (one semitone larger than perfect)

>> Diminished (one semitone smaller than perfect)

Seconds, thirds, sixths, and sevenths can be

>> Minor

>> Major (one semitone larger than minor)

>> Diminished (one semitone smaller than minor) or augmented (one semitone larger than major), though this is rare

Table 3-1 shows the most common interval sizes with their various qualities and their sizes in semitones. Though you can use this information to go deep into music theory, you'll find that the most useful application to blues is understanding how to construct the chords used in blues.

TABLE 3-1

Interval Sizes and Qualities

Interval Size	Interval Quality	Number of Semitones
Second	Minor	1
Second	Major	2
Third	Minor	3
Third	Major	4
Fourth	Perfect	5
Fourth	Augmented	6
Fifth	Diminished	6
Fifth	Perfect	7
Fifth	Augmented	8
Sixth	Minor	8
Sixth	Major	9
Seventh	Minor	10
Seventh	Major	11
Octave	Perfect	12

Keys

A musical *key* is named for a note that you can use to sing or play a melody, such as G, A-flat, or C-sharp. You call the note that names the key the *tonic note* (or just the tonic).

For instance, the key of G is named after the note G, and the key of A♭ is named after the note A♭. Which octave the G or A♭ is in doesn't matter; the note name refers collectively to all notes with an identical name. For example, in the key of C♯, all notes called C♯, no matter how high or low pitched, are collectively the tonic notes for that key.

Your ear senses the tonic as the tonal center. Melodies often start on the tonic note, move away to other notes, and then come back to the tonic. When you move away from the tonic note, you create a sense of movement and even of tension. When you move back to the tonic note, you feel as if the melody has come home to rest and that any feeling of tension has been resolved.

Scales

When you play in a particular key, you usually use a group of notes that includes some notes and excludes others. This group of notes is known as a *scale*. The simplest way to catalog the notes of the scale is to start on the tonic and then go to the next highest, which is also the next letter in the alphabet, and so on, until you reach the next tonic note an octave higher.

Most scales use all seven note names just once, and some of the note names may be raised by a sharp or lowered by a flat.

>> The scale of A major in ascending order is A B C♯ D E F♯ G♯ A. You can see that it uses all seven note names, but three of them are sharps.

>> The scale of A♭ major is A♭ B♭ C D♭ E♭ F G A♭. Again, this scale uses all seven note names, but four of them are flats.

Every note in the scale has an identity that's measured by its relationship to the tonic. These identities are called *degrees.* The tonic note is the first degree of the scale. The next highest note is the second degree, and so on. When you number the degrees of the scale this way, you're really describing the size of the interval between the tonic and the other degrees in the scale.

Many types of scales exist, and they're defined by the different interval qualities that exist between the tonic and each scale degree. For instance, minor scales always have a minor third degree, and major scales always have a major third degree. Blues uses a strange hybrid scale that varies according to context and doesn't fit any standard structure (in blues, the third degree of the scale is sometimes major and sometimes minor). Though musicians often use the term *blues scale*, they use it to describe several different scales, all of which work to play blues.

Probably the easiest and most comprehensive way to describe the scale used in blues is to start with the major scale and then add three notes to it, which are known as the *blue notes.*

You can use two different templates to describe or construct a major scale. You can

>> Use the pattern of semitones between the degrees of the scale, which is tone (that is, a whole tone), tone, semitone, tone, tone, tone, and semitone (often abbreviated as TTS TTTS).

>> Describe the quality of each scale degree.

Figure 3-7 shows both approaches together, applied to the C major scale.

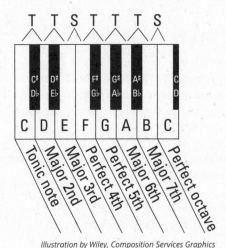

FIGURE 3-7:
Construction of a
major scale.

Illustration by Wiley, Composition Services Graphics

The three blue notes that are added to the scale are

>> The minor third (often called the *flatted third,* even when a flat isn't involved)

>> The diminished fifth (often called the *flat five*)

>> The minor seventh (often called the *flat seven*)

When you add these notes to the C major scale, you add E♭ (the flat third), G♭ (the flat five), and B♭ (the flat seven).

As you start playing blues on the harmonica, you'll find yourself using these notes, though sometimes you'll have to *bend notes* — that is, lower a note's pitch by moving your tongue inside your mouth. I show you how to bend notes in Chapter 11.

Chords and chord progressions

When you sound two or more pitches at the same time, you create *harmony.* Some harmonies are called *chords.* On the harmonica you can sound harmonies and chords by playing two or more holes at the same time.

Chords make a pleasing sound, but they're also an important element in how songs are structured and how you choose melody notes. This section walks you through the logic of how chords are constructed. I don't go into every possible kind of chord, just the ones you'll encounter most often in the context of the blues. I encourage you to seek out more information on chords and harmony in general because this knowledge will deepen your abilities to express yourself by playing all kinds of music.

Every chord is named for a note, such as C or G or E♭. That note is called the *root* of the chord. For example, to build a C chord, you start with the note C as the root of the chord.

The most basic type of chord is called a *triad* because it has three notes: the *root*, the *third*, and the *fifth*. To build a C triad, you follow these steps:

1. **Assign the number "1" to the root note.**

   If you're creating a C chord, then C is 1.

2. **Count five notes up from the root.**

   Counting up from C, you get C, D, E, F, and G.

3. **The notes numbered 1, 3, and 5 form a C triad.**

   So if C is 1 (the root), then E is 3 (the third), and G is 5 (the fifth).

Blues often uses a type of chord called a *seventh chord* (or 7th chord) because it includes a *seventh* along with the root, third, and fifth. To build a seventh chord, you start at the root, count up seven letter names, and then use the note numbers 1, 3, 5, and 7 to build the chord.

For example, to build a seventh chord on C, you count up seven notes, starting with the root. The letter names that correspond to 1, 3, 5, and 7 are C, E, G, and B.

However, the seventh chord formed by C, E, G, and B isn't the type of seventh chord used in blues.

REMEMBER

Let me explain. Chords are made up of intervals, and the quality of intervals contained in the chord determines the *chord type*. Several types of seventh chords exist, and the seventh chord used most often in blues is the *dominant seventh*. A dominant seventh chord built on C contains the notes C, E, G, and B♭. The distinctive sound of the dominant seventh chord is a signature sound in the blues.

Chords exist in several types that are determined by the qualities of the intervals between the chord's root and its other notes. Here are the most important chords to know for playing blues:

>> **Major triad**

- A major triad has a major third and a perfect fifth.

- The blow notes on a diatonic harmonica form a major triad.

- The draw notes in Holes 1 through 4 form another major triad.

>> **Dominant 7th chord** (often simply called a 7th chord)

- A dominant 7th chord is a major triad with an added minor seventh.

- The dominant 7th chord is the most commonly used chord in blues.

- The draw notes in Holes 1 through 5 of a diatonic harmonica form a dominant 7th chord.

>> **Minor triad**

- A minor triad has a minor third and a perfect fifth.

- The draw notes in Holes 4, 5, and 6 (and also Holes 8, 9, and 10) form a minor triad.

>> **Minor 6th chord**

- A minor 6th chord is a minor triad with an added major sixth.

- Draw 4, 5, 6, and 7 form a minor 6th chord.

- This chord is important in the sound of third position (see Chapters 14 and 15 for more on third position).

>> **Minor 7th chord**

- A minor 7th chord is a minor triad with an added minor seventh.

- Minor 7th chords aren't built into the diatonic harmonica.

- Minor 7th chords occur in some blues songs with a slightly expanded set of chord choices, such as "The Thrill Is Gone."

>> **Diminished triad**

- A diminished triad has a minor third and a diminished fifth.

- Draw 3, 4, and 5 (and also Draw 7, 8, and 9) form a diminished triad.

- Diminished triads are used occasionally in blues, often as a *passing chord,* a chord that appears briefly in passing between two chords that receive stronger emphasis.

>> **Augmented triad**

- An augmented triad has a major third and an augmented fifth.

- Augmented chords aren't built into the diatonic harmonica.

- Augmented chords occasionally appear in blues tunes influenced by gospel style.

A *chord progression* is a sequence of chords, progressing from one chord to the next. A few blues songs stay on a single chord for the whole song, but most start on the tonic chord (the chord built on the home note of the key), go to another chord, then another, and so on, and usually return to the tonic chord at the end.

Each chord in a chord progression is played by some combination of bass, guitar, and keyboards, and each chord lasts for a defined number of beats or bars before going on to the next.

A *chord chart* is a written map of a chord progression that shows each chord in a progression in sequence, along with diagonal slashes to show how many beats each chord lasts and bar lines to show how many bars the chord is played or how many chords occur within that bar. You can see a typical chord chart in Chapters 7 and 17.

Using chord shorthand with I, IV, and V

When you number the notes in a scale, you use Arabic numerals. But when you number the chords that you build on those scale degrees, you use Roman numerals.

For example, in the key of C, C is the tonic, or 1st degree of the scale. The chord you build on the 1st degree is the *I chord.* If you build a chord on the 4th degree of the scale, that chord is the *IV chord.*

You can build a chord on any degree of the scale. However, the three most important chords in blues are the I chord, built on the 1st degree of the scale; the IV chord, built on the 4th degree of the scale; and the V chord, built on the 5th degree of the scale. This is true regardless of what key you play in.

In blues (and in rock and country music), the I, IV, and V chords are the most often-used chords, and many tunes contain no other chords. Knowing what these chords are in any key — and, even more important, knowing which notes on your harmonica fit with any of these chords — is critical to playing blues well.

TECHNICAL STUFF

When you substitute Roman numerals for the actual names of chords (such as I, IV, and V instead of C, F, and G), you can talk about the structure of a tune without talking about a specific key. Musicians in Nashville use a version of this system called the *Nashville Number System* so that they can change a tune's key to suit a singer's preference without having to refigure all the details. Blues musicians don't generally use the Nashville system, but they do use the I-IV-V terminology to talk about musical structures.

Shaping Musical Statements

Musical statements are similar in many ways to spoken statements, especially poems. Individual notes are like words, and verses of a song are like stanzas of a poem. Each line of a poem is like a musical phrase.

Phrases

A musical *phrase* sounds like a spoken phrase. Each phrase is part of a longer statement, and it has a beginning and an end, often ending with a pause before the next phrase in the statement.

Phrases are usually either two measures or four measures in length. Within those measures, a phrase may have many fast notes, a few very long ones, or any other combination. A phrase may have a *pickup,* a short series of notes that begins before the two-measure or four-measure "container" for the phrase and that serves as an introduction.

The end of a phrase is marked either by a long, held note or by a rest, which may take up the last few beats of the two or four measures. A phrase may end before the end of the two or four measures, either holding a long note or leaving a rest to mark the end of the phrase.

Phrases often occur in pairs that sound like a question followed by an answer or in longer groups of three or four phrases, with all but the last one sounding inconclusive in some way. Sometimes you find that even a single phrase can have a two-part question-and-answer structure.

Verses and musical form

Every tune has a *form* that gives it shape. The form of a tune is comprised of two or more phrases, just as the stanzas of a poem contain two or more lines.

Blues uses certain standard forms, such as the 12-bar blues, the 8-bar blues, and Saints changes (the form of "When the Saints Go Marching In"). I describe 12-bar blues in Chapter 7 and both 8-bar blues and Saints changes in Chapter 17.

A tune's form usually remains consistent and is repeated several times, just as successive stanzas of a poem have a structure that stays consistent.

Form in blues tunes has two main characteristics:

>> **Length:** Length is gauged by the number of bars in the form. Common lengths include 8, 12, 16, and 32 bars.

>> **Chord progression:** Certain chord progressions are associated with some standard lengths, such as the chord progression that's standard for 12-bar blues. However, an individual tune may vary from a standard progression in some significant way that you need to know about. The bandleader may describe this to you, give you a chord chart showing the chord progression and how long each chord lasts, or simply surprise you.

The familiar terms *verse* and *chorus* both describe the form of a tune, and they're often used interchangeably. However, many songs have two or more *sections* with different chord progressions or melodies, and each section is described by a different name. For example, a song may have a verse, a separate chorus that sounds different, and maybe even a third section, such as a bridge that sounds different from either the verse or the chorus.

Most blues tunes stick to a form with just one section and repeat it several times. A few blues songs, however, have *bridges,* with a distinct chord progression and a different overall length from the main verse structure.

Communicating with Other Musicians

When you get together to play with other musicians, everyone needs to understand what he's going to play and how he's going to play it.

The details of what a blues musician plays is up to him. To fill in those details, he relies on knowledge of the general blues style and of its many substyles to choose and employ memorized patterns, often in spontaneous combinations. At the same time, all the musicians playing together listen actively to one another and adapt to what the others are playing.

But before all that tradition-based creativity can unfold, everyone needs to know certain basic information. To communicate this information, blues musicians use a shorthand code that communicates quickly and efficiently, though it can sound mysterious and even bizarre to the uninitiated. Here's a brief guide to that code.

Naming the key of a song

I've heard some very strange and awkward performances where different band members were playing in different keys and couldn't figure out what to do about it. So the first thing to communicate is what key the tune is played in. If the bandleader says the tune is in G, you pick up the harmonica you'd use to play in G.

Note that I didn't say to pick up a G harmonica to play in the key of G. When you play blues harmonica, the key of the song frequently doesn't match the key of the harmonica. This may sound strange, but an essential part of the sound of blues harmonica is playing in *positions,* which describe the relationship between the key of the harmonica and the key of the song. Depending on the character of the tune, you may choose among harmonicas tuned to several different keys to play that tune. (I explain positions in Chapter 12.)

WARNING

Some non-harmonica players know a little about positions, and, as you know, a little knowledge can be a dangerous thing. Instead of telling you the key of a song, they may try to help you by telling you the key of harmonica they think you should use. Always ask, "What key are *you* playing in?" Based on that information and the character of the song, you can then make your own choice about which key of harmonica to use.

Counting off to begin the song

To play together, musicians needs to know

>> The tempo (the speed of the beat) so they can play in synchronization.

>> When the first beat happens so they can all start together.

To communicate this information, the bandleader usually *counts off* two bars at the tempo of the tune, something like this: "One!" (pause) "Two!" (pause) "One, two, three, four!" On the next beat after the count-off, the whole band comes in, although sometimes the first few notes of the melody are played during the count-off.

Indicating tempo and rhythm

In the blues environment, you're not likely to see a bandleader defining how fast the beats go by in beats per minute, let alone using a metronome to demonstrate. More likely, the leader will describe a tune as fast, slow, or medium, even before she counts off the tempo. Band members may need to understand the general character of the tempo in advance so that they can prepare to play in a way that fits well with that tempo.

Musicians also need to know some basic information about the rhythmic character of the tune they're about to play. Does the beat divide into two equal parts (straight eighths) or into three (shuffle, or triplet feel)? In addition, the leader may describe a specific rhythmic style, or *groove,* such as Texas shuffle, New Orleans second line, rumba, or some other groove. Detailing the dozens of rhythmic styles is beyond the scope of this book, but you can learn about them by either hanging out at jam sessions or getting prerecorded backing tracks featuring a band playing in various rhythmic styles.

Conveying a song's arrangement

Sometimes when you play a song, you start at the beginning of a verse, play several verses, and then stop. But often you arrange the tune to make it more interesting. Blues uses several standard arranging devices. Understanding them and knowing what to call them helps you play along with a bandleader's ideas and also helps you communicate your ideas when you're the arranger. Arrangements in a blues tune may include

>> **An introduction,** or *intro,* often consisting of the last four-bar phrase of a verse (known as "starting at the V"). Sometimes the intro is played by the full band and sometimes by a solo instrument.

>> **An ending** (sometimes called an *outro*) consisting of a phrase at the end of the last verse that brings the music to a satisfying conclusion instead of just stopping cold. Blues has several standard endings, and you should be aware of them so you can join in (or keep quiet if you don't know them).

>> **Solo breaks,** which allow the singer to rest for one or more verses while one or more instrumentalists take solos. Solo breaks may be decided in advance or indicated by the bandleader on the spot as the band is playing the tune.

>> **Stops,** a series of short riffs that repeat several times, with each riff coming to an abrupt stop and a pause before the riff repeats. Each pause is filled by vocals or a solo instrument. Stops usually happen during the first 4 bars of a 12-bar blues tune but can happen in other parts of the verse as well.

>> **A vamp,** where the band plays for an indeterminate amount of time while waiting for something to occur, such as a singer walking across the stage to take the microphone or the singer or leader making a series of announce-ments. Usually, the band plays a short riff or a single chord with a repeating rhythm, or it repeats a short sequence of chords.

>> **A change of tempo or rhythmic style,** such as a fast tune that changes to a slow tempo for the song's ending or a tune in shuffle rhythm that changes to straight eighths or a Latin rhythm.

>> **Changes in volume,** such as dramatically dropping to a quiet sound level or building to a *crescendo* (an increase to a very loud volume).

>> **A change of key** at some point. Sometimes, changing the key of a song can give it new energy. For a harmonica player, this may mean a change of harmonica, so this is something you need to know about.

>> **A breakdown,** a segment of the tune where most of the band stops playing and just one or two players continue for awhile before the rest of the band joins in again.

2

Doin' the Crawl: Your First Harmonica Moves

IN THIS PART . . .

You start to play simple rhythms, get the hang of playing single notes, and then begin to master the elements of motion. As you learn patterns of notes, you start to develop your stock of licks and riffs and acquire an understanding of the building blocks of musical phrases.

Chapter **4**

Breathing Life into the Harmonica

This chapter is where you start to experience the harmonica, to feel it and know it. You situate the harmonica in your mouth, make sounds, and then get those sounds working together, using the most important elements in music — time and rhythm.

But first, like a bluesman about to go out on the road, you prepare to make the best use of your resources — your energy, your muscles, and your mind. No matter how new the task or how unfamiliar the skills that it requires, I help you prepare for success with a series of simple steps.

In this chapter you build the base for everything else you'll do when you play blues harmonica, so take it slow for awhile and groove on these essentials. The ingredients may look plain, but they add up to some mighty fine home cookin'.

Preparing Your Body and Your Mind

Your whole body plays the harmonica. That may seem surprising; after all, the harmonica is so small! But check it out:

>> Your arms and hands hold the harmonica and help shape the sound.

>> Your mouth, tongue, and throat focus, color, and inflect the sound.

>> Your air column, from your lips to your belly, shapes and amplifies the tiny vibrations of the reeds.

>> Your feet can tap time and your legs and hips can groove to the music.

>> Even if you stand still, your entire lower body supports the active upper body and holds a lot of energy in reserve.

By relaxing, aligning your posture, and focusing your breath, you activate all the power you need to get a big sound out of the harmonica.

Relaxing and getting ready

Whenever you try something new, you may start to worry. You may think, "I don't know anything about this; I'm clumsy; I'll mess it up!" That's natural, and the best way you can handle your anxiety is to relax, prepare, and take things slowly.

Throughout this book, you face new challenges. If you relax you'll have more focus and energy to meet each challenge. And if you have a strategy for meeting each challenge, you'll be able to face it with confidence.

TIP

Before playing, always spend a few minutes getting your mind and body into a relaxed state. You don't need to do anything illegal, though. The best way to relax is to align your posture and focus your breathing, as I detail in the following sections.

Aligning your posture

When you breathe, talk, sing, or play the harmonica, you use your *air column*. The air column starts above the waist and extends through the diaphragm, lungs, rib cage, throat, mouth, tongue, and lips. When you sit or stand up straight, you give your air column the room it needs to expand and contract. To get your posture in alignment, follow these steps:

1. **Stand up straight, with your arms relaxed at your side.**

   Imagine you're a marionette, dangling from a string attached to the top of your head. Your spine is straight, and your shoulders, arms, and legs are all relaxed and dangling.

2. **Now imagine that you're standing on a wide plain looking at a distant horizon.**

   Your head is erect, and you're gazing into the distance, not up or down.

3. **Inhale, slowly and deeply.**

   Let your chest and shoulders rise and your abdomen (the area between your ribs and waist) expand.

4. **Exhale, also slowly and gently, but let your ribs stay expanded while your abdomen slowly subsides.**

   Keeping your rib cage expanded is an important part of breathing for playing harmonica (and for speaking and singing). Doing so lets you breathe fully and quickly with very little motion and also helps you relax and feel confident.

5. **Keep breathing in and out gently and fully from the abdomen.**

   As you breathe, monitor your body sensations. Look for opportunities to relax and for tensions you may feel in these areas, from head to toe:

   - Forehead and scalp
   - Lips and jaw
   - Throat
   - Shoulders
   - Arms, hands, and fingers
   - Chest and abdomen
   - Pelvic area
   - Upper legs, knees, and calves
   - Ankles, feet, and toes

Focusing your breath

When you speak, sing, or play a wind instrument such as the flute, you use your breath to express yourself. You inhale quickly to fill your air supply, and then you exhale slowly as you make sounds.

When you play the harmonica, however, you do something unique: You inhale to make musical sounds. (You exhale, too, of course!) Half the notes built into the harmonica are *draw notes* (sounds you make by inhaling), and half the notes are *blow notes* (sounds you make by exhaling). When you play blues harmonica, you use more draw notes than blow notes, so one of the first things you want to do is get the hang of inhaling in a controlled way.

Inhaling and exhaling deeply, gently, and slowly prepares you to play both draw notes and blow notes on the harmonica. However, to fully prepare, do these three things:

>> **Breathe exclusively through your mouth.** Any air that doesn't go through the harmonica weakens your sound and makes you work harder to deliver air to the harmonica. To direct all air through your mouth, close your nasal passages.

>> Not sure how to do this? Imagine you're blowing up a balloon, something you can't do with air leaking through your nose. You can use an actual balloon or just press your lips to the back of your hand. Now try blowing up the balloon. Your cheeks should bulge out because the air has nowhere to go. If you try to inhale, your cheeks will suck in.

>> **Open your throat.** Your throat is a major gateway to your air supply. The best way to open it is to yawn. Try it; your throat will open way up. Of course, your lips and jaw will also open, so you need to isolate the open-throat part of yawning because you need to close your lips around the harmonica.

>> **Breathe softly and steadily.** Try the *warm hand exercise*. Place the palm of your hand 2 inches in front of your open mouth and breathe gently. If you can feel the warmth of your breath but not the wind, this is all the air you need to make sounds with the harmonica (though most of the time you'll use more air than this). Try this exercise a few times and see whether you can get the beginning of your breath to be as gentle as the sustained flow that follows, without any noticeable push of air at the start.

Adding the Harmonica

When you play the harmonica, the harmonica comes to you, not the other way around. It won't drip butter or barbecue sauce on your shirt, so don't be afraid to bring it right up into your face. In this section I show you the best way to connect that little box of reeds with your mind and body.

Getting the harmonica in your mouth

Playing the harmonica is like eating corn on the cob; you have to open your mouth wide and get it around the cob. Harmonicas don't make particularly good eating (no butter or sauce, right?), but they do respond well to the corncob treatment. Getting the harmonica deep in your mouth helps to keep air from escaping and helps you get a full, rich sound.

REMEMBER

Before you begin, make sure you have the harmonica right side up. The holes should face you, and the name of the harmonica should be on top. If the harmonica has hole numbers, hold it so that the numbers run from 1 to 10 from left to right.

To situate the harmonica in your mouth, do this:

1. **For now, hold the harmonica by the two ends with the fingertips of both hands.**

   In the section "Holding the harmonica" later in the chapter I show you the best way to hold the harmonica.

2. **Drop your jaw and open your mouth wide.**

3. **Keep your neck erect.**

   Don't crane it forward or backward; instead, act like you're looking at the distant horizon.

4. **Insert the harmonica in your mouth until the harmonica touches the corners of your mouth, where your top and bottom lips meet.**

5. **Let your jaw close gently and let your lips fall onto the harmonica's covers.**

   Remember to keep your jaw and lips relaxed.

6. **Feel the moisture of your lips where they touch the harmonica.**

   This moisture helps seal the harmonica and give it lubrication to glide right and left in your mouth.

Breathing gently and deeply

After you have the harmonica in your mouth (see the preceding section), it's time to breathe through it and start making some noise. Don't try to isolate a single hole for the time being. Just nestle the harmonica in your lips and let your breath flow through several holes at once. You'll get a pleasing combination of sounds called a *chord*. (For more on chords, check out Chapter 3.)

Here's how to do it:

1. **Make sure your nose is closed.**

2. **Inhale through the harmonica.**

   Start gently and inhale comfortably for a few seconds.

3. **Let your rib cage expand and your abdomen swell outward.**

   Listen to the sound of the harmonica as you inhale.

4. **Exhale gently and slowly.**

   Let your rib cage stay expanded while your abdomen subsides. The harmonica now makes a different sound. Listen and absorb that sound.

5. **Keep inhaling and exhaling slowly in a repeating cycle.**

   Listen to the sound the harmonica makes and notice how it feels in your hands and your mouth. This is the beginning of your blues harmonica experience.

REMEMBER

Listen for air leaking around your lips. If you hear a sound of air hissing, try to move the harmonica a little farther into your mouth to help your lips form a seal. But don't tense up your lips or bite down on the harmonica; relaxation is always important.

Holding the harmonica

In this section I show you the classic *grip* — the way you hold the harmonica. Your grip has a powerful effect on the sound of the harmonica. When you use the classic grip, you cup the harmonica, enclosing it in both hands.

Here's how you do it: Place your left thumb and forefinger along the ridges that run along the back of the harmonica's covers, as shown in Figure 4-1. (If you're left-handed, you may prefer to reverse these directions and hold the harmonica in your right hand.) Hold the harmonica lightly; it's not trying to get away from you. All you need is skin and tin, gentle contact between the skin of your hand and the tin of the covers (actually, covers are mostly stainless steel or chrome, but tin rhymes nicely).

TIP

If the right end of the harmonica extends past your fingertips, you may want to rest the left end of the harmonica on top of the webbing between your thumb and forefinger. That way you can enclose the harmonica in your hands for hand effects and also enclose a microphone (see Chapter 19 for more on microphones).

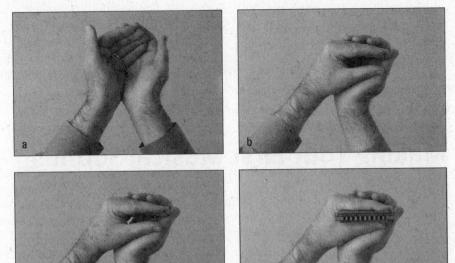

Photograph by Anne Hamersky

FIGURE 4-1:
Holding the harmonica in your left hand and forming a basic hand cup.

Though harmonica players occasionally hold the harmonica in one hand, they usually use both hands — the left hand to hold the harmonica and the right hand to enclose it. By completely enclosing the harmonica in your hands, you can control the sound that emerges in several ways:

>> You can make the sound dark and muffled by closing the cup or make the sound bright by opening it.

>> You can use your hands to make the harmonica "talk" by opening and closing your hands to form sounds like "ooh," "wah," and "wow" (more about this technique in Chapter 10).

>> You can enclose a microphone in your hands with the harmonica to concentrate the sound that goes into the microphone. (See Chapter 19 for more on microphones and amplification.)

You form the cup as shown in the second, third, and fourth photos in Figure 4-1. A few important things to note:

>> Keep the fingers of each hand together, like you could scoop up water in either hand.

>> Wrap your right hand around your left hand. Your left hand forms a U-shaped rim from the tip of the little finger to the tip of the thumb. Your right hand

contacts the edge of that rim along its entire length to seal the harmonica inside your hands.

>> Leave a slight opening at the back of the cup, below the little fingers, so that some sound can get out.

Making Your First Musical Sounds

Blues is all about rhythm, and rhythm is just sound arranged in time. Before you play licks, riffs, and melodies, you start by breathing with simple rhythms. To understand the basics of rhythm and the music symbols I use, check out Chapter 3.

In this section I show you how to play the basic rhythmic units — whole notes, half notes, and quarter notes — as well as how to balance your breath while playing and how to make some classic harmonica sounds.

Playing long, medium, and one-beat notes

Before you begin to play a song, you can set the *tempo*, or speed of the beat, by counting several beats at the desired tempo. You've probably heard a bandleader calling out "A-one, a-two, a-one, two, three, four!" at the beginning of a tune. He's *counting in* (or *counting off*) — setting the tempo so that everyone plays together in time.

To get you started, I set the tempo at 60 beats per minute, or 60 *bpm*. That gives you one beat per second, which is just slow enough to be comfortable. You don't even need a metronome to set this tempo; just count along with the seconds on your watch.

To represent beats, I use some music notation — not enough to hurt, mind you, just enough to get the job done:

>> **A quarter note** (a solid oval with a stem) lasts for one beat.

>> **A half note** (a hollow oval with a stem) is twice as long as a quarter note and lasts for two beats.

>> **A whole note** (a hollow oval with no stem) is twice as long as a half note and lasts for four quarters, or four beats.

The numbers above the notes are there to help you count beats as they go by. I include these numbers in the early chapters of the book, but as you get used to playing in time with the beat, you won't need them anymore. (Want to know more about counting beats? Check out Chapter 3.)

Now I want you to get several holes of the harmonica in your mouth and breathe, like I describe in the section "Adding the Harmonica" earlier in the chapter. However, this time I get more specific about which holes you play and how long you breathe:

>> **Focus on playing Holes 1, 2, 3, and 4 together.** Why? Partly because that combination sounds really good together, but also because the first four holes are where a huge amount of blues playing occurs.

>> **Measure how long you breathe by counting beats mentally as you play.**

You can listen and play along with Tabs 4-1, 4-2, 4-3, 4-4, and 4-5 on Track 2.

Playing half notes

To play the rhythm in Tab 4-1, do this:

1. **Inhale deeply and expand your rib cage as you breathe in. Then let your breath out and relax.**

2. **Bring the harmonica up to your mouth, aiming for the four holes on the left.**

3. **Place the harmonica in your mouth. Make sure that it touches both corners of your mouth, with your lips gently sealing the harmonica.**

4. **Use your watch or a metronome to find the desired tempo of 60 beats per minute.**

5. **Now count "one, two, three, four" to count yourself in, either mentally or out loud.**

6. **On the fifth beat, start inhaling in time with the beat.**

7. **Inhale for two beats and then exhale for two beats.**

   Keep repeating this sequence for several repetitions.

Sustain each breath through the full count of beats before you change breath direction. The sound should never stop, and neither should your breathing.

In Tab 4-1, you can see the repeating count of 1–2, 1–2 above the notes. These numbers help you count the length of each note in beats. Below the notes are arrows that tell you when to inhale and when to exhale.

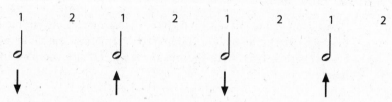

TAB 4-1:
Alternating draw and blow breaths for two beats each.

After playing Tab 4-1 for awhile, did you notice that you started to fill up with air or started to empty out? Even when you breathe in and out for an equal amount of time, you're likely to fill up with air as you play. Later I show you how to balance inhaled and exhaled air, but for now, pay attention to two things:

>> Make sure that air isn't leaking through your nose or lips.

>> Try to inhale and exhale with equal amounts of air flow.

Playing whole notes

In Tab 4-2 you sustain each breath for four beats, as shown in the beat count above each note.

REMEMBER

You need enough air to sound each note for four beats, so make sure to breathe gently when you first try playing whole notes. You can increase the air flow after you discover how much breath you need to sustain a note for four beats.

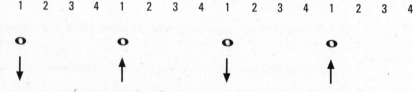

TAB 4-2:
Alternating draw and blow breaths for four beats each.

Playing quarter notes

In Tab 4-3 you play each breath for only one beat. You count the beats in groups of two; you inhale on the first beat and exhale on the second beat. Pay extra attention to starting each breath in time with the beat. Remember to breathe from your abdomen and sustain each breath for a full beat.

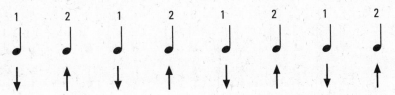

TAB 4-3:
Alternating draw and blow breaths for one beat each.

Repeating notes with articulation

When you repeat a note, you start it a second time. This new start is called an *articulation* because you create a new "article" in the form of a new note.

REMEMBER

When you repeat a note, you keep on breathing. You play a series of repeated notes on a single long breath, not by stopping and starting your breath in a series of puffs. You play two blow notes in a row on a single exhaled breath and two draw notes in a row on a single inhaled breath.

TIP

Try saying "kaakaakaakaa." You do this with one long, exhaled breath. Every time you make the "k" sound, you momentarily interrupt the flow of air by touching your tongue to the roof of your mouth. When you drop your tongue, the air flow resumes and you start a new note.

You've been saying "k" while you exhale for your whole life. But probably the only time you've ever said "k" while inhaling is when you've had the hiccups. So take a moment to get familiar with this sensation:

1. **Whisper "kaakaakaakaa" softly on an exhaled breath.**

2. **Now, try making the "k" sound without breathing.**

   Try it a few times and note the sensation of lifting your tongue and touching it to the roof of your mouth.

3. **Begin to inhale, gently and slowly as always.**

4. **As you draw breath into your mouth, gently raise your tongue to the roof of your mouth to make the "k" sound, and immediately let your tongue drop to let air continue to flow into your throat.**

5. **Repeat the "k" sound several times on a single inhaled breath until you start to feel familiar with the sensation.**

Try playing Tab 4-4, using the "k" sound to articulate each beat.

For more on the "k" sound, turn to Chapter 11, where you use this sound to bend notes.

TAB 4-4:
Articulating
repeated notes
with a "k."

Kaa-Kaa-Kaa-Kaa,   Kaa- Kaa-Kaa-Kaa,   Kaa-Kaa-Kaa-Kaa,   Kaa- Kaa-Kaa-Kaa.

Dividing the beat

When you play music, you often divide the beat into shorter notes, with two, three, or even four notes to the beat. Here you practice dividing the beat in two.

When you divide a quarter note in half, you get an *eighth note*. You can identify eighth notes in Tab 4-5 by the thick beam that binds each pair of eighth notes together. (For more on eighth notes, check out Chapter 3.)

When you count beats, you count the half beat as "and," as in "one, *and* two, *and* three, *and* four." When you write beats, you use numbers for the beats and the plus sign (+) for the "and."

Try playing Tab 4-5.

TIP

Look at the syllables under the breath arrows in Tab 4-5. Each breath starts with a simple "ah" because you don't need the "k" sound until you repeat the note.

Blues is very intuitive music, but it's not always straightforward. A good example of this paradox is the way you divide the beats into two parts. Sometimes you play *straight eighths* — you divide the beat into two parts that are equal in length. But when you play blues you often play *shuffle rhythm* (also known as *swing eighths*). When you play shuffle rhythm, the first part of the beat is twice as long as the second part; you're really dividing the beat into three parts.

PLAY THIS

On Track 2 you can hear Tab 4-5 played first with straight eighths and then in shuffle rhythm.

1 + 2 +   1 + 2 +   1 + 2 +   1 + 2 +   1 + 2 +

TAB 4-5:
Dividing the
beat in two.

Ah - ka - ka - ka,   Ah - ka - ka - ka,   Ah - ka - ka - ka,   Ah - ka - ka - ka,   Ah

Balancing your breath

When you play the harmonica, you don't always breathe in and out in equal amounts. As you play, you may often feel as if you're filling up with air and can't take in another molecule without floating away like a blimp. Or you may occasionally feel like you've expended all your air and are about to collapse into a heap, as if the big bang had suddenly kicked into reverse. In these situations, you need to balance your breath.

You can balance your breath before you start to play, between the notes, and even while you're playing a note.

TIP

>> **Before you start to play** you can inhale extra air if you know you're going to play a long series of exhaled notes. Or you can exhale more air than usual if you know you'll be playing a lot of inhaled notes.

To do this, start by finding your *balance point.* Inhale deeply and expand your rib cage. Then let your breath out and relax. Now you're at your balance point.

Now either inhale or exhale to compensate for the long blow or draw sequence, but not enough to make you feel uncomfortable. If you push yourself too far past the balance point, you'll feel physical distress, and you won't be able to play with confidence.

As you develop your breathing for harmonica playing, you can deliberately extend your breath supply — especially for blow notes — by pushing past the point of discomfort when you exhale, so that you can increase your ability to play long series of draw notes. After a while, your nervous system will get comfortable when you push past your accustomed limits.

>> **Between the notes** you can sometimes find pauses that occur naturally in the flow of the music, like the pause that you naturally take at the end of a phrase or sentence when you talk.

When you sneak a quick breath, you use the *jaw-drop breathing move.* This move allows you to avoid breathing air through the harmonica and making unwanted sounds. It also keeps the harmonica in your mouth so you can come back quickly to the holes you were just playing.

To do the jaw-drop breathing move, lower your jaw slightly, letting the harmonica rest on your lower lip. Inhale or exhale over the top of the harmonica, not through the holes. Raise your jaw again to resume contact between the harmonica and your upper lip, and continue playing.

Try out the jaw-drop breathing move by playing Tab 4-6. You play inhaled notes without interruption and start filling up with air pretty quickly.

 TAB 4-6:
Sneaking a breath with the jaw-drop breathing move.

Kaa - Kaa - Kaa - Kaa - Kaa - Kaa - Kaa - Kaa

TIP

Note the apostrophe-like sign just after the fourth beat. That's your breathing cue. Instead of continuing to inhale, drop your jaw just after the fourth beat and exhale, and then raise your jaw and continue to inhale.

>> **While you're playing a note**, you can open your nose to vent excess air during a blow note or to take in more air during a draw note. But be very careful not to make this a habit, as diverting air from the harmonica can weaken your tone and volume and reduce your control over the reed you're playing. If you're careful, though, you can minimize these effects when you vent air through your nose.

Try playing Tab 4-6. Open your nose to vent air during a blow note, and then close it again to inhale.

REMEMBER

When you play with your nose open, pay attention to the volume and tonal quality of the sound you make. Always strive to make your nose-open notes match the sound of the notes you play normally with your nose closed. Try playing Tab 4-7 to practice venting air through your nose.

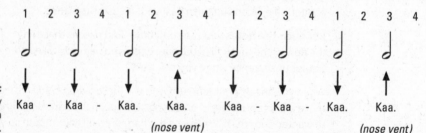

 TAB 4-7:
Venting air by exhaling through your nose.

Kaa - Kaa - Kaa. Kaa. Kaa - Kaa - Kaa. Kaa.

(nose vent) *(nose vent)*

 You can hear Tabs 4-6 and 4-7 on Track 3.

PLAY THIS

Chugging with train rhythms

By playing patterns of blow notes, draw notes, and repeated notes, you can imitate the rhythm of an old-time railroad train, complete with clattering wheels, puffing steam, and moaning whistle. The classic train imitation was a favorite showpiece of prewar rural harmonica players, and you can still hear echoes of the train tune in modern blues.

Some of the old-time train imitations are true feats of virtuosity, but I don't expect that level of playing from you — not yet, at least. I start you out with train sounds based on simple breathing patterns.

Tab 4-8 shows four different rhythmic breathing patterns. Play each one, repeating it until it becomes familiar. Then try combining the rhythms in sequence. When you combine them, repeat each one a few times for musical effect before moving on to the next.

REMEMBER

Use the "k" sound whenever you repeat a note. I left out the syllables in Tab 4-8 so that you can get used to adding them on your own.

TAB 4-8:
Four train
rhythms.

PLAY THIS

On Track 4, you can hear each of the rhythm patterns in Tab 4-8 and the whooping in Tab 4-9.

Whooping

When you make a sudden, short falsetto sound with your voice, you're *whooping*. Old-time blues harmonica players would play a *fox chase*, a rhythmic tune that sounds similar to a train imitation but depicts hunting with dogs instead of the sound of a train. To mimic the sound of dogs yelping, they'd replace a blow note with a whoop. Urban blues doesn't often take up the subject of hunting, but you may sometimes hear vocalizations such as moaning in between harmonica notes or phrases.

To whoop, drop the harp like you're sneaking a breath and then make a sound — a grunt, moan, bark, or whoop. You can fit a whoop into a sequence of notes by replacing one of the notes with a whoop. In Tab 4-9, the whoop replaces three blow notes where you see "WHOO."

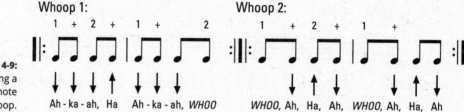

TAB 4-9:
Replacing a
blow note
with a whoop.

your tongue

» **Finding your starting hole and changing your breathing direction**

» **Moving from hole to hole and playing blues phrases**

Chapter 5

Moving Around with Single Notes

The harmonica is named for its capability to create harmony by sounding two or more notes at once. You can inhale or exhale in any group of holes and almost all combinations, or *harmonies*, will sound reasonably pleasing together. To play a melody, however, you need to play just one note at a time. When you do that, you're playing *single notes*, and you get single notes by isolating just one hole on the harmonica.

By the way, you may hear harmonica players talk about their *embouchure* (*awm-boo-shure*). This word comes from the French word *bouche*, which means "mouth," and it refers to whatever you do with your mouth to get a sound out of a wind instrument. Now that you've reached this part of the book, you can inform your friends that you've reached a new level of artistry and that you're deep in embouchure studies on the harmonica.

REMEMBER

Blues players never walk in a straight line, though, and their approach to embouchure is no exception. They have at least two different ways to play single notes, and they argue all the time about which one is best. Meanwhile, they find all sorts of ways to sneak harmonies in with single-note melodies (I get into that subject in Chapter 10).

Isolating a Single Note with Your Lips

When you play the harmonica, all the air you inhale or exhale goes through the harmonica. Your lips form a seal to keep air from escaping. They also determine how many holes are in your mouth, and therefore, how many notes you play at once.

To isolate a single note with your lips, you reduce the size of your mouth opening so that you direct air to just one hole. You can do this in a relaxed way, and with a little practice, you'll soon be playing single notes with your lips. This technique goes by several names, including *puckering*, *lip blocking*, and *lip pursing*. I prefer *puckering* and use that term in this book.

To get started with puckering, here I revisit the part in Chapter 4 where you get the harmonica in your mouth:

1. **Drop your jaw and open your mouth wide.**

2. **Insert the harmonica in your mouth until the harmonica touches the corners of your mouth, where your top and bottom lips meet.**

3. **Let your jaw close gently and let your lips fall onto the harmonica's covers.**

   Remember to keep your jaw and lips relaxed.

4. **Inhale gently, and continue to inhale as you perform the next steps.**

5. **Slowly raise your jaw.**

   You'll feel the harmonica being gently pushed out of your mouth. Important: Make sure to keep full-lip contact with the harmonica. Your upper lips, lower lips, and both corners should continue to form a relaxed, airtight seal with the harmonica.

6. **As your mouth opening shrinks, you'll be playing fewer and fewer holes.**

   Eventually, you'll be playing one hole and you'll hear only one note. If you get close and can't seem to isolate a single note, try moving the harmonica a tiny amount to the left or right, in case your mouth opening is straddling the border between two holes.

TIP

You don't need to squeeze your mouth into a tiny opening. Avoid tensing your lips, and avoid making a hole smaller than the hole in the harmonica, as doing so can obstruct airflow and make the harmonica unresponsive. Figure 5-1 shows how large your mouth opening can be and still isolate a single hole. Before taking this photograph, I played a single note and then maintained my mouth shape while moving the harmonica out of my mouth.

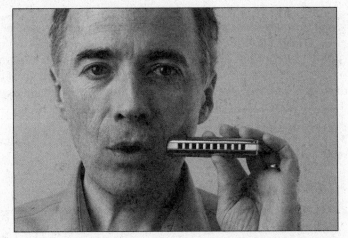

FIGURE 5-1:
Lips configured to play a puckered single note.

Photograph by Anne Hamersky

After you start to get the feel of playing a single note, try alternating between inhaled breaths and exhaled breaths. At first you may find that a neighboring hole starts to sound when you change breath direction. If that happens, pay attention to things you may be doing without thinking about them, and try to eliminate them:

>> Don't widen your lip opening or move your lips to the right or left.

>> Don't move the harmonica.

If the note sounds bad — choked, weak, or somehow wrong — tap any moisture out of the harmonica and then try playing the note again.

PLAY THIS

On Track 5 you can hear me isolating Hole 4 by starting with an inhaled chord, narrowing my embouchure to isolate the draw note in Hole 4, and then switching to Blow 4 and back to Draw 4.

Singling Out a Note with Your Tongue

Puckering is a straightforward and obvious way to play a single note. But many, perhaps most, blues harmonica players prefer to use another method, called *tongue blocking.* When you tongue block, you have several holes in your mouth, and you use your tongue to block the hole or holes you don't want to sound while leaving an opening at the right or left corner of your mouth for the holes that you do want to sound.

Tongue blocking allows you to keep your lips and jaw relaxed and keep the harmonica deep in your mouth, which promotes a rich tone. Just as important, tongue blocking allows for all sorts of special effects that you get by alternating between single notes and chords and by playing different combinations of the various holes that are in your mouth. (In Chapter 10 I describe the techniques you use to create these effects.)

Before trying a tongue-blocked single note, I want you to first get familiar with some of the physical sensations that can help guide you.

1. **Open your mouth as if to say, "ahhh."**

2. **Extend your tongue forward so that the tip of your tongue rests on your lower lip.**

Leave a space between your tongue and upper lips so that you can breathe through that opening. Also, pay attention to the right and left edges of your tongue. The edges of your tongue should be touching the right and left corners of your mouth.

3. **Lower your jaw by a tiny amount to open your mouth slightly wider.**

Keep contact between the left edge of your tongue and the left corner of your mouth. Let a gap open between the right edge of your tongue and the right corner of your mouth. You'll direct air through this gap to a single hole of the harmonica.

4. **Let your upper lip drop onto the surface of your tongue.**

The only place for air to move should now be the right corner of your mouth.

5. **Try breathing through the right corner of your mouth.**

Make sure that the opening is big enough that air can pass through easily. You shouldn't hear any sound or feel any pressure when you exhale or suction when you inhale.

Try simply breathing with a tongue block for awhile to get used to the feeling.

>> Remember to breathe only through your mouth and not through your nose.

>> Relax your jaw, lips, and tongue.

Figure 5-2 shows my tongue in position, ready to add a harmonica and play a tongue-blocked single note.

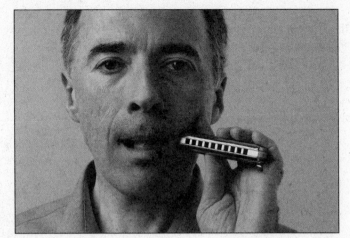

FIGURE 5-2:
Position of
lips and tongue
to play a
tongue-blocked
single note.

Photograph by Anne Hamersky

When you're ready to add the harmonica and isolate a single note with tongue blocking, do this:

1. Drop your jaw and open your mouth wide.

2. Place your tongue on your lower lip, with the left edge touching the left corner of your mouth, but with a gap between the right edge of your tongue and the right corner of your mouth.

3. Bring the harmonica up to your mouth and rest its bottom front edge on top of the tip of your tongue.

4. Insert the harmonica into your mouth until it touches both corners of your mouth.

5. Let your upper lip drop onto the harmonica's top cover.

6. Gently press your tongue forward so that the top surface of your tongue blocks all the holes except the one in the right corner of your mouth.

WARNING

Don't block holes using the tip of your tongue or the right or left edge of your tongue. Using the tip creates friction and drag when you try to slide the harmonica to the right or left and can abrade your tongue. Using the side edges makes several important tongue-blocking techniques difficult or impossible.

Now that you've formed a tongue block, try playing a note. Gently inhale or exhale. If you get a single note, congratulations! Now try breathing in the other directions, and again you may get a clear single note.

If you don't get an isolated note that sounds clear, you may need to make some adjustments.

» If you hear more than one note

- Try moving the harmonica slightly to the right or left in case you're straddling two holes.

- Try closing your mouth opening a tiny amount to bring the right corner of your mouth closer to your tongue and create a smaller opening.

» If the note sounds weak, muffled, or obstructed

- Tap any moisture out of the harmonica and try again.

- Try relaxing the tip areas of your tongue. Don't press hard on the holes, as doing so may push your tongue into obstructing the hole you want to play.

- Try opening your throat as if you're yawning, and make sure the back of your tongue isn't humped up close to the roof of your mouth and narrowing the airflow.

- Try relaxing your jaw or widening your lip opening to allow the opening in the right corner of your mouth to be big enough.

If you get a single note when you breathe in one direction but not in the other direction, make sure you're not changing your mouth formation or moving the harmonica when you change between inhaling and exhaling.

PLAY THIS

On Track 5 you can hear me playing tongue-blocked single notes in Hole 4.

Making Your First Moves

To play a note, first you find the hole where that note is located. When you get there, you either inhale or exhale to play the note you want. Optionally, you can alter the pitch of the note by bending it (see Chapter 11 for more on bending).

When you play a melody, you move from one note to another. To do that on the harmonica, you can

» Change the direction of your breath to sound a different reed.

» Move to another hole.

» Change both the hole and your breath direction.

You can also bend a note to alter its pitch as I describe in Chapter 11, but first you need to find the right hole and breathe in the right direction.

Finding your starting hole

You may know that a tune starts in Hole 4 and that the holes on most harmonicas are numbered, but you can't actually see the numbers under your nose as you play. So how do you find your starting hole? You can

>> **Count up as you play.** To do this, start at Hole 1 (which has no notes to its left) and play one continuous breath as you move the harmonica to the left, counting holes as you go until you reach your destination. (You can do this by counting down from Hole 10 if it's closer to the hole you're looking for.)

>> **Match the note you're hearing.** Listen to your target note on a recording or sound it on a keyboard or guitar while you try to find the same note on your harmonica.

>> **Memorize the physical location of the note.** If you always hold the harmonica the same way, you can eventually memorize the feel of where the note is on the harmonica in your hands.

For now, try finding your starting hole either by counting up from Hole 1 as you breathe or by matching the note you hear.

Changing between inhaled and exhaled notes

After you find your starting hole, you have to play the right starting note, which is either a blow note or a draw note. So your first job is to know which direction to breathe in and then do it. To play the next note, you can do one of several things:

>> Repeat the note you just played (see Chapter 4 for info on repeating a note).

>> Change the direction of your breath between inhaling and exhaling (a *breath change*).

>> Move to another hole (a *hole change*).

>> Simultaneously make both a hole change and a breath change.

In this chapter I take you through hole changes and breath changes, but you don't do both of them at once until you get to Chapter 6.

Playing your first single note blues

Your first blues song is "I Wanna Get Close to You," as shown in Tab 5-1. The singer delivers the melody while you add a nice harmony by playing some long notes. All you have to do is stay in Hole 4 and alternate between inhaled and exhaled notes.

TAB 5-1:
"I Wanna Get
Close to You."

TIP

You can play this song with a pucker embouchure or with a tongue block. I recommend that you try both.

To play the notes, look at the tab below the music notation. It tells you the sequence of action you perform on the harmonica — which hole to play and whether to blow or draw.

To get the timing correct, you can do one of three things:

» **Read the notation.** If you can read rhythmic notation, follow the rhythm and the tab at the same time.

» **Count the beats.** Coordinate your actions with the beat numbers written above the music:

1. Play your first note (Draw 4) starting on Beat 1 and continue through Beat 2.

2. In Beats 3 and 4, you play Blow 4.

3. In the next bar, you return to Draw 4 for Beats 1 and 2 and then rest for Beats 3 and 4.

4. Repeat Steps 1 through 3 two more times.

» **Follow the lyrics.** The words to the song are written under the tab. Start each new tabbed note at the same time as the word that appears underneath it. Most of the notes last for more than one syllable, though, so don't change breath every time you hear a new syllable.

To prepare for playing this song, first listen to the track a few times. As you listen, try counting beats out loud or following the written lyrics and observing the word that coincides with each new harmonica note. Then turn off the music, find Hole 4, and try playing the draw-blow-draw-rest sequence a few times before you try playing along with the track.

REMEMBER

If you haven't gotten the hang of single notes yet, don't worry. This song will sound fine, even with a little unintended harmony bleeding in from neighboring holes. But keep working on your single notes anyway.

When you feel ready to play along with the track

1. **Find your starting note (Draw 4) and sound it.**

2. **Turn on the music and listen for the count-in.**

   The beat after you hear "four" is where you start playing.

3. **Play through the tune with the recording a few times.**

   If you feel like you've made a mistake, don't stop. Keep going and keep playing. After a few tries you'll be groovin' with the band.

PLAY THIS

You can listen and play along with this tune on Track 6.

TIP

You can break your long notes into shorter notes that start with each new syllable of the lyrics so that you're more in sync with the singer. To do this, apply the note repetition techniques I show you in Chapter 4 to sound the syllables written below the lyrics in Tab 5-1. To hear the song played this way, listen to the second version of "I Wanna Get Close to You" on Track 6.

Playing Your First Blues Phrases

If you've worked through the preceding section, you've played a blues song with just two notes. Now it's time to start getting around on the harmonica to play more notes and shape them into short phrases.

Moving to a neighboring hole

Now that you've worked out a little with *breath changes* (changing between inhaled and exhaled breaths) in the preceding section, it's time to tackle *hole changes*, where you play a note in one hole and then move to another hole to play another note.

When you change holes, make the transition smooth by following these principles:

>> **Keep the harmonica in your mouth as you change holes.** That way you don't disturb the seal between your lips and the harmonica, alter the shape of your single-note embouchure, or lose your place on the harmonica.

>> **Breathe continuously as you change holes.** You want one note to flow into another, and this can't happen if you stop breathing between notes. Also, you get audible feedback if you breathe while you move from one hole to another — you can hear when you arrive at the hole you're moving to.

In Tab 5-2, you play a series of two-bar phrases that include hole changes and breath changes.

>> For now, ignore the brackets and titles above each two-bar phrase.

>> Get familiar with each phrase on its own before you play them all in sequence. Repeat each one several times until you're familiar with it and can play it without stopping.

>> Take a moment to breathe at the end of each two-bar phrase. Remember to drop your jaw with the harmonica resting on your lower lip and to breathe over the top of the harmonica.

TAB 5-2:
Two-bar phrases
with hole
changes.

PLAY THIS

You can listen and play along with the phrases in Tab 5-2 on Track 7.

Question-and-answer phrases

Often, two musical phrases form a pair. The first phrase sounds like it's asking a question, and the second phrase sounds like it's providing an answer. Sometimes, the answer doesn't sound conclusive, though, and the next phrase restates the question, with another answer that has more finality. This back-and-forth dialogue helps give form to musical statements and also holds your interest as a listener — you feel like you're hearing a conversation.

Look back at Tab 5-2 again. Each phrase is labeled as either a question or an answer. Note that Question 1 always precedes the answer. That pairing of first question and answer doesn't always happen in question-and-answer phrases, but it helps bring the music to a more final conclusion.

Always listen for question-and-answer phrasing in the music you hear, and try to include it when you make up your own blues phrases.

Finalizing your musical statement

Blues songs often have three large phrases in each verse. The first two are similar, and both leave the question hanging. But then the third phrase sums everything up and drives the verse to a conclusion, or "brings it on home," as blues musicians sometimes say.

Tab 5-3 is a full 12-bar blues verse. The first four bars contain a question with an inconclusive answer. The second four bars contain a different question that echoes the first one and then receives a similar answer. The last four bars are really one long phrase that drives the verse home to a conclusion by using longer sequences of notes that traverse a wider stretch of holes and employ fewer resting points that contain long notes.

You can listen to Tab 5-3 on Track 8.

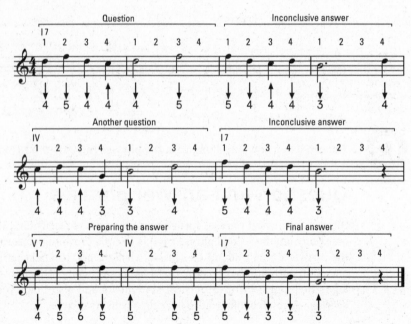

TAB 5-3:
A 12-bar blues verse with question-and-answer phrases.

Chapter 6

Creating Blues Harmonica Licks and Riffs

C offee and cream are wonderful on their own, but put them together and they are, as the French say, *formidable!* Your harmonica playing also becomes *formidable* when you can simultaneously move from one hole to another while changing between inhaled and exhaled breath directions.

In this chapter, you start synchronizing hole changes and breath changes. Then I introduce you to licks and riffs, the building blocks of blues melody. I also show you a powerful way to connect existing building blocks and to generate new ones by using pathways.

Combining Breath Changes and Hole Changes

In Chapter 5, I show you some simple phrases that require you to either change your breath direction or move from one hole to another, but never both at once. Now it's time to synchronize these actions so you can really get moving on some blues licks.

Taking your first step

In Tab 6-1, you prepare your first synchronized hole change and breath change. First you take an indirect note, using simple moves to reach the notes you're about to combine. Then, making your decisive move, you combine two actions into one:

1. **You start with a simple breath change in a single hole, going from Draw 4 to Blow 4 and then back to Draw 4.**

2. **Then you make simple hole changes on a single inhaled breath, going from Draw 4 to Draw 3 and back again.**

3. **Now that you've marked out the territory, combine a hole change with a breath change: Go from Draw 3 to Blow 4 and then go back and forth a few more times.**

PLAY THIS

You can hear and play along with Tab 6-1 on Track 9.

TAB 6-1:
Combining a breath change and a hole change.

As you make these daring leaps, you may get unexpected results:

>> You may change holes before you change breath direction. You'll reach your target hole and sound a note that you didn't intend to play.

>> You may change breath direction before you change holes. You'll sound an unintended note in your starting hole before you move anywhere.

Strive to change breath direction and hole simultaneously so that the only notes you hear are Draw 3 and Blow 4. However, if you do hit an unintended note, listen to the effect; you may like it and want to use it later when you're not trying for a precise, clean change.

TIP

Always listen to the effects that you create through mistakes or actions you stumble on without meaning to. Although no reliable statistics have been compiled, I wouldn't be surprised if at least 50 percent of all great blues harmonica playing effects were discovered by accident.

To hear the Draw 3-Blow 4 move in real-life blues, listen to the introductions to two Little Walter tunes, "My Babe" (played on a B♭ harp) and "Blues with a Feeling" (played on a D harp). Though Walter adds some fancy frills, he uses the same basic move between Draw 3 and Blow 4.

Extending the pattern

In this section you try the same move from the preceding section but you start in a different hole. Tab 6-2 takes you traveling through the area between Hole 3 and Hole 6.

1. **In the first line, you go directly to the move you made at the end of Tab 6-1.**

2. **In the second line, you shift one hole to the right and make the same move between Draw 4 and Blow 5.**

TAB 6-2: Extending the hole change–breath change pattern in "Pent-up Demand."

3. **In the third line, you shift one more hole to the right and make the same move between Draw 5 and Blow 6.**

4. **In the fourth line, you step back through the notes you just played to arrive at your starting move.**

You can hear and play along with Tab 6-2 on Track 10.

PLAY THIS

Tab 6-3 is "Easy Strides," a blues tune that uses the actions from Tabs 6-1 and 6-2.

You can hear Tab 6-3 on Track 11.

PLAY THIS

TAB 6-3: "Easy Strides."

Getting Acquainted with Licks and Riffs

When you play the blues, you use short sequences of notes called *licks* and *riffs* as building blocks for longer musical statements.

Both riffs and licks usually emphasize the notes of the chord being played in the background. Blues musicians often emphasize the notes of the home chord (the I chord), even when another chord is being played; blues tends to stick close to home in this way.

You can emphasize a note in several ways:

>> By playing the note on the beat instead of between two beats.

>> By playing the note on one of the strong beats in the bar (the first and third beats).

>> By holding the note for a long time.

>> By repeating the note.

>> By using a special effect, such as a bend, to bring attention to the note.

>> By playing the note louder than other notes.

Sometimes, instead of emphasizing a note that belongs to the underlying chord, you emphasize a note that creates tension, such as a non-chord tone or a blue note (see Chapter 3 for more on blue notes). Tension creates interest and a sense of movement. When you resolve a tension note to a chord tone, you create a sense of relief.

Discovering five common blues riffs

Riffs often help define the signature sound of a tune, and you usually repeat them several times in a verse of a song. Examples include a catchy rhythmic bass line that immediately identifies a tune before you hear the melody or a repeated melodic line played by melody instruments behind a singer.

Tab 6-4 shows you five of the most common riffs that most blues musicians know. Some of these riffs include bent notes; to play those, you may want to develop your bending skills with Chapter 11.

>> The first riff is a common bass line that's also often played by melody instruments. It uses the home note as both the lowest note (Draw 2) and the highest note (Blow 6) and places both home notes on the strong first beat.

- » The second riff is a common swing-era, big-band riff that has also been used in harmonica instrumentals such as Snooky Pryor's "Boogie" and, in a slightly altered version, Little Walter's "Juke." Like the first riff, it begins and ends on the song's home note, rising to place the final home note on the first beat of the bar.

- » John Lee Hooker often used the third riff, as did the band Canned Heat, notably on the song "On the Road Again," featuring the harmonica of Alan "Blind Owl" Wilson. Sonny Boy Williamson II also used this riff for the instrumental backing to his song "Help Me."

- » The fourth riff is often played behind a singer, who sings between each riff. Muddy Waters' "Hoochie Coochie Man," featuring Little Walter on harmonica, is probably the most famous of many songs to use this riff.

- » The fifth riff also punctuates statements by a singer. Bo Diddley used this riff most famously in "I'm a Man," with Billy Boy Arnold on harmonica.

PLAY THIS

You can hear all the riffs in Tab 6-4 on Track 12.

Getting your licks in

Licks tend to be shorter than riffs, and you can play them anywhere within a song and combine them with other licks in different sequences at will. Often a solo by a guitarist or harmonica player is just a showy, well-crafted series of licks.

TIP

In Tab 6-3, the first three notes you play in the first bar form a lick that you repeat in the second bar and then extend into a longer lick in the third and fourth bars. In the second four bars, you play different notes, but you also play a three-note sequence, repeat it, and then extend it into a longer lick. In the last four bars the pattern of short bursts is replaced by a long, seamless musical line that lasts most of the four bars.

Every blues instrument — from the guitar to the piano to the harmonica — has its characteristic licks that are convenient to play on that instrument and sound good. Every blues musician knows dozens, perhaps hundreds, of standard licks and has probably made up a few as well. And each player strings licks together in her own individual way. Over time you'll absorb a lot of standard licks just by listening to blues records and performances and then picking up a harmonica and trying to imitate what you hear.

Building Licks and Riffs with Pathways

When you want to get from one place to another, you might map out your route. Different routes let you see different sights, and you may make several stops along the way to visit different people or businesses. Each of those stops can be its own mini-trip. On some days you may traverse only one or two parts of the route, and on other days you might go the whole distance.

When you play blues, different licks are like those mini-trips, and a *pathway* is the entire route. Each pathway may have its own mood or character, like the sights along a particular route. Sometimes each step along a pathway employs the same set of breath and hole changes, just moved one hole to the left or right for each leg of the journey.

In this section I show you a few key pathways, and by playing them you'll discover how to play several common, useful licks that you often hear when you listen to other harp players. You can also use pathways to explore and to come up with your own original licks.

Creating a pathway

Tab 6-5 shows a pathway that I'll call Pathway No. 1. It extends from Draw 1 to Draw 6. It ends at Hole 6 because Holes 7 through 10 follow a different note layout. To follow this pathway, you use a consistent series of actions.

To go up in pitch, you use a repeating pattern of draw, then shift, and then blow:

1. **You play a draw note in your starting hole.**

2. **You shift one hole to the right and play a blow note.**

3. **After the blow note, you can stay in the same hole and start the sequence again with another draw note.**

To come down, you use a pattern of draw, then blow, and then shift:

1. **You draw and then blow in the same hole.**

2. **Then you shift one hole to the left and repeat the sequence.**

Pathway No. 1

First lick   Second lick

Third lick   Fourth lick

TAB 6-5:
Pathway No. 1.

Tab 6–5 also includes some licks derived from Pathway No. 1.

You can hear Tab 6–5 on Track 13.

PLAY THIS Most of Tab 6–1 follows Pathway No. 1.

Tabs 6–2 and 6–3 both follow Pathway No. 1 but move around along the pathway to create licks and longer lines.

In Tab 6–2

» Each of the first two measures contains a one-bar lick, and the last two bars contain a longer lick that uses the same back-and-forth movement.

>> The second and third lines do the same things as the first line, using different pairs of holes but all along the same pathway.

>> The last line continues to follow the pathway but strings several one-bar licks together to create a longer line. Each of the first three one-bar licks uses identical moves but plays them in a different pair of holes, shifting one hole to the right each time.

In Tab 6-3, you can see the method I use in Tab 6-2 to construct a 12-bar blues melody: short licks and then longer extensions, ending in an extended line that follows the same path.

TIP

A famous harmonica instrumental that follows Pathway No. 1 pretty closely is Big Walter Horton's "Easy."

Tab 6-6 shows another, shorter pathway that can generate several blues licks, together with a few of the common licks that follow that pathway.

PLAY THIS

You can hear Tab 6-6 on Track 14.

By the way, if you go around talking to other harmonica players about "Pathway No. 1" or "Pathway No. 2," you'll probably get some strange looks. These pathways aren't inscribed in some secret book of blues rules. I'm just using these names as convenient labels.

Finding short pathway licks

Most pathways contain chord notes and non-chord notes that act as connectors between the chord notes. Short licks concentrate on as little as one chord note and one non-chord note or perhaps as many as three of each. When you explore a pathway, try to

>> Concentrate on a short stretch of the path.

>> Emphasize chord notes but also experiment with emphasizing non-chord notes.

>> Play around with different beginning and ending notes for the lick. The beginning and ending note can be the same — you can go away from your starting note and come back to it.

>> The lick can move in one direction — up or down — or can move both up and down.

TAB 6-6:
Pathway No. 2.

>> You can leap from point to point on the path. You're not required to always proceed step by step through the scale.

>> You can keep repeating the same series of notes, cycling around in a rhythmic way.

Remember, paths aren't rigid; they're simply ways to explore the notes in your harmonica.

Extending pathway licks into longer lines

Many shorter licks follow one of the two pathways I describe in the earlier "Creating a pathway" section. However, when you create longer musical lines, you may or may not follow a single pathway. You might start on one pathway and end on another. No rules exist, and you're free to mix and match to the extent of your creativity. The whole idea of pathways is to make the infinite possibilities a little easier to explore, not to trip you up with rules.

When you create a longer line, think of where you want it to start, how long you want it to run, and where you want it to end. Then try using the different pathways from the beginning note to the ending note. The more you do this, the more you'll be able to identify what other players are doing when you hear them.

Chapter **7**

Progressing Through the 12-Bar Blues

You can give a bluesy tinge to styles such as rock, jazz, bluegrass, and country by adapting blues techniques to those styles. But when the blues goes home, takes off its shoes, and relaxes, it plays songs that lend themselves to a natural, easy expression of bluesy feelings. Most of those songs follow a form called the *12-bar blues*. In addition to being 12 bars in length, the 12-bar blues has its own internal logic. After you grasp that logic and use it to shape your phrases, playing the blues will seem as natural as talking. Even if you don't yet have a large vocabulary, you'll quickly start to feel like a fluent speaker.

The Three Parts of 12-Bar Blues

A verse of 12-bar blues has three parts, and each part is 4 bars long. Each part does several things:

>> It advances the narrative of the words.

>> It builds on the previous part.

>> It prepares the following part.

Some 12-bar blues just use one background chord that plays behind the entire tune. However, most blues tunes have a *chord progression*, or sequence of chords. Each part of the blues verse starts with a different chord, and that helps you know where you are in the verse. Musicians have come up with thousands of variations and sophisticated elaborations on the 12-bar blues chord progression. However, here I stick with the most basic, down-to-earth version. It uses just three chords, which I identify by their relationships with one another, using roman numerals:

>> The I (one) chord, which is also the *home chord* that's identified with the song's key

>> The IV (four) chord, four scale steps above the I chord

>> The V (five) chord, five scale steps above the I chord

(For more on chords and how they're built, have a look at Chapter 3.)

Figure 7-1 shows a 12-bar blues as a *chord chart*, which shows you the chord progression of a tune and how long each chord lasts. Each diagonal slash represents one beat, with the vertical bar lines marking the end of each 4-beat bar. The chords in parentheses are optional. They don't occur in the very simplest version of the 12-bar blues, but players use them very often.

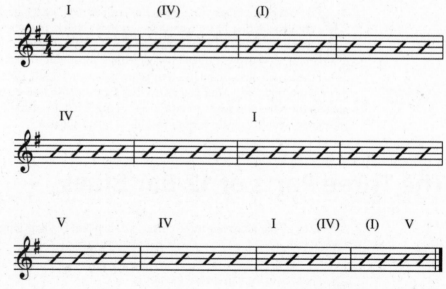

FIGURE 7-1:
Chord chart for a 12-bar blues verse.

Illustration by Wiley, Composition Services Graphics

Setting the stage with the first part

The first part of a 12-bar blues verse is often called the I (the "one") because it establishes the I chord and often stays on that chord for all 4 bars. This is where you make your first instrumental statement or sing the first line of the verse. With the same chord for 4 whole bars, you're free to make your opening statement without having to think too much about what's happening in the background.

But what's that IV chord doing in parentheses in the second bar in Figure 7-1? That's an *early IV*. The guitar player got impatient and decided to give you a little advance taste of the IV chord that's coming up soon, but then he went back to the I chord and behaved himself for the third and fourth bars. The early IV is in parentheses because it's optional; the band may play it in some verses and not in others, even within the same song.

Going somewhere with the second part

The second part of the blues verse is often referred to as the IV (the "four") because it starts on the IV chord before going back to the I chord. This *chord change* from the I to the IV is the first significant change in background chords that happens in the verse.

When you sing over the second part of the verse, you usually repeat the words that you just sang over the I chord. You also sing the same melody notes — almost. I go into more detail about this later in the chapter.

Though the first part of the verse stays on the I chord for the entire 4 bars, the second part spends 2 bars on the IV chord and then 2 bars back on the I chord. The chords start to go by faster as the verse progresses.

Raising the roof and taking it home with the third part

The third part of the blues verse starts on the V chord, so it's often called the V (the "five"). When you sing over it, you usually sing different words that form a conclusion to the statement that was repeated over the verse's first two parts. Sometimes, the third part of the tune uses the same melody as the first two parts, but usually, the melody changes for this part.

The V chord adds tension that pulls you back in the I chord's direction, but by resisting, you create some energy near the end of the verse. Instead of just plunging directly back to the I chord, the V moves down to the IV after just one bar for one more bar, and finally back to the I. So now the chords are coming even faster, spaced only one bar apart.

I call this stepping down from the V to the IV and back to the I the *comedown* because, well, you're coming down through the chords.

When you land on the I chord, though, you're not done. The verse's last two bars are called the *turnaround*, which can happen a few different ways:

>> In the simplest form of the turnaround, you just stay on the I chord for the remainder of the verse.

>> Almost always, though, you end with the V chord, which often comes on the second half of the second beat of the last measure.

>> In the most elaborate form of the turnaround, shown in parentheses in Figure 7-1, you cycle through a quick succession of chords that last only 2 beats each and end on the V chord, spiking a little extra tension.

Note how the rate of chord change speeds up through the verse, from 4 bars, to 2, to 1, to every half bar. This accelerating rate of change stirs up energy that helps propel the song into the next verse, where you can spend the first part just hanging out on the I chord again for 4 bars.

Relating Each Part of the Verse to the Harmonica's Chords

Each chord in a 12-bar blues has a counterpart on the harmonica. As each chord plays in the background, you can play licks and riffs that feature that chord's notes. This approach sounds logical, and sometimes you'll use it. But people, can I get a witness? I'm talking about the blues here. The blues can play nice and be sensible, but the blues always finds its own spin — its own little wrinkle that makes the music even more blues but never, ever moves in a straight line.

In the following sections I try to describe how the blues and the harmonica interact to create music in the 12-bar blues verse. In attempting to describe this mystery, vast fortunes have been lost, clearheaded philosophers have lost their minds, and whole armies have vanished, never to be seen again. But sometimes it takes a fool (or is that a dummy?) to find the hidden treasure. Here goes.

The magnetic lure of the home chord

Blues has a tendency to emphasize the notes of the home chord even when other chords are playing. This practice may have a historical root in combining African chants that fit with a single home chord (or no chord at all) and adding chords to them. Playing the home chord's notes against other chords can have several different effects:

» Emphasizing the home chord while other chords are playing can create a drone-like, hypnotic effect that works well with some blues songs.

» Sometimes, the home chord's notes just sound good. (Wanna hear a long, complicated explanation using music theory? Maybe another time.)

» Sometimes, the home chord's notes also belong to another chord being played.

» Sometimes, the notes of the home chord clash with the chord being played, creating tension (and excitement) that you resolve by moving to another note.

» Sometimes, you *inflect* the home chord's notes — you lower (or sometimes raise) them slightly in pitch — so they fit better with the chord being played. In the next few sections I show you how to inflect the home chord when you play over the IV and V chords.

REMEMBER

In this chapter I relate the 12-bar blues to the harmonica when you play it in second position, such as playing in the key of G on a C harmonica. In Chapters 12, 13, and 14, I discuss playing 12-bar blues in first and third positions, the other two often-used positions.

The I chord and the first phrase

When you play over the I chord, you focus on the notes of the home chord. Figure 7-2 shows the home chord's notes in second position.

In Holes 1 through 6, these notes are mostly draw notes that bend down — perfect for bluesy wailing, which is why most players concentrate on that region of the harmonica.

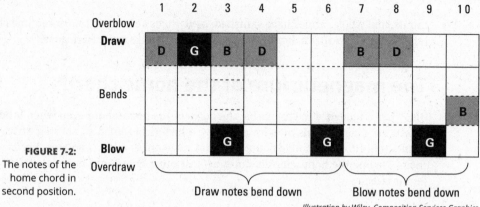

FIGURE 7-2:
The notes of the
home chord in
second position.

Illustration by Wiley, Composition Services Graphics

Leaning on the pretty notes

Along with the home chord's notes, you can add some notes that lend a cheerful feeling to your licks and riffs. This group of five notes is called the *major pentatonic scale.* Figure 7-3 shows the major pentatonic scale on the harmonica.

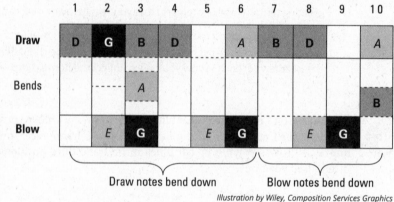

FIGURE 7-3:
The home chord
with cheerful
added notes
(the major
pentatonic scale).

Illustration by Wiley, Composition Services Graphics

Tab 7-1 shows some typical licks and riffs you can play over the I chord using the major pentatonic scale.

PLAY THIS

You can hear and play along with Tab 7-1 on Track 15.

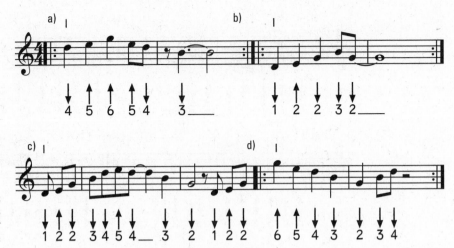

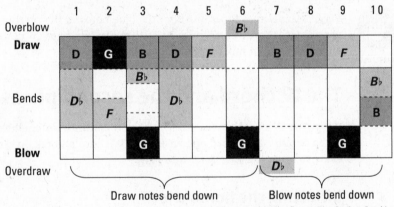

TAB 7-1:
Licks and riffs using the major pentatonic scale.

Getting funky with the blue notes

When you want a more hard-edged, darker sound, you can focus on the blue notes, adding them to the notes of the home chord. You can see the blue notes added to the home chord on the harmonica note layout in Figure 7-4.

	1	2	3	4	5	6	7	8	9	10
Overblow						B♭				
Draw	D	G	B	D	F		B	D	F	
Bends	D♭	F	B♭	D♭						B♭ B
Blow			G			G			G	
Overdraw							D♭			

Draw notes bend down   Blow notes bend down

FIGURE 7-4:
The blues scale.

Illustration by Wiley, Composition Services Graphics

Tab 7-2 shows some typical licks and riffs you can play over the I chord while focusing on the blue notes.

PLAY THIS

You can hear and play along with Tab 7-2 on Track 16.

TAB 7-2:
Licks and riffs
focusing on the
blue notes over
the I chord.

REMEMBER

Players sometimes focus on either the blue notes or the pretty notes of the major pentatonic. However, no rules exist that say you have to use one or the other, and players often mix them together freely.

The IV chord and the second phrase

When the IV chord comes along, you can continue to emphasize the I chord's notes or you can instead emphasize the IV chord's notes. In both instances, you can also bring the blue notes into play.

Inflecting the home chord

During the IV7 chord, you lower the 3rd degree of the scale (B to B♭). The IV7 chord contains the flat 3 (a blue note), and the nonflat 3 may clash.

In second position, you can play the flat 3 by

» Bending Draw 3 down a semitone in the low register.

» Playing a 6 Overblow in the middle register (you can't bend Draw 7 down).

» Bending Blow 10 down two semitones in the high register.

You're not required under penalty of law to flatten the 3rd degree of the scale during the IV chord. Some players claim that you must always do this. But listen to harmonica greats such as Little Walter and you'll hear them breaking this "law" when it suits them. As always, your ear must be the final judge of whether to flatten the third.

Figure 7-5 highlights the home chord with notes inflected to fit the IV chord.

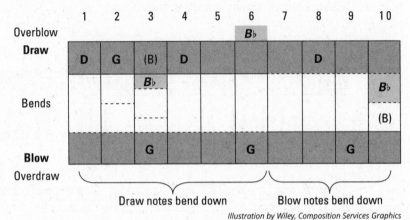

FIGURE 7-5:
Home chord notes inflected to fit the IV chord.

Illustration by Wiley, Composition Services Graphics

Tab 7-3 shows a few licks first played over the I chord and then inflected and played over the IV chord.

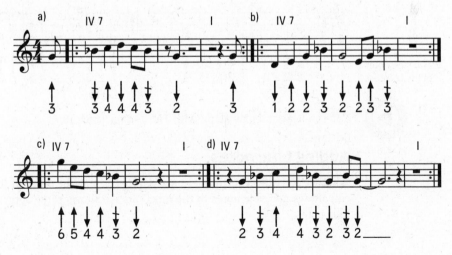

TAB 7-3:
Inflecting licks over the IV chord.

You can hear and play along with Tab 7-3 on Track 17.

PLAY THIS

Playing the notes of the IV chord

When your guitarist or piano player goes to the IV chord, you can play the IV chord's notes instead of staying with the I chord. When you play in second position, all the harmonica's blow notes are part of the IV chord. You can connect the notes of the chord using whatever notes lie in between them. Tab 7-4 shows some licks based on the blow chord's notes.

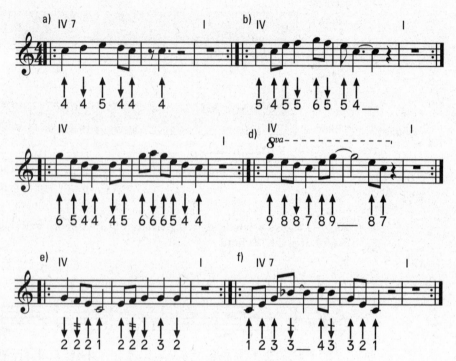

TAB 7-4:
Playing the notes of the IV chord.

You can hear and play along with Tab 7-4 on Track 18.

PLAY THIS

Adding blue notes

Whether you inflect the home chord's notes or play the notes of the IV chord, you can always add blue notes to the mix. Tab 7-5 shows some approaches to adding blue notes.

TAB 7-5:
Playing blue
notes over the
IV chord.

TIP

The flat 3 blue note works as part of the IV7 chord, but the flat 7 and flat 5 clash with it — in a good way. You can resolve the tension created by these notes by moving down a semitone. The flat 5 goes down to the 4th degree of the scale (the root of the IV chord), and the flat 7 goes down to the 6th degree of the scale (the third of the IV chord).

PLAY THIS

You can hear and play along with Tab 7-5 on Track 19.

The V chord and the third phrase

When you play in second position, the harmonica gives you a full I chord (Draw 1, 2, 3, and 4) and a full IV chord (all the harmonica's blow notes). But it doesn't give you a "correct" V chord, only a sort-of version. Yet that sort-of version can be very powerful. But players also master the deep bends in Holes 2 and 3 so they can create the notes of a proper V chord.

Inflecting the home chord

During the V7 chord you can create the third of the chord (F♯). When you do this, you can either lower the 1st degree of the scale (G) or raise the flat 7 (F). In second position you can play the third of the V chord by

>> Bending Draw 2 down a semitone in the low register.

>> Playing a 5 Overblow in the middle register.

>> Bending Blow 9 down a semitone in the high register.

You can see this on the note layout in Figure 7-6.

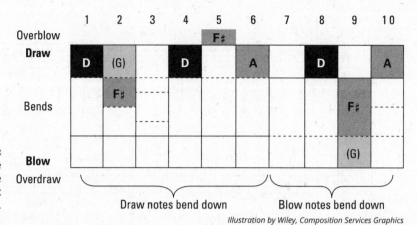

	1	2	3	4	5	6	7	8	9	10
Overblow					F♯					
Draw	D	(G)		D		A		D		A
Bends		F♯							F♯	
Blow									(G)	
Overdraw										

Draw notes bend down   Blow notes bend down

Illustration by Wiley, Composition Services Graphics

FIGURE 7-6:
Inflecting the notes of the home chord to fit with the V chord.

TIP

You don't always need to play the third of the V chord. You can just play the flat 7 of the scale, a blue note, for a harder-edged sound. You can even play the 1st degree of the scale, though it tends to clash. Again, try all three possibilities. Each one may sound best in a particular situation.

Tab 7-6 shows some licks you can play when you inflect the home chord over the V chord.

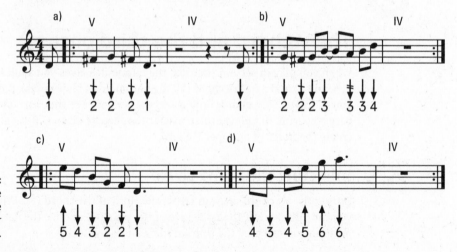

TAB 7-6:
Inflecting the notes of the home chord over the V chord.

PLAY THIS

You can hear and play along with Tab 7-6 on Track 20.

Digging in with the blue notes

The flat 5 blue note is a semitone below the V chord's root note. If you bend Draw 1 or Draw 4 to play this blue note, you can release the bend to arrive on the root note in a powerful way.

The flat 3 blue note clashes with the fifth of the V chord, but you can play it for a hard-edged sound and then move down a semitone. You can do this by bending Draw 3 down a semitone for the flat 3 blue note and then bending it down one more semitone.

The flat 7 blue note is a semitone below the third of the V chord. This clash is at the heart of the blues sound. Play this blue note unapologetically by wailing on Draw 5, on Draw 2 bent down two semitones, and on Draw 9.

Figure 7-7 shows the notes of the V chord (D, F♯, and A) together with the blue notes. Tab 7-7 demonstrates all three blue notes played against the V chord.

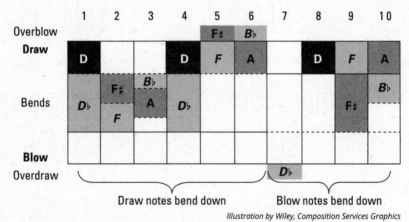

Illustration by Wiley, Composition Services Graphics

FIGURE 7-7:
Blue notes against the V chord.

PLAY THIS

You can hear and play along with Tab 7-7 on Track 21.

Exploring the notes of the V chord

Instead of inflecting the I chord or leaning on blue notes, you can play licks and riffs that outline the V chord's actual notes. In second position, some of the V7 chord's notes aren't built in, and you have to bend notes to get them. Traditional blues players often bend Draw 2 and 3 to create those notes and sometimes bend Blow 9 as well. More recently, players have started using 5 Overblow instead of relying on the blue note in Draw 5. Tab 7-8 shows some licks and riffs you can play using the V chord's notes.

TAB 7-7: Blue notes against the V chord.

TAB 7-8: Exploring the notes of the V chord.

PLAY THIS

You can hear and play along with Tab 7-8 on Track 22.

Dodging through the fast-changing chords of the last part of the verse

The chords change quickly during the comedown and the turnaround in the third part of the blues verse. How do you navigate through them without playing a wrong note? Doing this is a little like shooting the rapids in a raft — you hang on for dear life and try to avoid the big rocks while the water hurls you forward.

During the comedown, the V and IV chords each last a full bar, so you have four beats to lean on a chord note or a blue note, inflect the I chord, or play a lick that outlines the chord of the moment.

When the turnaround comes, though, the chords last only two beats each. That's the stretch where you can either coast on long notes or whip up some froth with a fast series of notes without thinking too much about how they fit with the chord. The important thing is that you drive toward a conclusion and then land on the V chord at the very end.

Tab 7-9 shows you a few different ways of getting through the blues verse's home stretch.

PLAY THIS

You can hear and play along with Tab 7-9 on Track 23.

Playing tunes to explore these approaches

When you listen to a blues harmonica player, you may hear her staying with one approach, whether it's chasing each chord, inflecting the home chord, or leaning on blue notes. However, much of the time, a player varies her approach to create variety. But to get a feel for each approach, try playing the following tabs. As you get familiar with hearing and playing them, you'll start to notice how the best players use, mix, and vary these approaches.

TIP

Try using some of the licks in the rest of the chapter to fashion your own verses, adapting them to each part of a 12-bar blues verse.

Tab 7-10 stays on the home chord through a verse of 12-bar blues.

TAB 7-9: Shooting the rapids on the home stretch.

TAB 7-10: Staying on the home chord through a 12-bar blues in "The Denver Coast."

PLAY THIS

You can hear and play along with Tab 7-10 on Track 24.

Tab 7-11 follows the outline of each chord through a 12-bar blues.

PLAY THIS

You can hear and play along with Tab 7-11 on Track 25.

TAB 7-11: Following the chords through a 12-bar blues in "Boppin' the Beat."

Tab 7-12 inflects the home chord through a verse of 12-bar blues.

PLAY THIS

You can hear and play along with Tab 7-12 on Track 26.

Tab 7-13 leans on the blue notes through a verse of 12-bar blues.

PLAY THIS

You can hear and play along with Tab 7-13 on Track 27.

TAB 7-12: Inflecting the home chord through a 12-bar blues in "White on Rice."

TAB 7-13: Leaning on the blue notes through a 12-bar blues in "Mud Crawl."

Shaping Your Statements in 12-Bar Blues

Knowing how to relate the three parts of the 12-bar blues verse to the harmonica's notes is the *what* of playing 12-bar blues. The *how* is even more important, and in this section I show you the *how* of shaping your statements. Every musical statement has a beginning, an end, and some kind of relationship with what goes before and what comes after. When you play blues phrases, licks, riffs, and melodies, the easiest way to understand how they begin and end and relate to one another is to start with the beats of the bar and where each statement begins and ends in relation to those beats.

If the bar's first beat is the strongest beat, then beginning or ending a musical statement such as a lick, riff, or melody on that strong beat makes for a strong statement. Blues players often do start statements — riffs especially — on the first beat. However, blues players often start and end statements in two characteristic ways that don't involve starting on the first beat. I explain these two ways in the next sections.

Leading into the first beat with a pickup

A *pickup* is a short series of notes that leads up to a note played on the first beat of a bar. When you arrive at the first beat, you can do one of three things:

>> **Land:** Arrive on the first beat and end there, either hitting the note and stopping or holding the note for several beats.

>> **Bounce:** Arrive on the first beat and then repeat the note a few times.

>> **Extend:** Arrive on the first beat and then extend the statement by continuing with other notes.

Tab 7-14 shows all three approaches to arriving on the first beat after a pickup. Note that the pickup usually starts after the third beat of the preceding bar.

PLAY THIS

You can hear and play along with Tab 7-14 on Track 28.

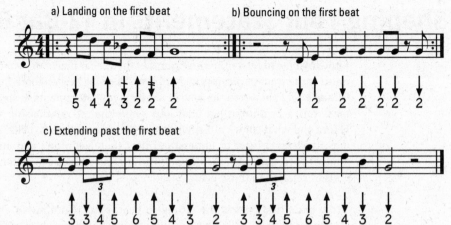

a) Landing on the first beat   b) Bouncing on the first beat

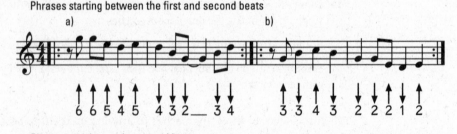

c) Extending past the first beat

TAB 7-14:
Using a pickup to
the first beat.

Starting after the first beat

Blues statements often begin after the first beat, either between the first and second beats for a more casual, swinging feel or directly on the second beat for a
more insistent effect. Statements that begin this way don't often end on the first
beat. Tab 7-15 shows statements starting after the first beat.

PLAY THIS

You can hear and play along with Tab 7-15 on Track 29.

Phrases starting between the first and second beats

a)   b)

Phrases starting on the second beat

c)   d)

TAB 7-15:
Starting after the
first beat.

Combining both approaches with riff-and-vocal phrasing

Many blues songs alternate between a riff played by the band and a line of vocal. The riff uses a pickup to land on the first beat, and then the singer starts after the first beat, as shown in Tab 7-16, where the vocal rhythm is shown in notes with x-shaped note heads.

You can hear and play along with Tab 7-16 on Track 30.

Listen to blues songs and harmonica instrumentals and try to identify when a phrase starts on the beat, when it starts with a pickup to the first beat (and what happens after the first beat), and when it starts after the first beat. Then try to incorporate these approaches into your own playing.

TAB 7-16:
Riff-and-vocal phrasing in "Are you Lyin'?"

3
Beyond the Basics: Getting Bluesy

IN THIS PART . . .

You delve deeper into the resources the harmonica offers for playing blues, such as bending notes and making your notes sound richer and fuller with tongue-blocked enhancements. You also work on opening up the harmonica's low and high registers for exploration, find out how to apply special texture effects such as warbles, and discover how to make the harmonica "talk" with your hands.

IN THIS CHAPTER

» Sounding notes clearly in the low and high registers

» Discovering the unique possibilities of the low register

» Navigating the notes of the high register

Chapter 8

Working with the Low and High Registers of the Harmonica

The ten holes of the diatonic harmonica divide into three distinct but overlapping *registers*, as shown in Figure 8-1. Each register covers four consecutive holes and is distinguished by

- A unique note layout
- Unique note-bending possibilities
- A distinctive way of responding to your breath

	Low register				Low register			High register		
Hole	1	2	3	4	5	6	7	8	9	10
Draw	D	G	B	D	F	A	B	D	F	A
Blow	C	E	G	C	E	G	C	E	G	C

FIGURE 8-1: The three registers of the diatonic harmonica (C-harp).

Illustration by Wiley, Composition Services Graphics

To really master the harmonica's expressive potential, take some time to get familiar with all three registers:

» **The low register:** This register covers Holes 1 through 4. It was originally designed to provide chords to accompany melodies played in the middle register, and it has notes missing from the scale. However, the low register is where most blues playing is focused, and it's also the register with the juiciest note-bending possibilities.

» **The middle register:** The middle register covers Holes 4 through 7. It was originally designed to be the main focus of melody playing. The middle register provides a complete scale, and its reeds respond more easily than those of the low and high registers. However, blues players use it as a seamless extension of the low register.

» **The high register:** The high register covers Holes 7 through 10. It was originally designed to provide an upper extension to the middle register for melody playing. This register has the most confusing note layout. Perhaps for that reason, blues players have traditionally used the high register the least, except for first position blues (see Chapter 13 for more on first position). However, modern players use the high register more and more in their second and third position playing as well.

The rest of this chapter shows you how to get the most from the high and low registers.

Getting Low and High Notes to Sound Clearly

Most players have no trouble getting notes to sound clearly in the harmonica's middle register, but they often experience difficulty in getting notes to sound clearly in the low and high registers. You can approach these problems in three different ways:

» **Blame the instrument.** Though you may have gotten a bad instrument, most harmonicas are just fine straight from the factory. Before you fling your harmonica into the trash while muttering curses under your breath or spend big bucks getting a technician to adjust your harp, try working on your playing technique.

>> **Use excessive force.** When a note seems reluctant to sound, especially in the high register, some players try to force the note to sound by breathing hard and attacking the note strongly. Yet you can get the note to sound far more easily if you know how to persuade it into responding.

>> **Work on your technique.** Use the advice in the next two sections to improve the response and sound of your notes in the low and high registers.

The dying cow syndrome in the low register

Draw 1 and especially Draw 2 are notes that have a frustrating tendency to sound like dying cows or foghorns with clinical depression. Instead of sounding clearly, they moan, and not in a good way. How can you get them to cheer up?

The problem is that you're *pre-bending* the notes. Though you may spend weeks of effort trying to learn to bend notes down (see Chapter 11 for more on bending), that moaning sound you hear from Draw 1 and 2 is you bending the note without meaning to and without even knowing how — hence the term *pre-bending*.

TIP

When you pre-bend you usually obstruct the flow of air at some point between your lungs and the harmonica. Try playing Draw 1 or 2 and then removing the harmonica from your mouth as you continue to breathe. If you hear any sound of air moving, you're obstructing airflow.

To remove obstructions to airflow and get Draw 1 and 2 to sound clearly, try these actions:

>> **Make sure you're not obstructing the hole with your lips or tongue.**

   The opening in your lips needs to be slightly bigger than the hole you're playing to allow air to flow easily between your mouth and the harmonica.

>> **Make sure that your tongue isn't obstructing the flow of your breath.**

   Your tongue should lie like a rug on the floor of your mouth. Air should be able to flow freely over the top of your tongue. Pay special attention to the area where you make the sound "k." If your tongue is humped up in this area, it can bend the note down, so make sure that this area is open.

   If you're tongue blocking, air should be able to flow freely past your tongue's free side.

>> **Make sure your throat is open.**

   Try yawning. When you yawn you open up your throat to easily move a lot of air between your mouth and lungs without obstruction.

>> **Lower your jaw.**

Doing this can open up more space inside your mouth and can help prevent pre-bending.

>> **Breathe deeply from your abdomen.**

Your abdomen should expand outward when you inhale and contract slightly when you exhale. The more you use your abdomen, the more air you can move, and this allows a reed to sound more easily.

TIP

As you work on getting Draw 1 and Draw 2 to sound clearly, here are a few helpful hints:

>> **Give yourself an example of the sound you're trying to achieve.**

Blow 3 produces the same note as Draw 2, so alternate between the two and work on making Draw 2 match the sound of Blow 3.

>> **Make sure the reeds aren't clogged with saliva.**

An obstructed reed can sound as if you're pre-bending, so periodically tap the moisture out of the reeds by holding the harmonica holes down in one hand and tapping the holes lightly against the palm of your other hand.

>> **Try playing Draw 1 and 2 on other keys of harmonica.**

If you have harmonicas in lower keys, such as G, A, or B♭, or in higher keys, such as D, E, or F, try playing Draw 1 and Draw 2 on those harmonicas. You may find that you pre-bend only within a certain range of keys. Playing harmonicas in keys where you don't pre-bend can at least let you get accustomed to playing those notes without frustration and may help you overcome pre-bending in the keys where it affects your playing.

Reluctant notes and squeals in the high register

At the best of times, dogs and cats aren't fond of the high-frequency energy that the harmonica emits. But even humans can be distressed by the shrill, metallic sounds that you can get from the harmonica's high register. Sometimes, you may find that you can't get any sound at all from those stubborn high reeds unless you use a lot of breath force.

Oddly, you can get the high reeds to sound easily — and even make sweet sounds — by using a gentle approach to let the notes float out instead of wrestling the reeds into submission under protest.

To get the high notes to sound clearly, try these actions:

>> **Keep your lips open to let air flow easily.**

All the harmonica's holes are the same size, even the ones in the high register. So don't pinch your mouth opening to play high notes. Instead, make sure that your mouth opening is as big as you can make it and still get a single note.

If you're tongue blocking, make sure that the edge of your tongue isn't crowding the hole.

>> **Drop your jaw.**

When you lower your jaw, you open up your oral cavity. Doing this helps air to flow easily.

>> **Pay attention to the tip of your tongue.**

If you're puckering, rest the tip of your tongue on the floor of your mouth, lightly touching your lower lip or the back of your lower teeth.

If you're tongue blocking, tuck the tip of your tongue under the front edge of the harmonica, with plenty of space between the top of your tongue and the roof of your mouth.

>> **Pay attention to the K-spot.**

For easy airflow, lower the part of your tongue that touches the roof of your mouth to make the "k" sound. (For more on the K-spot, see Chapter 11.)

>> **Keep your throat wide open.**

Try yawning and notice how your throat opens wide. Try to keep your throat open as you play.

>> **Breathe gently and deeply from your abdomen.**

Feel your abdomen expand as you gently inhale and contract as you gently exhale.

Unlocking the Power of the Low Register

The low register was designed for playing several holes at once to supply chords. When you play blues, you couple that chordal strength with your ability to select notes with your tongue and the expressive power of bending notes.

Making sense of the missing notes

The middle register provides all seven notes of the C major scale. But in the low register, the notes F and A are missing, and the note G is duplicated, appearing in both Draw 2 and Blow 3.

The low register was designed to provide the two most basic chords in the key of C — the C major chord (consisting of C, E, and G) and the G major chord (G, B, and D). The note G appears in both chords, while F and A don't appear in either chord.

The simplified set of notes in the low register allows for strong chordal effects and for deep draw bends in Holes 2 and 3 (more on this in Chapter 11).

REMEMBER

The strong, flexible G chord in Holes 1 through 4 forms the basis for most blues harmonica playing. Instead of playing the harmonica in C and using the blow chord as home base, blues musicians play it in G and use the draw G chord in the first four holes as home base. G is five notes up the scale from C, and when you play a harmonica in a key five steps above its labeled key, you're playing in second position. For more on positions, check out Chapter 12.

Working with the duplicated note

Draw 2 is the home note of the home chord when you play in second position. This note bends down and is surrounded on both sides by notes that support it. Blow 3, by contrast, doesn't bend and is surrounded by notes that belong to a different chord. For those reasons, you might conclude that you'd want to avoid Blow 3, and some harmonica players do exactly that.

However, Blow 3 is a very useful alternative to Draw 2, because

>> You can play Blow 3 when you're filled up with inhaled air and need to get rid of it while playing.

>> You can use Blow 3 for convenience and smooth note transitions when you're moving to or from other blow notes. Tab 8-1 shows some licks that make good use of Blow 3.

- Lick a) is the "I'm a Man" riff that often punctuates the vocal lines on songs of bravado and machismo.

- Lick b) uses Blow 3 in a rhythm that's based on the *pull-off* technique I describe in Chapter 10 and is often heard in Chicago blues harmonica playing.

- Lick c) is one that Sonny Boy Williamson used in many different variations.

- Lick d) follows a pathway heard in Sonny Boy II's "Help Me" and is often used as well by Paul Butterfield.

TAB 8-1:
Licks that use
Blow 3.

PLAY THIS

You can hear and play along with Tab 8-1 on Track 31.

Exploiting the strengths of the low register

When you play in the low register, you can concentrate on its strengths (and also on its challenges), which include

» Combining the draw notes as chords.

» Applying the tongue textures I describe in Chapter 10 to the draw chord (and also to the blow chord).

» Using the four consecutive draw notes of the home chord as the basis for creating licks and riffs (see Chapter 6 for more on this).

>> Bending the notes of the home chord to give them expression.

>> Inflecting the notes of the home chord to fit with other chords by bending them (see Chapter 7 for more on this, and see Chapters 13 and 14 for info on adapting the low register to the chords used in first and third positions).

>> Bending the notes of the home chord to access missing notes and blue notes.

Demystifying the High Register

The high register is awfully high and piercing sounding, and that's the first reason you may not want to spend much time there. In addition, navigating its strange note layout can make you feel like you've made a wrong turn in the dead of night on a road that's miles from nowhere. You may feel like slamming on the brakes, pulling a quick U-turn, and making a hasty escape.

Over the years, several prominent players have fearlessly explored this mysterious area and found some real treasures. Little Walter, Sugar Blue, and Charlie Musselwhite are only a few of the many players who have blazed trails for the rest of us to follow.

Making sense of the blow-draw shift

The one really confusing thing about the high register is its unique note layout, as shown in Figure 8-2.

In the low and middle registers, the draw note in each hole is **higher** than the corresponding blow note.

In the high register, the draw note in each hole is **lower** than the corresponding blow note.

Hole	1	2	3	4	5	6	7	8	9	10
Draw	D	G	B	D	F	A	B	D	F	A
Blow	C	E	G	C	E	G	C	E	G	C

FIGURE 8-2: The unique note layout of the high register.

Illustration by Wiley, Composition Services Graphics

In any of the holes from Hole 1 through Hole 6, if you first blow and then draw, the note goes up in pitch when you draw. But in Holes 7 through 10, the note goes down instead of up. To go up in pitch from a blow note, you have to first shift one hole to the right and then draw.

Why do the notes shift? Simple arithmetic. The scale has seven different note names. Three of them are blow notes, so the other four have to be draw notes (unless you leave some notes out, as is done in the low register). Eventually, the blow and draw notes get out of alignment, and that's what happens in Hole 7, at the beginning of the high register.

TIP

One way to get used to the high register's note layout is to play some simple action patterns to help you form an association between the sounds you're looking for and the actions that produce those sounds. Tabs 8-2, 8-3, and 8-4 take you through some actions to gain a footing in the high register.

Tab 8-2 takes you through an easy action sequence that uses a simplified five-note scale called the *pentatonic scale*.

Tab 8-3 walks you through the complete scale, first focusing on the draw notes and then focusing on the blow notes.

Tab 8-4 focuses on a harder-edged five-note scale that you start in the low register and carry up through the high register and then back down.

TAB 8-2:
Five-note scale in
the high register.

TAB 8-3:
The complete scale in the high register.

TAB 8-4:
Hard-edged five-note scale from low to high and back.

PLAY THIS

You can hear and play along with Tabs 8-2, 8-3, and 8-4 on Tracks 32, 33, and 34.

Adapting riffs and licks to the high register

The high register differs from the other two registers in two important ways:

» The draw notes in the high register are shifted one hole to the right, requiring you to change your breathing patterns to duplicate melodies you play in the low and middle registers.

» The high register draw notes don't bend down, but the blow notes do. You can't get the same bends as in the other registers, but you have new bending possibilities to explore.

Tabs 8-5 and 8-6 are two consecutive verses of a 12-bar blues tune played in the high register. I call it "Piping Blues" because it's reminiscent of the old country blues practice of playing a sort of high-pitched panpipe known as *the quills.*

Both verses use licks that are similar to licks typically played in the low and middle registers but with the patterns of hole changes and breath changes adapted to the high register. Tab 8-6, the second verse, also includes some high blow bends, so you'll want to get your sea legs with high blow bends so you can tackle that verse.

TAB 8-5:
"Piping Blues,
Part 1."

PLAY THIS

You can hear Tabs 8-5 and 8-6 on Track 35.

TIP

Look for tabs in other chapters that don't involve draw bends and try adapting them to the high register by shifting the blow notes one hole to the left (or, if you prefer to think of it another way, by shifting all the draw notes one hole to the right).

TAB 8-6:
"Piping Blues,
Part 2."

To hear what some of the harmonica greats have done with the high register in second position, check out Little Walter's "Mellow Down Easy," Big Walter Horton's "Walter's Boogie," Sonny Boy Williamson II's "Nine Below Zero" (the version on Chess Records), Paul Butterfield's "Small Town Talk," and Magic Dick's tour de force on the J. Geils tune "Whammer Jammer." (I talk about the high register in first position in Chapter 13 and in third position in Chapter 14.)

Chapter 9

Modulating and Punctuating Your Sound

To get harmonica reeds to vibrate, you move air through the harmonica. With luck and skill, you can get the air moving in the right direction and through the right holes. Of course, you could do that with a hose coupled to an air blower — maybe a hair dryer or a vacuum cleaner.

But household appliances just can't shape sound with the sensitivity and musicality you can achieve with your lungs, throat, tongue, and hands. In this chapter I show you how to develop finesse in shaping the air that you breathe through the harmonica.

Starting and Stopping Notes with Articulation

When you end one note and start another, that new note is a new article, so the specific method you use to begin or end a note is called *articulation*. You can articulate a note on the harmonica simply by starting or stopping your breath, but you can make the job much easier by keeping your breath in motion, and you can make the note more interesting and distinctive by using your tongue, throat, or diaphragm to start or end a note.

REMEMBER

The farther away from the harmonica that you articulate a note, the more air you move, giving more oomph to the note and less crispness to the articulation.

In the next few sections, I start at the top of the chain, where you get crisp articulations with your tongue, and then I work down through the throat and diaphragm.

Making "p" sounds with your tongue

When you speak, you make the sound "p" by closing your lips together. But with a harmonica keeping your lips apart, you have to find another way to make the "p" sound. Why does this matter? Because when you use tongue-blocking techniques (see Chapters 5 and 10 for more on tongue blocking), the tip of your tongue is on the harmonica and can't easily make "t" or "l" sounds to articulate notes. For that reason, the sound I call *tongued P* is a valuable substitute when you tongue block.

To make the sound of tongued P, do this:

1. **Play a single note with a tongue block.**

2. **Press your tongue forward slightly until its right edge contacts the right corner of your mouth.**

   Your tongue will also press the harmonica forward slightly, and the airflow will stop. You can think of this as a total tongue block — your tongue blocks all the holes.

3. **Now start breathing and retract your tongue so that the air starts flowing through the harmonica.**

   You'll hear the note start with a crisp "p" sound.

You can use tongued P to both begin and end notes. Try using it to make a note *pop* — to both begin and end with a "p" sound.

Tab 9-1 uses tongued P to begin notes, to end them, and to pop them. The syllables under the tab indicate the "p" articulations.

PLAY THIS

You can hear and play along with Tab 9-1 on Track 36.

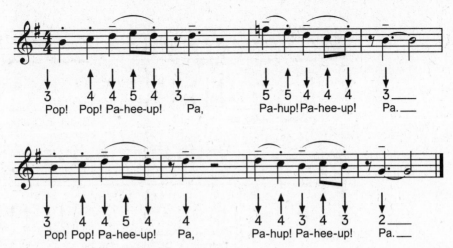

TAB 9-1:
Using tongued P.

Forming "t" and "l" sounds

When you play with a pucker, you can use the tip of your tongue to make crisp, rapid "t" and "l" sounds.

When you make a "t" or an "l" sound, you touch the tip of your tongue to the roof of your mouth. But these sounds differ in ways that you can use to good advantage:

» **The "t" sound completely stops the flow of air.**

Try forming the sound "tut" as you play a note. Your tongue will create a crisp attack and then completely stop the note.

Try saying "tatatatatata" as you play a note. Each "ta" will sound like a separate repetition of the note.

» **The "l" sound lets the airflow continue but alters the sound.**

Try saying "lalalalalala" as you play a note. Each "la" will sound like a repetition of the note but won't sound as strongly marked as the repetitions you create with "ta."

» **The combination of "t" and "l," as in the word "little," allows you to make rapid repeated articulations with ease.**

Try saying "little-ittle-ittle-ittle-ittle-ittle" as you play a note.

You can also articulate groups of three notes by using the syllables "tittle-ta, tittle-ta."

Tab 9-2 is a blues that uses "t" and "t-l" articulations.

You can hear and play along with Tab 9-2 on Track 37.

PLAY THIS　Try playing Tab 9-1, substituting "t" sounds for "p" sounds.

Creating the "k" sound

You make the sound of "k" with the surface of your tongue, humping it up to touch the roof of your mouth and momentarily stop the flow of air. The "k" sound doesn't produce as crisp an articulation as "p" or "t," but it's still useful.

When you tongue block, you can repeat "k" rapidly without the harp bumping forward and backward in your hands, which happens when you use tongued P.

Try playing Tab 9-1, substituting "k" sounds for "p" sounds.

Combining "k" sounds with "p" and "t"

You can deliver articulations more rapidly with two articulation points than you can with one. You usually use rapid articulations when you repeat a single note.

You can do this by alternating "k" with "p" or "k" with "t."

>> Try alternating "k" with "p" when you tongue block.

>> Try alternating "k" with "t" when you pucker.

You can also articulate groups of three repeated notes with combinations of "k" with "t" or "p," such as

>> t-k-t, t-k-k, and k-k-t

>> p-k-p, k-p-k, and p-k-k

Each combination delivers a slightly different texture of articulations. Experiment with these and use the ones you like.

You can hear combined articulations on Track 38.

PLAY THIS

Try playing Tab 9-2, replacing the "tittle" sound with "t-k" and "p-k" combinations.

Making cough sounds

Your *glottis* (also known as your vocal cords) is a pair of fleshy folds that sits on top of your windpipe. Like a harmonica reed, your glottis vibrates in response to your breath to supply sound for speech, song, grunts, and any other vocal sounds you make. Unlike a harmonica reed, your glottis can also completely close off the flow of air. This action is called a *glottal stop*.

Follow these steps to get going with glottal stops. Each exclamation mark represents a glottal stop.

1. **Say "!uh! uh," as if you're refusing a bad deal whispered from a dark alley.**

   Notice what your throat did to make the "!" sound? That's a glottal stop.

2. **Try whispering "!uh, !uh, !uh, !uh, !uh"; start each syllable with a glottal stop.**

   Keep your rib cage and abdomen still when you do this. Concentrate on the action in your throat, in exactly the same place that sound comes from when you say "aaaaaaah."

3. **Now pick up a harmonica and start playing a blow note. Then add a series of glottal stops to the sound by whispering "!uh, !uh, !uh, !uh, !uh."**

   You should hear a series of repeated notes, each one beginning with a glottal stop.

4. **Now try using a series of glottal stops on an inhaled note.**

You can repeat glottal stops (also called *throat articulation*) very rapidly if you do them gently. Because they leave your mouth cavity open, they have a fuller sound than tongue articulation but are less crisp sounding.

PLAY THIS

To hear throat articulation, listen to Track 39.

Try playing Tabs 9-1 and 9-2 using throat articulation.

Adding heft with the diaphragm thrust

You can articulate notes by thrusting air up from the bottom of your lungs. This type of attack, called a *diaphragm thrust*, starts at the bottom of your air column. For that reason, it moves a lot of air and creates a lot of emphasis but completely lacks crispness. If a tongue articulation delivers the crispness of hitting a snare drum with a hardwood stick, then a diaphragm thrust is like hitting a deep bass drum with a cushion-tipped baton.

Your *diaphragm* is the sheath of muscles beneath your lungs that pumps air in and out. To feel it moving, do this:

1. **Place your hand on your abdomen at the highest point, just below your rib cage.**

2. **Say "huh!"**

   Notice how the area under your hand seems to suddenly push in and then relax? That's an exhaled diaphragm thrust.

3. **Now inhale suddenly, as if you're surprised.**

   Do you feel your diaphragm suddenly bulge out and then subside? That's an inhaled diaphragm thrust.

If you try these thrusts with a harmonica, you may hear a strong note attack that dies away quickly. To sustain a note after a diaphragm thrust, you need to keep your breath moving and temper the strength of the thrust so that you don't use all your lung capacity just starting the note. Instead of just saying "huh!" try lengthening it to "haaaaaaah."

TIP

As you gain the ability to sustain a note following a diaphragm thrust, try applying thrusts to the beginnings of phrases and repeated notes and chords. Try substituting thrusts for other articulations and notice the effect. You can add a diaphragm thrust to throat or tongue articulations to add oomph to those attacks.

PLAY THIS

To hear diaphragm thrusts, listen to Track 39.

Making Vowel Sounds

The harmonica can mimic the vowel sounds of human speech. Some old-time players even played showpieces that imitated sounds such as dogs yelping and children asking questions or crying. With a harmonica in your mouth, you can't use your lips to form vowels, but you can use your tongue and your hands very effectively.

Forming tongue vowels

When you use your tongue to form vowels, you may be tempted to get your lips in on the act. Here I walk you through an exercise to isolate the vowel sounds in your tongue:

1. **Open your mouth slightly, as if you're going to say "uh."**
2. **Point your index finger up at your nose and place it gently on your upper and lower lips.**

   If you start moving your lips, your finger will feel them moving, so keep them still.

3. **Now say "aaa" and then extend it into "eee" and then back to "aaa," alternating between the two sounds like this: "aaa-eee-aaa-eee-aaa-eee-aaa."**

4. **Notice what your tongue is doing.**

When you say "aaa" it's lowered, but when you say "eee," the middle part of your tongue (about an inch back from the tip) is raised toward the roof of your mouth.

5. **Now try playing a note on the harmonica and alternating between "aaa" and eee" sounds.**

TIP

You may find that the note bends down in pitch when you form the "eee" sound with your tongue while playing a note. (I dunno, maybe this is a warning and not a tip.) If you already know how to bend and don't want this effect, try to keep your tongue from narrowing the airflow when you say "eee." If you haven't yet mastered bending, though, you've got a head start!

Shaping hand vowels

In Chapter 4 I show you how to form a cup with both hands enclosing the harmonica. By holding the harmonica in one hand and moving the other hand by large or small amounts, you can change the cup's shape to produce vowel sounds and vibrato.

You can make the sounds "wah" and "ooh" with your hands by opening and closing your cup. Here's how:

1. **Start by playing a sustained note with your hands closed around the harmonica.**

2. **As you play the note, pull your right hand away from the harmonica.**

Don't change the formation of your hand; just remove it quickly. You should hear the sound of "wah."

3. **Now quickly move your right hand back into position, enclosing the harmonica.**

You should hear a sound like "ooh."

4. **Try going back and forth between the "wah" opening sound and the "ooh" closing sound.**

TIP

Try bending the note down as you open your hands to play the "wah" sound and then releasing the bend as you close your hands. Move your hands slowly and bend slowly for a slinky effect.

PLAY THIS

You can hear the sound of tongue and hand vowels on Track 40.

Undulating Your Sound with Vibrato

All sound is vibration, but the word *vibrato* is Italian, and that makes it especially musical. Seriously, though, vibrato adds a layer of modulation to a sound. If you think of a sustained note as a straight line streaming along the horizon, vibrato puts a wave in the straight line and makes it undulate in a regular, repeating cycle. That undulation gives the note a voice-like quality that sounds warm and emotional. You can make a note undulate in several ways:

>> By making the pitch fluctuate up and down slightly (some musicians insist that this is the only "true" vibrato).

>> By making the volume fluctuate slightly, getting louder and softer (some musicians call this *tremolo,* though that word has several different meanings).

>> By changing the note's tone color or vowel sound (also called tremolo by some harmonica players).

All types of vibrato have two essential characteristics that you can control to vary the effect:

>> **Depth:** The more your vibrato changes the sound of a note, the greater its depth. Sometimes a very shallow, subtle vibrato is best, but other times a really strong, deep vibrato is more effective. Always listen to the effect you create with the depth of your vibrato and experiment to find what sounds best at any given moment.

>> **Rate:** You can make your vibrato fluctuate slowly or quickly. You can learn to time it and even synchronize it with the divisions of the beat.

Avoid letting your vibrato fluctuate at a fast, erratic rate.

WARNING

When you first start to learn a new vibrato technique, you may find it challenging to control the rate. However, you can develop your skill with a systematic approach. Here's how:

1. **At first, perform each pulsation as a separate, individual action, whether it's a movement of your tongue, throat, hand, or diaphragm.**

    Get familiar with performing the action and with the sensation of doing it and the resulting sound.

2. **When you're familiar with the individual action, start doing a series of repeated actions at a slow, steady rate.**

3. **When you can reliably do the action at a slow rate, try speeding up the rate.**

4. **As you become familiar with performing a series of repeated actions, you can stop initiating each individual action and instead just set the series in motion.**

The following sections take you through the different ways to create vibrato.

Tongue vibrato

Tongue vibrato is perhaps the easiest vibrato to learn and control. It's equally effective on blow notes and draw notes, and you can use it with both tongue blocking and pucker embouchures. That said, blues players tend to favor throat vibrato and hand vibrato. When bending notes, some players have difficulty producing a throat vibrato and use tongue vibrato instead.

Tongue vibrato creates a changing vowel sound but can also add a subtle variation in pitch.

Here's how you do it: Try saying "yayayayayayaya." Notice how your tongue rises close to the roof of your mouth for the "y" sound and then drops for the "a" sound. When you use this motion for tongue vibrato, you keep your tongue's range of motion near the roof of your mouth for two reasons:

>> **Controlling depth:** When you keep the range of motion small, you also keep the change in sound small and subtle. You should experiment with the different sounds you get, but you'll likely want to avoid exaggerated changes in vowel sound.

>> **Adding pitch variation:** When you keep your tongue close to the roof of your mouth, you can create a small amount of air pressure when you exhale and suction when you inhale, similar to when you bend a note. This change in the airflow allows you to exert a small amount of pitch variation, along with the change in tone color that the tongue vibrato produces.

PLAY THIS

To hear tongue vibrato, listen to Track 41.

Throat vibrato

Throat vibrato changes the volume of the sound passing through your throat. It can also pull your soft palate and tongue into the action to create a slight bending effect to vary the note's pitch.

To prepare for throat vibrato, first master throat articulation. While throat articulation uses your glottis to interrupt your airflow and cut it into separate bursts, throat vibrato uses your glottis to partially close and massage the stream of air rather than cut it into separate bursts. To smooth your articulations into vibrato, do this:

1. **Play a long, inhaled breath on Draw 4 and start using throat articulation to break the breath into a series of notes, at a rate of three to four notes per second.**

2. **Pay attention to the sound between the bursts and make sure that the sound never stops; connect the dots between the attacks with continuous sound.**

3. **Now try to ease off on the attacks so that the sound becomes even more continuous and the attacks turn into something more like nudges.**

To add pitch variation to throat vibrato, bring your tongue and soft palate close together. You do this at the "nggg" spot, the point where you say "ng," as in "sing." To get the hang of it, try this:

1. **Say "nggg."**

   Notice where your tongue and soft palate are touching, in an area somewhere between your mouth and throat.

2. **Hold your tongue and soft palate in contact and start to inhale through your mouth (not through your nose, though).**

   Pull the air through the "nggg" spot, opening it just enough to let the air through.

3. **Try playing Draw 4 with this narrowed "nggg" spot.**

   If the note bends down or refuses to sound, open up the "nggg" spot a little to allow the note to sound.

4. **Play Draw 4 with throat vibrato and add the "nggg" spot.**

   Experiment with this combination to add a slight bend to your throat vibrato.

PLAY THIS

To hear throat vibrato, listen to Track 41.

Hand vibrato

When you use your hands to create vibrato, you cup the harmonica in both hands, as I describe in Chapter 4. To work this cup for a subtle vibrato, do this:

1. **Leave a slight opening between your two hands, along the edges of the palms.**

2. **With your thumbs together, keep the hand holding the harmonica steady; the harmonica shouldn't move.**

3. **Rock your cupping hand (the hand that isn't holding the harmonica) from the wrist to make the opening between the edges slightly larger and then smaller in a repeating cycle.**

   Keep the fingers of your cupping hand together and don't change its shape; let the wrist motion do the work. Listen for a change in the sound as you move your hand.

4. **Try making the opening between your hands larger by rotating your wrist farther.**

   Listen for the point where the sound changes dramatically. Stay in this area and work the change by moving slightly over the area.

5. **For each note on the harmonica, repeat Step 4 to find the "sweet spot" where the sound changes the most.**

   You'll find the sweet spot for low notes with a small hand opening, but for high notes you'll need to open your hands wider to find the sweet spot.

For a more pronounced vibrato, move your forearm from the elbow to completely remove your right hand and then replace it.

PLAY THIS

To hear hand vibrato, listen to Track 41.

Combining different vibratos

You can combine hand vibrato with tongue or throat vibrato. Rather than trying to do both at the same rate, you can do them at two different rates, with the faster vibrato being colored by the slower one. For instance, Sonny Boy Williamson II made very effective use of slower hand vibrato with faster throat vibrato. Listen for it on his recordings.

You can also use your tongue to vary vowel sounds while you play a throat vibrato.

PLAY THIS

You can hear the effect of combined hand and throat vibrato on Track 41.

Chapter **10**

Enriching Your Sound with Textures

B lues musicians have a saying: "It ain't what you do; it's the way how you do it." In other words, the "way how" you play a note is just as important as which note you play.

When you play a melody note in one hole of the harmonica, you can enhance that note with the help of the notes in neighboring holes. You can use the neighboring notes to emphasize the beginning of the melody note and to make the melody note sound bigger. You can also use the neighboring notes to create interesting rhythmic textures. These enhancements are a central part of the blues harmonica sound and are just as important as the technique of bending notes (though bending seems to have a better public relations team; see Chapter 11 for the full scoop on bending).

Most of the techniques I show you in this chapter are *tongue-blocking* techniques. When you tongue block, you use your tongue on the harmonica's holes to select, group, and alternate the notes you play. To employ these techniques, you first need to have a command of tongue-blocking basics, which I describe in Chapter 5, so you may want to review those basics to prepare to work with these enhanced tongue-blocking techniques.

Playing Warbles and Shakes

When you rapidly alternate between two notes in neighboring holes, you're playing a *warble*, which is also called a *shake* or, as Little Walter called it, a *quiver*.

WARNING

Don't confuse a warble with a *trill*, as some players do. Trills have a dissonant, clashing sound due to the combination of notes involved, whereas warbles sound harmonious and smooth.

You can play a warble with either a pucker embouchure or a tongue block; how you isolate a single hole doesn't matter, as long you're able to rapidly alternate between two holes. When you play a warble,

>> The note in the hole on the left is usually the main note, and the note on the right is the added note.

>> You usually start with the note on the left, move to the note on the right, and then continue moving back and forth between the two holes.

>> You play both notes on a single, sustained breath that creates a fluid, continuous sound.

>> By playing both notes you create a harmony, and by alternating between them instead of playing them both at once you create a rhythmic texture.

You can use any of four different techniques to alternate between the two notes:

>> **Jaw flick:** Flick your lower jaw from side to side.

>> **Tongue flick:** Select two holes with your lips and flick the tip of your tongue from side to side to alternate between them.

>> **Head shake:** Hold the harmonica steady and shake your head from side to side.

>> **Hand warble:** Hold your head steady and move the harmonica from side to side with your hands.

The jaw flick is used in Irish music for quick, single alternations. Country blues great Sonny Terry used a tongue flick. However, most blues harmonica players use either the head shake or the hand warble, or both simultaneously. They constantly argue over which method is the best. Among the greats, Big Walter Horton was often observed using the head shake, while Little Walter Jacobs expressed a strong preference for the hand warble. On this one, I'm with Walter (Little Walter, that is).

Doing the hand warble

I find that I have much more control over the speed and intensity of a warble when I use the hand warble. Here's how you do it:

1. **Hold the harmonica in both hands, using the classic grip I describe in Chapter 4.**

   Notice that your right hand is bent slightly backward at the wrist.

2. **Play Draw 4, sustaining your inhaled breath for the entire sequence that follows.**

3. **Unbend your right wrist slightly.**

   When you do this, your right hand presses your left hand and the harmonica to the left, sliding Hole 4 out of your mouth and Hole 5 into your mouth so that you're now playing Draw 5. (Remember, continue to sustain your inhaled breath.) Notice that when you unbend your right wrist, your left wrist bends slightly backward.

4. **Allow your right hand to release the pressure, letting your left hand spring back and carry the harmonica back to its starting position, returning you to Hole 4.**

Remember, let your right hand drive the motion and let your left hand respond passively as a spring.

TIP

Work on this move slowly until you can accurately move just one hole by using your right hand to gently nudge the harmonica and then release the pressure. After you get the hang of this move, try repeating it at a steady rate, first slowly and then at increasing speed.

Varying the sound of a warble

You can vary the sound of a warble in four different ways. By mastering these warbling techniques and then combining them, you can emulate the warbles you hear from the Chicago blues masters.

>> **Vary the speed of the warble.** You can play a slow or fast warble, or you can change the speed of a sustained warble, either slowing it down or speeding it up.

>> **Bend the note down and then release it while you sustain a warble.** Normally, you target the note on the left for bending. However, when you do a warble on Draw 5, the note to the right, Draw 6, bends more readily and contributes more to the bending effort.

>> **Allow the two notes to bleed together for a *wet warble* or keep them separated for a *dry warble*.** To play a dry warble (sometimes called a *clean warble*), you start with the note on the left isolated and then move far enough to isolate the note on the right. You never play both notes at once.

For a wet warble (also called a *dirty warble*), you sound both notes at once at least part of the time. To do this, you start by playing the note on the left and then move to the right far enough to include the right note but not so far to exclude the left hole.

During a sustained warble you can vary the sound between wet and dry, either gradually or suddenly.

>> **Change the vowel sound between bright and dark.** You darken the sound by dropping your tongue to open up the chamber inside your mouth, and you brighten the sound by lifting your tongue toward the roof of your mouth and forward toward your teeth.

TIP

You can more easily create pronounced contrasts between bright and dark sound with a pucker because you have a greater range of tongue motion when your tongue isn't placed on the harmonica's holes. When you tongue block, you can assist the front of your tongue by lowering your jaw for a darker sound or by raising it for a brighter sound. You can also heighten the brightening effect by wrinkling up your nose as if you smell something unpleasant.

PLAY THIS

You can hear a basic warble between Draw 4 and 5 — with bends and with variations in speed, wetness, and brightness — on Track 42.

Warbling along a melody line

Tab 10-1, "Walkin' and Warblin'," is a blues tune that adds warbles to a melodic line. In the tab, the stack of diagonal lines beside the hole number indicates a warble between that hole and the neighboring hole to the right.

First, get the hang of playing the melody line without the warbles. Then take the melody notes one at a time and get acquainted with warbling on each of the notes. Finally, try playing the melody with the warbles added.

PLAY THIS

You can hear Tab 10-1 on Track 43.

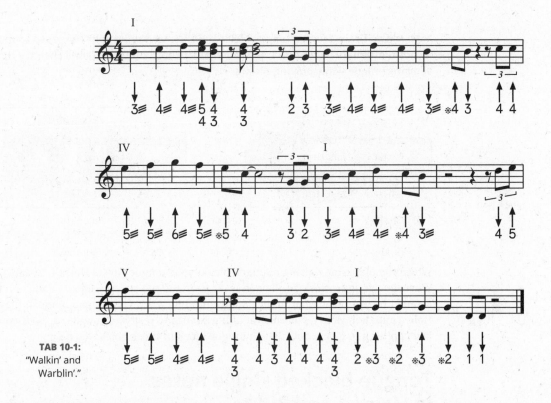

Mastering Tongue Action

The harmonica was designed so that you can use tongue blocking to play both a melody and chords that accompany that melody. When you tongue block, you have several holes in your mouth, typically four. To play melody notes, you use your tongue to block all the holes except the one in the right corner of your mouth (I describe how to do this in Chapter 5). To switch to a chord, you lift your tongue off the blocked holes by retracting it away from the harmonica. Figure 10-1 shows the alternation between single note and chord when you use this technique. This technique of alternating between chord and single note using your tongue is the basis for the tongue vamp, pull-off, slap, and hammer techniques, all of which I cover in this section.

Later in this section, I show you how to produce additional techniques and effects with your tongue on the harp, including shimmers and splits (playing notes on both sides of your tongue), along with rakes and tongue switches, which you produce by moving your tongue from side to side.

Try playing Draw 4 with a tongue block and then retracting your tongue to sound a chord. Alternate between a single note and a chord on Draw 4, and then try the same technique while playing Blow 4.

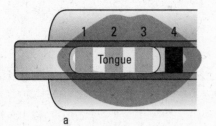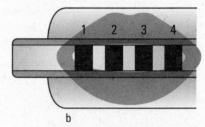

FIGURE 10-1:
Alternating between a tongue-blocked single note and a chord.

Illustration by Wiley, Composition Services Graphics

When you play Hole 4 using a tongue block, your tongue covers Holes 1, 2, and 3. When you tongue block to play Hole 3, your tongue covers Holes 1 and 2 and extends to rest on the harmonica's left end. But when you tongue block to play Hole 2 and then Hole 1, you run out of harmonica to rest your tongue on. So if you have nothing to block, how do you tongue block in those holes? Read on.

Tongue-blocked single notes in Holes 1 and 2

To tongue block and play Holes 1 and 2, use your lips to seal the area where your tongue extends past the harmonica's left end.

1. **Play Draw 4 using a tongue block.**

2. **Now slide the harmonica to the right in your mouth, moving to Draw 3, then Draw 2, and then Draw 1.**

3. **As the harmonica exits the left corner of your mouth, let your upper and lower lips close behind it like a zipper, gently touching your tongue to create an airtight seal.**

4. **Sustain Draw 1 for a moment and then slide the harmonica to the left to return to Draw 4.**

   Let the harmonica's left edge push your lips apart while you maintain an airtight seal.

Figure 10-2 shows the approximate position of your tongue and lips when you tongue block to play Hole 1.

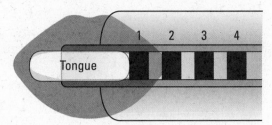

FIGURE 10-2:
Tongue blocking
to play Hole 1.

Illustration by Wiley, Composition Services Graphics

TIP

You can play Holes 1 and 2 by two additional methods. Some players switch to a pucker to play these holes, while others switch to a *left-side tongue block*, where you place the opening in your mouth on the left side of your tongue instead of the right side. I recommend that you learn both alternative methods. Most of the tongue-blocking techniques I describe in this chapter work best when you tongue block with an opening on the right side of your tongue.

Tongue vamps

The word *vamp* can mean many things, but here I concentrate on just one meaning that has nothing to do with sexy ladies or pasty-faced people with pointy eyeteeth. When you play a melody note with your tongue on the harp and then sustain your breath as you lift your tongue off the harp, the notes in the holes you uncover form a chord that's added to the melody note. When you play a melody with each note landing on the beat, you can lift your tongue between beats to add chords on the off beats. When you do this, you're playing *tongue vamps*. Figure 10-1 shows the basic sequence of tongue actions on the harmonica's holes to alternate between a single note and a chord.

Try playing a sustained Draw 4, alternating several times between a single note and a chord. Then do the same with Blow 4. When you have the feel for this action, try playing Tab 10-2. Each asterisk after a note (*) indicates a chord that you play by lifting your tongue.

PLAY THIS

You can hear and play along with Tab 10-2 on Track 44.

Pull-offs

Pull-offs are similar to vamps but incorporate two refinements:

>> Pull-offs are brief and percussive.

>> A pull-off can be in a different breath direction and in a different hole from the single note that precedes it. For instance, you might follow Blow 4 with a pull-off in Draw 1, 2, and 3.

TAB 10-2:
"The Tongue
Vamp."

Here's how you play an inhaled pull-off:

1. **Play a single note with your tongue on the harp.**

2. **Close the gap between the right edge of your tongue and the right corner of your mouth so that all the holes are blocked, and then start to inhale.**

   Because your tongue is blocking all the holes, a tiny amount of suction builds up.

3. **Retract your tongue and allow all the holes in your mouth to sound.**

   The sudden release of built-up air suction creates a percussive effect.

4. **Quickly cut off the sound by closing your throat.**

   You do this the same way you make the sound "uh" when you say, "uh-uh."
   (This is called a *glottal stop*. I cover glottal stops in detail in Chapter 9.)

When you play a pull-off, you perform Steps 2, 3, and 4 almost instantaneously. Getting the hang of this can take some time, but the result is worth it.

Tab 10-3 is a 12-bar blues that uses pull-offs. Because each pull-off may be in a different breath direction and hole from the melody note that precedes it, I can't use a shorthand symbol to show the pull-off. Instead, I show each pull-off as a separate chord, with a dot above the tabbed note to indicate the glottal stop cutoff.

PLAY THIS

You can hear and play along with Tab 10-3 on Track 45.

TAB 10-3:
"Pull-off Blues."

TIP

You can hear pull-offs used to devastating effect by Sonny Boy Williamson II (also known as Rice Miller) on his classic recording of "Help Me."

Tongue slaps

When you play a *tongue slap*, you slap your tongue onto the harmonica as a way of starting a single note. So a tongue slap is sort of the opposite of a pull-off.

Imagine that you're about to play Draw 4 with a tongue block but you forget to put your tongue on the harp and you get a chord instead. Thinking quickly, you recover almost instantly and slap your tongue down on the harp to sound that isolated Draw 4. But you still hear a chord very briefly, as if the chord was a way of starting the note. That's the effect you get when you play a tongue slap. Figure 10-3 shows the sequence of tongue placement for a slap.

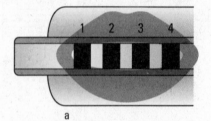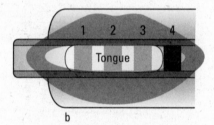

FIGURE 10-3: Tongue slap sequence.

a

b

Illustration by Wiley, Composition Services Graphics

A tongue slap is a way to *attack*, or start, a note. When you hear that brief vestige of a chord as you attack the note, the chord adds fullness to the sound and adds texture to the beginning of the note as it transitions from a complex sound to a simpler one. Tongue slaps are widely used in blues.

Try starting Draw 4 with a slap and then starting Blow 4 with a slap. Alternate several times between Draw 4 and Blow 4, starting each new note with a slap. When you feel that you have the slapping action down, try playing Tab 10-4. I indicate a slap with an asterisk below the tab.

You can hear and play along with Tab 10-4 on Track 46.

PLAY THIS

Hammers

Try saying "lalalalalalala." When you do this you create a texture in the sound "aaaa" by repeatedly touching your tongue to the roof of your mouth. However, your tongue never completely interrupts the "aaaa" sound. Rather, your tongue adds texture to a sustained sound.

TAB 10-4:
"Tongue Slap
Blues."

When you play a *hammer*, you create a similar effect to "lalalalalala," but you do so by touching your tongue repeatedly and rapidly to the harmonica's holes (refer to Figure 10-1). Each time your tongue touches the holes, you switch from a chord to a single note in the right corner of your mouth. The single note sounds the whole time.

Playing a hammer is closely related to both vamping and slapping; all three use the same basic action of using your tongue to move between a single note and a chord. A hammer is like playing a slap rapidly and repeatedly.

TIP

The hammer sounds best when you have four holes in your mouth, though when you play a hammer with Hole 3 as your single note, you have to settle for playing just three holes.

Try playing Draw 4 with a tongue block and rapidly moving your tongue on and off Holes 1, 2, and 3. Then try the same action in Blow 4. When you feel like your hammer action is ready, try playing Tab 10-5. I indicate a hammer with a pair of asterisks below the tab for each hammered note.

PLAY THIS

You can hear and play along with Tab 10-5 on Track 47.

TAB 10-5:
"Hammer Blues."

Rakes

When you play a *rake*, your tongue is on the harp but isn't anchored to one spot. You have three or four holes in your mouth, and you rake the tip of your tongue from side to side across the holes, so that the combination of holes in your mouth is constantly changing. When you do this, make sure that you feel your tongue's edges tapping the corners of your mouth as your tongue flicks from side to side. By reaching the corners of your mouth, you know that your rake is covering the entire range of holes in your mouth. You can see the basic action of a rake depicted in Figure 10-4.

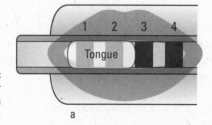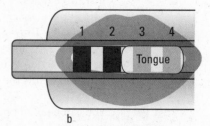

FIGURE 10-4:
Moving your tongue to play a rake.

a   b

Illustration by Wiley, Composition Services Graphics

TIP

Though most tongue-blocking techniques are best performed with the tip of your tongue tucked under the harmonica's front, you may find that for rakes, and for shimmers and splits that cover only three holes (see the following sections), pointing the tip of your tongue up instead of down allows it to glide more easily and do a better job of defining which holes are blocked at any given moment.

To try applying rakes to a tune, play Tab 10-6. Note that the tab shows the highest hole involved in each rake, with a stack of wavy lines below the tabbed note.

TIP

Listen to the different textures you get with hammers and with rakes. Though many blues harmonica players prefer to play hammers, some players, notably including Little Walter, preferred to play rakes instead.

TAB 10-6:
"Rake Blues."

PLAY THIS

You can hear and play along with Tab 10-6 on Track 48.

Splits

When you play a *split*, you split a chord apart into two widely separated notes on the left and right sides of your tongue.

With several holes in your mouth — typically from three to five — you use your tongue to block out the middle holes, leaving only the holes in the corners of your mouth open, as shown in the left-hand part of Figure 10-5. When you play a split you create harmonies that would otherwise be impossible, including octaves (for more on octaves, see Chapter 3).

REMEMBER

In a split, the note in the right corner of your mouth is the melody note, and the note in the left corner is the supporting note.

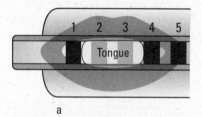 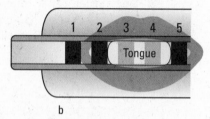

FIGURE 10-5:
The split (a) and the locked split (both a and b).

a   b

Illustration by Wiley, Composition Services Graphics

To play a split, do this:

1. **Start with several holes in your mouth and play them all together as a chord (play a blow chord or a draw chord; either one will work).**

2. **Then bring your tongue forward to block the holes.**

   Normally, to play a single note, you'd feel your tongue's left edge touching the left corner of your mouth while the right corner would be open. But when you play a split, both corners need to be open, so make sure that neither of your tongue's edges is touching the corners of your mouth.

3. **Listen for the sound of the chord to change to a thinner texture of a high note and a low note.**

4. **Change your breath direction but don't move your tongue or lips.**

   You should now hear a different combination of two widely spaced notes.

Blues harmonica players often use a split that covers four holes, with the two middle holes blocked. They often employ this split as a *locked split,* keeping this exact configuration as they move around among different holes on the harp. The two splits shown in Figure 10-5 illustrate a locked split.

Tab 10-7 is a simple blues melody that you play with a locked split. Most of the splits in this tune are *octaves* — one note reinforced by the same note an octave lower. After you listen to the track, you'll find it very easy to identify by ear whether you're playing an octave split. However, one of the splits — the one that combines Draw 5 with Draw 2 — is a very dissonant sound that blues players use deliberately.

You can hear and play along with Tab 10-7 on Track 49.

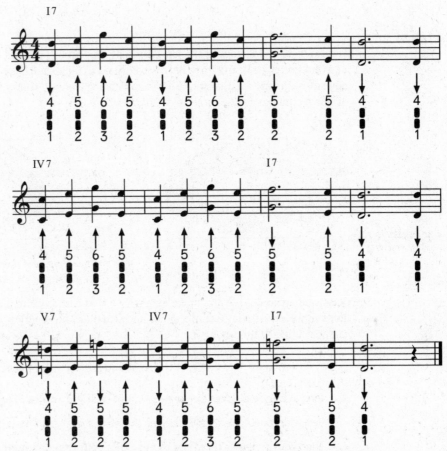

TAB 10-7:
"Blues with a Locked Split."

You can combine a split with a hammer by rapidly alternating a chord with a split instead of with a single note, as shown in Figure 10-6.

Try playing Tab 10-7 again, but this time with hammered splits instead of simple splits.

You can hear and play along with Tab 10-7 played with hammered splits on Track 49.

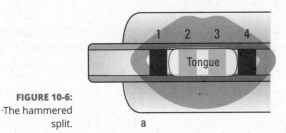
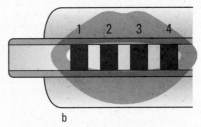

FIGURE 10-6:
·The hammered
split.

a

b

Illustration by Wiley, Composition Services Graphics

You can play melody out of the left corner of your mouth instead of the right corner, and switch back and forth between corners to make quick leaps between melody notes that are far apart on the harmonica. Figure 10-7 shows the basic motion of this technique, called *corner switching.*

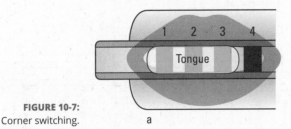
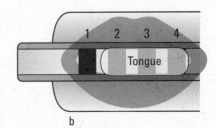

FIGURE 10-7:
Corner switching.

a

b

Illustration by Wiley, Composition Services Graphics

Classical harmonica players make extensive use of corner switching. Blues players don't make a systematic study of corner switching, but every now and then you can hear Little Walter using it.

To switch a melody note between the right and left corners of your mouth, do this:

1. Play a tongue-blocked single note out of the right corner of your mouth.

Feel your tongue's left edge touching the left corner of your mouth.

2. Slide your tongue's tip to the right so that your tongue's right corner touches your mouth's right corner and your tongue's left edge breaks contact with your mouth's left corner.

You should hear a lower note sounding out of the left corner of your mouth.

Tab 10-8 is a blues tune played with corner switching.

You can hear and play along with Tab 10-8 on Track 50.

PLAY THIS

TAB 10-8: "Corner Switching Blues."

Shimmers

A *shimmer* is just a corner switch played quickly and repeatedly. The effect is similar to a rake, but you play fewer notes and you can be more selective about which notes you play. When you play a rake, you may include four or five notes. Sometimes, not all the notes fit with the chord played in the background on guitar or piano. However, when you play a shimmer, you can select only the notes that fit. You do this by keeping the tip of your tongue on the harp and covering all the holes except one — either the hole in the right corner of your mouth or the one in the left corner. To alternate between corners, you can nudge your tongue slightly to the right or left and also move your jaw slightly, just enough to shift the opening in your mouth between the right and left corners.

Try playing Tab 10-7 with shimmers instead of with locked splits. You play the same notes but you switch back and forth between them by moving your tongue.

PLAY THIS

You can hear and play along with the shimmer version of Tab 10-7 on Track 49.

Try playing each of the tabs in this chapter and either substituting one technique for another (such as substituting hammers for rakes or warbles) or adding techniques such as slaps. When you do this, you get better at playing all these techniques, and you also start discovering new ways to use them.

Chapter **11**

Bending Notes: A Classic Part of the Blues Sound

When you *bend* a note, you change how fast it vibrates. You can make some notes on the harmonica vibrate more slowly or go down in pitch — you bend those notes down. You can get other notes to vibrate faster or go up in pitch — you bend those notes up.

You can bend notes to access notes that aren't built into the harmonica, especially the *blue notes* that help give blues its distinctive character. You can also use bending purely for expression — that whining, sliding sound of a note bending up or down can really steam up the windows.

Bending notes is a signature sound of the blues, and in this chapter, I guide you through the mysterious mouth actions you use to bend notes.

Acquiring the Knack

On the diatonic harmonica, some notes bend down while others bend up, and some notes bend farther than others (see the section "Mapping All the Bends," later in the chapter, for an overview of the harmonica's bending resources). For all these bends, you use the same basic technique and adapt it to each situation.

When you first start bending, though, you may feel as if each bend is completely different and enormously challenging. But take heart — as you strengthen your bending abilities, the differences will seem smaller and the similarities will seem larger.

REMEMBER

Bending isn't a feat of strength or a show of force, and it won't ruin your harmonica if you do it right. When you bend a note, you don't literally bend thick iron bars or break through stout walls. You simply set up a favorable condition that persuades the note to change pitch. Playing the harmonica with too much force always wears out the reeds, whether you bend notes or not, so always look for ways to get results with the minimum effort.

Tuning your mouth and activating the bend

Each harmonica reed is tuned to a specific pitch, but you can get it to produce slightly higher and lower pitches within a narrow range. When you bend a note, you select one of the pitches that the reed can produce, and then you position your tongue to do two things:

» You tune your mouth to the note you want.

» You activate the bend.

So how do you do either of those things? That's where the *K-spot* comes in. You use the K-spot whether you're bending a note up or down, whether you're inhaling or exhaling, and whether the tip of your tongue is on the harmonica (tongue blocking) or free to move (puckering). (See Chapter 5 for more on using tongue blocking or puckering to play single notes.)

Finding the K-spot

The K-spot tunes your mouth and activates the bend. To start exploring your K-spot, try saying the syllable "kuh."

Notice what happens inside your mouth:

1. **Your tongue humps up to the roof of your mouth, about halfway back from the tip along its length.**

2. **Your tongue momentarily blocks the flow of air between that point and the front of your mouth.**

3. **Air pressure builds up behind the blockage.**

4. **When you lower your tongue, the explosive rush of air makes the sound you hear as "K."**

The place where your tongue touches the roof of your mouth to make the "K" sound is the first place where you form a K-spot.

When you form a K-spot and use it to bend notes, you make a slight but critical change to the action of saying "K." Here's what you do:

1. **As you exhale gently, raise your tongue toward the roof of your mouth as if to make the "K" sound.**

2. **Instead of blocking the airflow completely, leave a tiny passage for the air to get through between your tongue and the roof of your mouth.**

   Hold your tongue in that position and continue to exhale.

3. **You'll experience air pressure trying to push your tongue away from the roof of your mouth.**

   Let your tongue stand its ground against the air pressure. This air pressure is important. If you don't experience it, you won't be able to bend a blow note.

4. **You'll hear a hiss of air rushing through the narrow passage between your tongue's surface and the roof of your mouth.**

Congratulations — you've successfully created a K-spot. But before you can put it to work, you need to do a few more things, including closing off your nasal passages, inhaling through your K-spot, exploring the roof of your mouth, and sliding your K-spot backward and forward along the roof of your mouth.

Closing off your nasal passages

To bend notes, you need to close off your nasal passages and breathe entirely through your mouth. When you do this, you direct all your air to the harmonica, giving you maximum control over the harmonica without wasting any air. For bending, closing off your nasal passages is especially important. If you haven't yet mastered this skill, flip to Chapter 4 for more info.

Inhaling through your K-spot

Most of the bends you play will be draw bends, so you need to be able to inhale through your K-spot. To get acquainted with inhaling through your K-spot, try this:

1. **As you inhale gently, raise your tongue toward the roof of your mouth as if to make the "K" sound.**

2. **Form the K-spot between the top surface of your tongue and the roof of your mouth, and continue to inhale.**

3. **You'll experience suction pulling your tongue to the roof of your mouth.**

    If you yield to it, the suction will collapse the narrow air passage and stop the airflow. Hold fast against the suction and keep the passage open.

    Suction is an important indicator that your K-spot is activating the draw bend. If you don't experience it, you won't be able to bend a draw note.

4. **You'll hear a hiss of air rushing through the narrow passage between your tongue's surface and the roof of your mouth.**

Exploring the roof of your mouth

To tune your mouth, you need to slide your K-spot along the roof of your mouth. That roof has a definite contour, and knowing the contour gives you landmarks to help you place your K-spot. Before sliding the K-spot around, take a moment to explore the roof of your mouth with the tip of your tongue.

1. **Touch the tip of your tongue to the place where your front teeth meet the roof of your mouth.**

2. **Slide the tip of your tongue back along the roof of your mouth as far as you can without discomfort (swallowing your tongue would be dramatic, but it probably wouldn't help you bend a note).**

    You should notice a contour in the roof of your mouth:

    - The roof stays level (more or less) immediately behind your front teeth. I call this the *front porch* (I know, very scientific).

    - Behind the front porch, the roof rises to a sort of rounded dome shape. I call this the *dome*.

    - Behind the dome is another more or less level area that I call the *back porch*. This is where you place your tongue to make the K-sound.

    - Behind the back porch, the roof ascends again and feels kind of soft. This is your *soft palate* (or *uvula*, if you want at least one real anatomical term). I'm going to call it the *backyard*.

You can see the contour of your mouth's roof in Figure 11-1, with the *hard palate* (the hard part of the roof), the front porch, the dome, the K-spot, and the soft palate. I refer to these various locations as you explore using your tongue to bend notes.

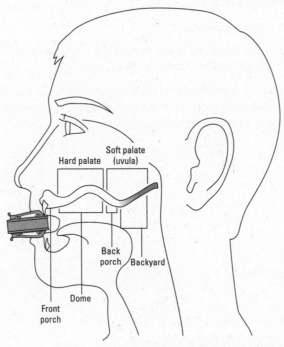

FIGURE 11-1:
The contour of the roof of the mouth.

Illustration by Wiley, Composition Services Graphics

Moving your K-spot forward and backward

You need to be able to move your K-spot forward and backward in your mouth because doing so is one of the two main ways that you tune your mouth.

>> Placing your K-spot forward in your mouth toward your front teeth makes your oral cavity smaller and tunes it to a higher note.

>> Placing your K-spot in the back of your mouth toward your throat makes your oral cavity larger and tunes it to a lower note.

When you want to bend a note, move your K-spot to the right place on the front-to-back continuum and engage (the bend, that is, not a warp drive — bending ain't rocket science).

To tune your mouth to low notes, move your K–spot back along the roof of your mouth:

1. **Begin inhaling and engage your K-spot, starting at the back porch (where you normally say "K").**

   Figure 11-2 shows this placement.

   If you're puckering, the tip of your tongue will simply hang in air, pointed forward and perhaps in a slight downward direction.

   If you're tongue blocking, the tip of your tongue will be on the harp, but you can still make the "K" sound and move your K-spot. I go into more detail when you come to actually trying to bend a note.

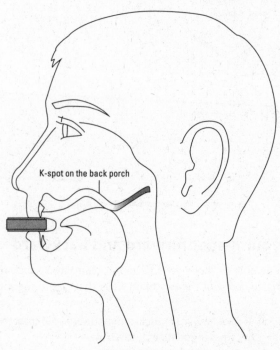

K-spot on the back porch

FIGURE 11-2:
Placing your K-spot on the back porch.

2. **Make sure you can feel suction in the air moving across your tongue.**

   Listen to the sound of the air rushing through your K-spot. It should sound something like "uhh."

3. **Slide your K-spot back along the roof of your mouth, making sure that you continue to feel suction.**

   Figure 11-3 shows how your tongue placement will change.

4. **Listen to the change in the sound of the air moving.**

    As your tongue slides backward, the sound should shift from "uhh" to "ooh," and the noise should sound as if it's getting lower in pitch.

5. **Slide your K-spot forward and return to your starting point.**

    Listen to the vowel sound of the rushing air change from "ooh" back to "uhh" and the noise rising in pitch.

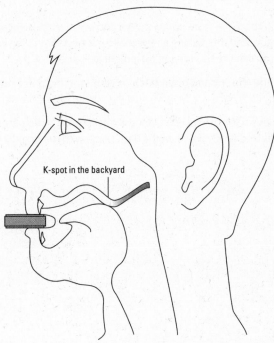

K-spot in the backyard

Illustration by Wiley, Composition Services Graphics

FIGURE 11-3:
Moving your K-spot into the backyard.

To tune your mouth to high notes, you advance your K-spot toward your front teeth. To slide your K-spot forward, try this:

1. **Start with an inhaled breath, engaging your K-spot at the back porch location, as shown in Figure 11-2.**

2. **Feel the suction between your tongue and the roof of your mouth, and listen for the "uhh" vowel in the sound of rushing air.**

3. **Start to slide the suction point forward.**

You may notice the vowel sound of the rushing air changing from "uhh" to "eee" and the noise rising in pitch.

You may also notice that the suction point slides forward on your tongue, closer to the tip, and that your tongue's tip rises toward the roof of your mouth as well.

4. **Continue to slide the suction point under the dome and then to the front porch.**

When you reach the front porch, the suction point will be right above the tip of your tongue, and the rushing air will make a sound something like "thh" (as in "thick"). You can see this tongue placement in Figure 11-4.

5. **Slowly slide the suction point back to your starting place on the back porch.**

As you move back, the suction point will travel from the tip of your tongue to the middle and finally arrive on the back porch with the original K-spot.

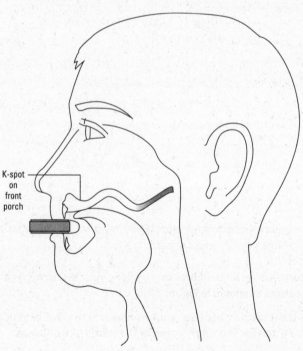

K-spot
on
front
porch

FIGURE 11-4:
Moving your
K-spot to the
front porch.

Illustration by Wiley, Composition Services Graphics

Bending with a tongue block

When you tongue block, your tongue's tip touches the harmonica and isn't free to move. This makes bending with a tongue block a little trickier to learn, but with a little effort you can get the hang of it.

Tongue-blocked bending is worth the effort to learn because it lets you combine bending with the tongue-blocking techniques I describe in Chapter 10. As you learn to recognize tongue-blocking techniques when you hear them, you'll also start to notice how often the great players bend while they use such tongue-blocking techniques as hammers and slaps.

I give you specific tips on bending with a tongue block in each of the sections on bending in the middle, low, and high registers.

Finding your first bends in the middle register

Everyone is unique. You may find your first bend in any hole on the harmonica, and you may even have your best early success on a harp in a key other than C. However, most new players seem to find their first bends in Holes 4, 5, or 6, so I start there.

Finding the sweet spot

When you first start to bend, you don't yet know where the *sweet spot* for the bend is located. The sweet spot is that precise location on the roof of your mouth where your K-spot activates the bend for the specific note you're trying to bend.

So how do you find the sweet spot in the dark? It's not like your mouth has frets like a guitar that you can feel. It's more like the smooth neck of a violin where you can slide into a note.

Luckily, you know where you normally say "K," on the back porch behind the dome in the roof of your mouth. So start there. Pick up your harp and get ready to bend. Cue up the Apache drums, 'cause here we go, Geronimo:

1. **Find Hole 4 on your harmonica and play a clear, isolated draw note.**

2. **As you inhale, raise your tongue to the roof of your mouth as if to say "K," and form the K-spot.**

    Your tongue is channeling the airflow between the surface of your tongue and the roof of your mouth. You feel suction trying to pull your tongue against the roof of your mouth and collapse the air passage. You resist and keep the air flowing.

3. **Maybe the note went down in pitch, and maybe not; time to try moving your K-spot.**

   Slide your K-spot backward in your mouth, slowly and in tiny amounts. Make sure you maintain the suction.

4. **Slide your tongue forward, returning to your original position, and then slowly move it forward, still maintaining the suction.**

Did I mention that you should maintain the suction? That's very important, but I don't mean that you should suck hard. Sucking more just sucks more. Suction doesn't cause the bend to happen. It's just a sort of dashboard light that tells you the bending system is engaged. After you have the suction going, the important thing is to move around and find that sweet spot that will make the bend sing out.

You may need to try this process a number of times over several days before you get a result, so don't get discouraged. Only a very few lucky souls get a note to bend on the first try.

When you first start bending notes, you may use a lot of breath and move your tongue farther back in your mouth than you knew was possible. But as you learn, you'll find you can bend with a very low airflow and without swallowing your tongue.

When you bend, always hear mentally the sound that you're going for. Before attempting a specific bend, listen to that bend on the audio track so that you know what to aim for.

Tongue-blocked bends in the middle register

Figure 11-5 illustrates bending middle-register notes with a tongue block. The front of your tongue is on the harp, and the K-spot is in its usual place on the back porch. You can reach most middle-register bends using a combination of techniques:

>> Slide your K-spot slightly forward or back.

>> Raise or lower the area of your tongue between the high point of your K-spot and the low point of your tongue's tip. Raising your tongue makes your oral cavity smaller, for bending higher notes. Lowering your tongue makes your oral cavity larger, for bending lower notes.

For your first bend, listen to Track 51 to hear the sound of draw bends in Hole 4, 5, and 6.

Though Draw 4 may be your lucky hole, try bending Draw 5 and Draw 6 as well. Everyone is different, and any one of these holes may be your gateway hole that opens up the bending universe.

When you can get bends going in one of the three holes, apply yourself to the other two. When you can get bends in Holes 4, 5, and 6, you're ready to play your first bending tune.

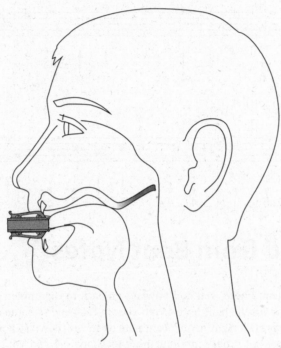

FIGURE 11-5:
Bending midrange notes with your tongue on the harp.

Illustration by Wiley, Composition Services Graphics

Your first bending tune: "Fishing Line Blues"

"Fishing Line Blues" (Tab 11-1) uses bends in Holes 4, 5, and 6. In this tune, you always play bends the easy way: You start with the note unbent, bend it down by sliding your K-spot back in your mouth, and then release the bend to let the note rise to its original pitch by sliding your K-spot forward again.

PLAY THIS

You can hear and play along with Tab 11-1 on Track 52.

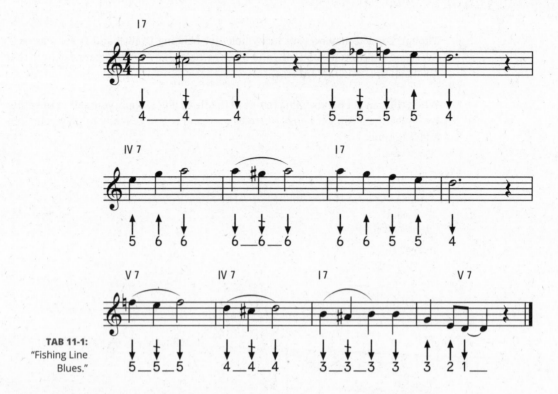

TAB 11-1:
"Fishing Line
Blues."

Moving to and from Bent Notes

When you bend a note, you don't always go back to the unbent note. Sometimes you just end with the bent note or move from the bend to some other note. Other times you may start right in on a bent note by sliding down to it or not playing the unbent note at all. These are your next missions, should you choose to accept them (and I know you will).

Stopping a bent note and starting it again

To slide down to a bent note and then end the note bent, try this:

1. **Play a draw note — either 4, 5, or 6.**

2. **Form a K-spot right on the edge between the back porch and the dome.**

   Make sure to feel the suction.

3. **Slide your K-spot back until the note bends down and then stay in that spot.**

Make sure you still feel the suction. Notice how the vowel sound shifts from "eee" to "ooo."

4. **Now stop breathing, but don't move your tongue.**

The bent note will end without sliding back up to the unbent note.

5. **Keep your tongue exactly where it is and start breathing again.**

The suction should resume and the bent note should start again.

6. **Try starting and stopping the bent note several times, repeating the bent note without ever playing the unbent note.**

You can see these moves tabbed out for Holes 4, 5, and 6 in Tab 11-2.

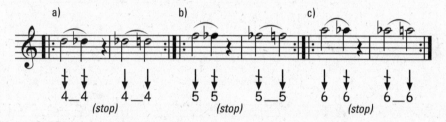

TAB 11-2:
Stopping a bent
note and starting
it again.

PLAY THIS

You can hear Tab 11-2 on Track 53.

Stopping a bend and moving on

After you play a bent note you might go anywhere. I'm going to stick with two obvious possibilities:

» Moving between a draw bend and a blow note in the same hole.

» Moving between a draw bend and an unbent draw note one hole to the left.

The following steps are key to successfully moving between a draw bend and another note:

1. **As you end the bent note, drop your tongue just enough so that the suction goes away.**

If you continue to inhale in the same hole, you'll hear the unbent note. Don't slide your tongue forward or back in your mouth. Just lower your tongue directly downward by a tiny amount.

2. **As you drop your tongue, change to the other note.**

Either continue to inhale and move one hole to the right or switch from inhaling to exhaling.

3. **When you move from the other note back to the bent draw note, simply raise your tongue — it's already in the right place — and resume the suction.**

Tab 11-3 shows the steps for moving to and from bends in Holes 4, 5, and 6.

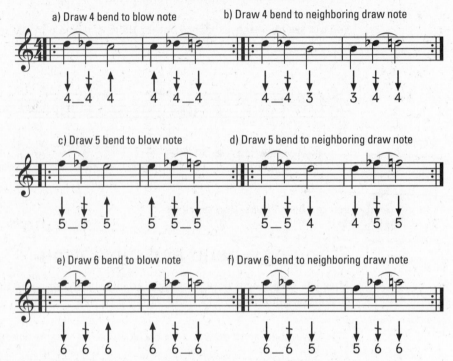

TAB 11-3:
Stopping a bend and moving on.

PLAY THIS

On Track 53 you can hear Tab 11-3.

Your second bending tune: "All Choked Up"

"All Choked Up" (Tab 11-4) is a blues tune that lets you practice ending and starting notes in a bent condition in Holes 4, 5, and 6.

PLAY THIS

You can hear and play along with Tab 11-4 on Track 54.

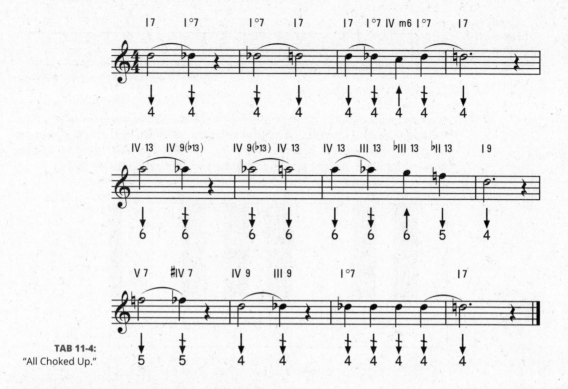

TAB 11-4: "All Choked Up."

Mapping All the Bends

On the diatonic harmonica, some notes bend down while others bend up, and some notes bend farther than others. You use the same basic technique for all bends, but you need to adapt that technique to each note. I take you through the entire harp in the next few sections, but first I map all the available bends on a harmonica in standard tuning.

Some harmonicas are tuned to alternate tunings, with different note layouts that result in different bending possibilities from the standard tuning I deal with in this book. Some of the popular alternate tunings you can buy include natural minor, harmonic minor, melody maker, and country tuning.

REMEMBER

On all keys of harmonica, the notes in corresponding holes bend by the same amount. For instance, Draw 2 always bends down two semitones on a C-harp, a G-harp, an E♭ harp, and so on. The note names may differ, but each note behaves the same way as its counterpart in the same hole on the same breath in another key of harmonica.

TIP

Figure 11-6 shows all the notes that are built into a C-harmonica.

FIGURE 11-6:
The note layout
of a diatonic
harmonica in C.

	1	2	3	4	5	6	7	8	9	10
Draw	D	G	B	D	F	A	B	D	F	A
Blow	C	E	G	C	E	G	C	E	G	C

Illustration by Wiley, Composition Services Graphics

However, some of the letter names are missing. And if you compare the notes on the C-harmonica with the notes on a piano keyboard, as shown in Figure 11-7, you can see that all the black-key notes are missing as well. You can create all these missing notes by bending; the next two figures show you where the notes are hiding.

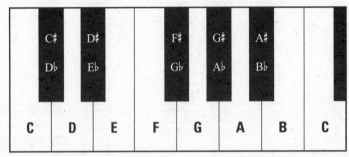

FIGURE 11-7:
A piano keyboard
with all the notes
in all possible
scales.

Illustration by Wiley, Composition Services Graphics

Figure 11-8 shows the notes you can get by bending down on a C-harmonica. A few important things to note:

>> In any hole, the higher note bends down almost to the lower note. The distance between them determines how far the note bends down.

>> In Holes 1 through 6, the draw notes bend down.

>> In Holes 7 through 10, the blow notes bend down.

Figure 11-9 adds the notes that bend up on a C-harmonica to the notes that bend down. A few things to note:

>> In Holes 1 through 6, you can play *overblows,* blow notes that sound one semitone higher than the draw note in each hole.

>> In Holes 7 through 10, you can play *overdraws,* draw notes that sound one semitone higher than the blow note in each hole.

Although Figure 11-9 doesn't show it, skilled players can bend the overblows and overdraws up to even higher notes.

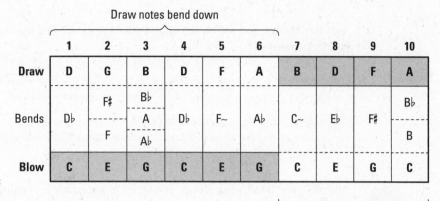

Draw notes bend down (spanning columns 1–6)

	1	2	3	4	5	6	7	8	9	10
Draw	D	G	B	D	F	A	B	D	F	A
Bends	D♭	F# F	B♭ A A♭	D♭	F~	A♭	C~	E♭	F#	B♭ B
Blow	C	E	G	C	E	G	C	E	G	C

Blow notes bend down (columns 7–10)

FIGURE 11-8: The notes you can create by bending down.

Illustration by Wiley, Composition Services Graphics

	1	2	3	4	5	6	7	8	9	10
Overblow	E♭	A♭	C	E♭	G♭	B♭				
Draw	D	G	B	D	F	A	B	D	F	A
Bends	D♭	F# F	B♭ A A♭	D♭	F~	A♭	C~	E♭	F#	B♭ B
Blow	C	E	G	C	E	G	C	E	G	C
Overdraw							D♭	F	A♭	D♭

FIGURE 11-9: The notes you can get by bending up.

Draw notes bend down (columns 1–6) · **Blow notes bend down** (columns 7–10)

Illustration by Wiley, Composition Services Graphics

TIP

Appendix A shows the complete note layouts for all 12 keys of diatonic harmonica, including all bends.

Playing Your Bends in Tune

When you bend expressively, you may just swoop down and back up in pitch in a continuous glide that doesn't need to land on a note that anyone can identify.

However, at least half the time you'll bend with the intent of landing on a specific note in the scale. When you do that, you need to play your bend in tune with what your ears expect and with what other instruments are playing. You can be out of tune in two ways:

>> Your bend is sharp or slightly higher in pitch than the note you're trying to play. In this case, you're not bending the note down far enough.

>> Your bend is flat because you've bent it down too far and gone past the note you're aiming for. (In Hole 3 you can actually bend down to another note entirely, which can be on pitch but still be the wrong note.)

WARNING

Whenever you bend a note down, you face a hidden danger of going too far. All the note layouts in the preceding section show that a particular note bends down one, two, or three semitones. The reality is that each of these notes bends down slightly farther, just enough to make you sound out of tune if you take the bend all the way to the bottom. So even though it may *feel* great to slam the pedal to the metal and go all the way on a bend, it doesn't always *sound* great.

So how do you make sure to play your bends in tune?

>> Listen to the musicians you're playing with and match their pitch when you bend. You'll get better at this as your bending skills develop.

>> Practice bending while sounding a reference pitch for the bent note you're aiming for. The reference pitch can come from you (or a patient friend) hitting a key on the piano, or from a recording or a tone generated by an app on your computer, tablet, or phone.

>> Practice your bends using a tuner so that you can see from the needle or readout whether you're in tune and whether you need to lower or raise your pitch to get there.

>> Use specialized software such as the Bendometer, which knows all the bends in every hole of every key of harmonica and gives you immediate feedback on how far you're bending a note and whether it's in tune or not. (To try out or purchase the Bendometer, see www.harpsoft.com).

Bending in the Low Register

The draw bends in Holes 1, 2, and 3 are at the heart of blues harmonica playing. They're also challenging to learn because they're the lowest-pitched bends on the harp and because, in the case of Draw 2 and especially Draw 3, they bend over a wide range.

Rather than deal with these bends in numerical order, I take them in approximate order of difficulty.

When you want to bend low notes, you need to increase the size of your oral cavity to tune it to a low note. You can do this in three different ways and can choose based on whether you're puckering or tongue blocking.

>> You can lower your jaw to increase the volume of your oral cavity. This works with both puckering and tongue blocking.

>> You can move your K-spot back along your soft palate. This works well when you're puckering.

>> You can lower your tongue between the K-spot and the tip, as shown in Figure 11-10. This is effective when you're tongue blocking because you can't slide your K-spot back very far. To compensate, you lower the floor of the cavity rather than move a wall back.

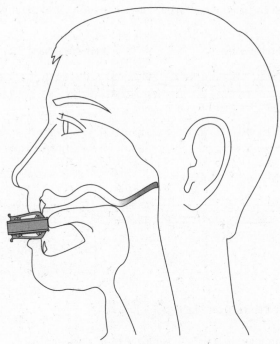

FIGURE 11-10: Bending low notes with your tongue on the harp.

Illustration by Wiley, Composition Services Graphics

Hole 2 bends

Draw 2 bends down two semitones. Both the shallow, one-semitone bend and the deeper, two-semitone bend are useful in the blues, though many players forget about the shallow bend and just plunge down for the deep one.

To get going on bending Draw 2

1. **Start with a clear Draw 2 and then activate your K-spot in the back porch area, making sure that you feel suction in the K-spot.**

2. **Slowly slide the K-spot back and listen for a change in pitch.**

At first you may get a tiny micro-bend or the full deep bend. You may also get a strange, shuddering, braying sound. That sound means you're right on the back edge of the sweet spot for the bend, so move your K-spot forward a tiny amount. Listen to Tab 11-5 to get the sound in your ears, and then work on finding these bends.

Tab 11-5 gives you four short, basic workouts on Draw 2 bends. If you repeat each one until you can do them all, you'll be ready for a lot of great blues playing.

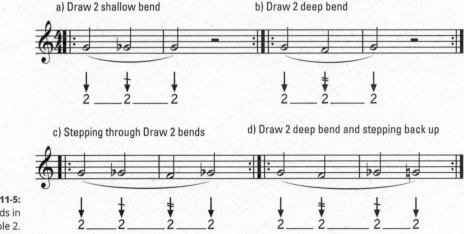

TAB 11-5:
Draw bends in
Hole 2.

PLAY THIS

You can hear Tab 11-5 on Track 55.

When you can play the bends in Hole 2, extend your control by

>> Stopping the note while it's bent and then starting it again as a bent note.

>> Moving from bent Draw 2 to Blow 2 and then back to bent Draw 2.

>> Moving from bent Draw 2 to unbent Draw 1 and then back to bent Draw 2.

Hole 1 bends

The draw bend in Hole 1 is a shallow bend like the one in Draw 4, but it's an octave lower. This is the lowest bend on the harp, so to achieve it you need to make an especially large oral cavity. In addition to sliding your K-spot back, dropping your jaw may be helpful to achieve this bend. Tab 11-6 gives you some Draw 1 bends to practice.

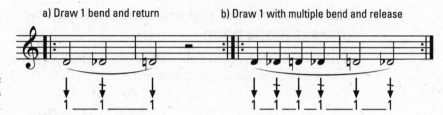

a) Draw 1 bend and return   **b) Draw 1 with multiple bend and release**

TAB 11-6: Draw bends in Hole 1.

PLAY THIS

You can hear Tab 11-6 on Track 55.

When you can play the draw bend in Hole 1, extend your control by

>> Stopping the bent note and starting it again.

>> Moving from bent Draw 1 to Blow 1 and then back to bent Draw 1.

>> Moving from bent Draw 1 to unbent Draw 2 and then back to bent Draw 1.

Hole 3 bends

Draw 3 is the widest-ranging bend on the harp and the most difficult to control and master. But the glorious sounds you can get are totally worth the effort.

When you first try to bend Draw 3, you may get several results. You could get a shallow, tiny bend, or you could find yourself plunging all the way to the bottom of the bend as if it were a powerful magnet and you were wearing iron shoes. Here's the key to mastering this bend:

1. Find the sweet spot that lets you grab on to the bend.

Remember that it's a higher note than Draw 2 and a lower note than Draw 4, so you need to place your K-spot farther forward than you would for Draw 2 but farther back than you would for Draw 4.

2. When you find the sweet spot, don't let it run away or pull you along.

Move your tongue slowly and deliberately, maintain the suction, and try to slide smoothly down to the bottom and back up to the top.

Your first experience with bending Draw 3 may lead you to find the shallow, one-semitone bend or the deep, three-semitone bend. You may even find the two-semitone bend that's right in the middle. After you make your first attempts, listen to the three different bends on Track 55 and try to identify which of the three bends your attempt sounds most like. Then work with one of the following sections to strengthen that bend before moving on to the others.

Skimming off the top with the shallow, one-semitone bend

If your first bend sounds like the shallow, one-semitone bend on Track 55, use the short workouts in Tab 11-7 to reinforce it.

TAB 11-7:
One-semitone draw bend in Hole 3.

PLAY THIS

You can hear Tab 11-7 on Track 56.

When you can play the one-semitone bend in Draw 3, extend your control by

>> Stopping the bent note and starting it again.

>> Moving from the bent note to the blow note in the same hole and then back to the bend.

>> Moving from the bent note to the unbent draw note one hole to the right and then back to the bent note.

Bottom feeding with the deep, three-semitone bend

If your first bend sounds like a deep, three-semitone bend, strengthen it with the short workouts in Tab 11-8.

When you can play the three-semitone bend in Draw 3, extend your control by

» Stopping the bent note and starting it again.

» Moving from the bent note to the blow note in the same hole and then back to the bend.

» Moving from the bent note to the unbent draw note one hole to the right and then back to the bent note.

PLAY THIS

You can hear Tab 11-8 on Track 56.

a) Plunge directly down to the deep bend and then return.

b) Slide smoothly down to the deep bend and then slide back up.

c) Plunge directly down to the bend, and then step back up by semitones.

d) Step down by semitones to the deep bend and then step back up again.

TAB 11-8:
Three-semitone draw bend in Hole 3.

Balancing in the middle with the two-semitone bend

The two-semitone bend in the middle can be hard to play in tune. The deep, three-semitone bend seems to act like a magnet, pulling the middle bend downward. Use the short workouts in Tab 11-9 to develop your control of this elusive but important bend.

PLAY THIS

You can hear Tab 11-9 on Track 56.

When you can play the two-semitone bend in Draw 3, extend your control by

» Stopping the bent note and starting it again.

» Moving from the bent note to the blow note in the same hole and then back to the bend.

» Moving from the bent note to the unbent draw note one hole to the right and then back to the bent note.

a) Move directly down to the
two-semitone bend, and then return.

b) Move to the two-semitone bend,
go to the blow note, then back to
the bend and then release.

c) Go to the two-semitone bend, then bend
down one more semitone, then return to
the two-semitone bend, then release.

d) Alternate between the two-semitone
and the one-semitone bends.

TAB 11-9:
Two-semitone
draw bend in
Hole 3.

Your third bending tune: "Tearing and Swearing"

"Tearing and Swearing" (Tab 11-10) is two verses long, giving you plenty of opportunities to work on your low-register bends.

PLAY THIS

You can hear and play along with Tab 11-10 on Track 57.

In Chapters 13 and 14 I give you more low-register bending workouts in first and third positions.

TIP

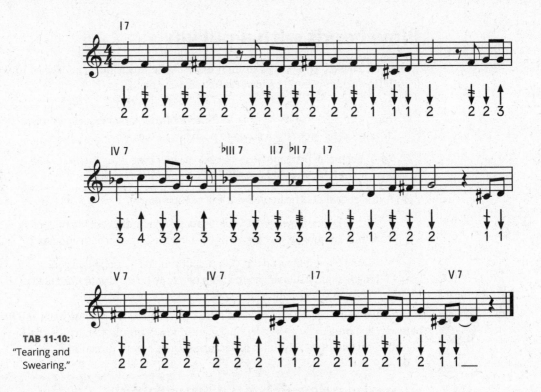

TAB 11-10: "Tearing and Swearing."

Bending in the High Register

The bends in the high register are all blow bends. These bends can be very expressive, but they're challenging to learn because you have to place your K-spot far forward in your mouth and because you must position your K-spot much more precisely than with lower-pitched bends. It's easy to zoom right past the sweet spot for a high bend.

Before trying high blow bends, first master bending Draw 6. Draw 6 is only slightly lower in pitch than Blow 7, the next highest bendable note, so the placement of your K-spot for Draw 6 is just slightly back from the sweet spot for bending Blow 7.

TIP

This book is written so you can do everything on one harmonica in C. But high blow bends are, well, high. If you use a lower-pitched harp, such as a G, a Low F, or even a Low D, you'll have a much easier time mastering high blow bends because those bends will be lower pitched and easier to control.

Blow bends with a pucker

When you pucker, you place the high blow bends much farther forward in your mouth than when you play a lower-pitched draw bend.

>> You raise your tongue's tip close to the roof of your mouth but curved slightly downward, as if forming a scoop to push the air forward.

You'll feel the air pressure pushing back on your tongue, as if your tongue were trying to push a rubber ball forward into the harmonica.

>> Your K-spot should be in the front half of your tongue.

- For the lowest blow bends, your K-spot should be at about the midpoint along your tongue, positioned just behind the front rim of the dome.

- For the highest blow bends, your K-spot should be just behind your tongue's tip, positioned on the front porch, just behind your front teeth.

TIP

If you have a Low F harp and can bend the Draw 6 on it, try moving back and forth between bending Draw 6 on the F harp and Blow 8 on the C-harp — the K-spot placement is identical. The only difference is your breath direction.

Blow bends with a tongue block

With the tip of your tongue tucked under the harmonica's front edge, you can control blow bends quite well, but you use a different method to create a tiny chamber that you can tune to the high notes you're bending down.

You raise the level of your tongue up toward the roof of your mouth to shrink your oral cavity. You can also raise your tongue along the front face of the harp to block the space immediately behind your front teeth. Figure 11-11 shows this tongue placement inside your mouth.

You may feel air pressure through the entire shallow air passage, not just at the K-spot. However, you'll feel as if you're working the pressure to push on the reed, just as you do with puckering for the high blow bends.

Hole 7 bends

Hole 7 gives a shallow bend of less than a semitone. It's also the lowest-pitched blow note that bends, so it's the easiest place to start.

Tab 11-11 gives you three workouts to help you gain control of bending Blow 7.

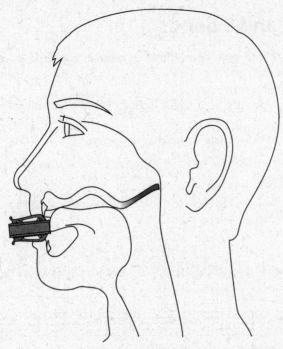

FIGURE 11-11:
Bending high notes with your tongue on the harp.

Illustration by Wiley, Composition Services Graphics

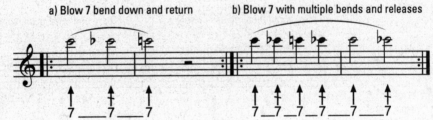

a) Blow 7 bend down and return   b) Blow 7 with multiple bends and releases

TAB 11-11:
Hole 7 blow bends.

7 ____ 7 ____ 7   7 __7 __7 __7 ____7 ____7

When you can play the Blow 7 bend, extend your control by

>> Stopping the bent note and starting it again.

>> Moving from bent Blow 7 to Draw 7 in the same hole and then back to the bend. (You'll be moving by smaller pitch amounts than Western music — and ears — normally measures, so it will sound kind of weird!)

>> Moving from bent Blow 7 to unbent Blow 6 and then back to bent Blow 7.

You can hear Tab 11-11 on Track 58.

PLAY THIS

Hole 8 and 9 bends

Blow 8 and 9 both bend down by one semitone. Tab 11-12 gives you three short workouts for each hole.

When you can play the blow bends in Holes 8 and 9, extend your control by

» Stopping the bent note and starting it again.

» Moving from the bent note to the draw note in the same hole and then back to the bend.

» Moving from the bent note to the unbent blow note one hole to the right and then back to the bent note.

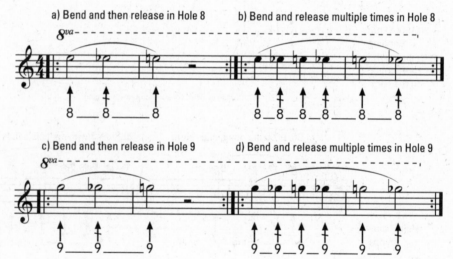

TAB 11-12:
Hole 8 and
9 blow bends.

PLAY THIS

You can hear Tab 11-12 on Track 58.

Hole 10 bends

Blow 10 is like Draw 2; it bends down two semitones. And as with Draw 2, players tend to zoom past the shallow, one-semitone bend and go for the glory of the deeper, two-semitone bend. But that shallow bend is worth cozying up to on a cold night.

Blow 10 is also the highest-pitched note on the harp, with a short, stubby reed that takes some very precise persuasion to get it to loosen up. Your K-spot is right behind your tongue's tip, which teeters on the edge of the front porch, trying to find a sweet spot that's narrower than the grooves between the floorboards. This takes a delicate touch, but when you do get the sound of this bend, you'll be glad you made the effort!

Tab 11-13 takes you through the various ways you can bend Blow 10. You may not master all of them right away, but work on them over time.

When you can play the bends on Blow 10, extend your control by

» Stopping the bent note and starting it again.

» Moving from bent Blow 10 to Draw 10 and then back to the bend.

» Moving from bent Blow 10 to unbent Blow 9 and then back to the bent note.

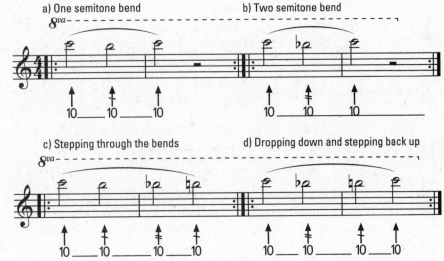

TAB 11-13:
Blow bends in
Hole 10.

PLAY THIS

You can hear Tab 11-13 on Track 58.

Your fourth bending tune: "Wailin' High"

Here's "Wailin' High" (Tab 11-14), a 12-bar blues that lets you sneak into those high blow bends and then cut loose and wail!

PLAY THIS

You can hear and play along with Tab 11-14 on Track 59.

TAB 11-14: "Wailin' High."

Bending on the Chromatic

The chromatic harmonica has a strange reputation. Folks sometimes say that you can't bend notes on a chromatic or that, even if you could, polite folks know better — bending is unnecessary, bad for its reputation, and leads to an early grave.

None of this is true. Even if it were, no self-respecting blues musician would sacrifice expressiveness for the sake of respectability. So have no fear. If you've decided to add a chromatic harp to your kit, you may as well get the most out of it and start bending notes on it.

But, you may say, the chromatic has all the notes built in, so why bend? Though it's true that you don't need to bend to supply missing notes, bending helps give you the voice-like expressiveness that makes the harmonica so attractive in the first place.

The uniqueness of bending on the chromatic

The chromatic has a unique set of bending abilities, and it can bend very expressively:

>> The draw notes and blow notes all bend down, except in the top few holes, where only the draw notes bend.

>> You can bend notes on the chromatic even farther than you can on a diatonic — as many as four or five semitones on a well-adjusted harmonica in the hands of an adept player.

>> You can't bend notes up on a chromatic, though.

However, the folks who counsel sober propriety and cold baths for the chromatic are right about one thing: The chromatic demands to be treated in a more ladylike fashion than the diatonic.

It's not that the chromatic cares if you use vulgar language or belch at the table. What the chromatic does require is to be treated gently. You can attack notes on a diatonic much harder than you can on a chromatic. You can play a chromatic just as hard, but you have to do it with finesse, by moderating your note attacks.

When it comes to bending on the chromatic, though, the chromatic requires not only gentleness but firmness. I explain by comparing bending on the chromatic with bending on the diatonic:

>> When you bend the draw notes on a diatonic, most of the suction is localized around the narrowed airflow passing through your K-spot. When you bend the high blow notes, you may notice air pressure along the front part of your tongue as well.

>> When you bend draw notes on the chromatic, the suction fills up the entire oral cavity between your K-spot and your front teeth. And when you bend blow notes, the air pressure also fills up the oral cavity.

TIP

To get acquainted with bending on the chromatic, I recommend that you work on your diatonic bending first and then apply what you learn — with gentleness and firmness — to both draw and blow bends throughout the range of the instrument.

REMEMBER

When pressure or suction occurs in a larger area, your tongue has to work a little harder to withstand it. That's the firmness I refer to. It doesn't mean you have to generate more suction or pressure, just that you need to manage and shape the pressure or suction that you do generate. And especially, you don't need to blow or suck harder; that makes the chromatic clam up and stop sounding. That's the gentleness part.

Chromatic bending tune: "Blue Blossoms"

Tab 11-15, "Blue Blossoms," is a 12-bar blues that uses expressive bends on the chromatic. The little curved lines in front of some of the tabbed notes indicate that you start the note slightly bent and then release the bend as you start to play the note. After you take some time to develop your bending finesse on the chromatic, put it to use by playing this tune.

PLAY THIS

You can hear and play along with Tab 11-15 on Track 60.

TAB 11-15:
"Blue Blossoms."

Bending Notes Up with Overblows and Overdraws

On the diatonic harmonica, bending notes up uses the same basic techniques as bending notes down, but the results it produces may seem very strange, as if you've entered an alternate universe where the laws of motion and gravity have all been reversed.

» A bent-up note pops up to a higher note instead of sliding down to a lower note.

» In Holes 1 through 6, you can bend draw notes down, but you can also pop up to higher notes on an exhaled breath. These are called *overblows*.

» In Holes 7 through 10, the blow notes bend down, while you can pop up to higher notes on an inhaled breath. These are called *overdraws*.

WARNING

Some players are confused and mistakenly assume that the term *overblow* refers to bending the high blow notes down. Those bends are called *high blow bends* or simply *blow bends*.

Why bending up is useful

Overblows and overdraws (collectively referred to as *overbends*) supply notes that are missing on the diatonic harmonica. The notes called *blue notes* are important to the sound of blues, and though some of them are built into the harmonica, you have to produce others by bending notes. But you can't get all the blue notes by bending notes down. For some of them, you have to play overblows and overdraws. The very first recorded overblow (by Blues Birdhead in 1929, on a tune called "Mean Low Blues") did exactly that — it produced a blue note that would have been impossible to play any other way.

Still, playing overbends takes dedication to master. Many of the current models of harmonica overblow reasonably well in the middle register straight from the box, but they require some careful setup to overblow — and especially to overdraw — well over their entire range. Getting a pure overbent note without additional weird sounds takes some work, and overbends tend to be slightly flat in pitch, so you need to bend them up slightly to play them in tune.

How bending up works

Reeds normally act like doors closing. When you inhale to play a draw note, the draw reed is pulled into its slot in the reedplate and then springs back, repeating this cycle as it vibrates. Likewise, a blow reed is pushed into its slot and springs back. When reeds act this way, they act as *closing reeds* and sound the notes they're intended to produce.

However, you can get a reed to move away from its slot before it springs back. This action is called *opening reed* action. A reed acting as an opening reed does something very curious — it sounds a pitch nearly one semitone higher than its opening pitch. This is the phenomenon that produces overblows (draw reeds opening in response to exhaled breath) and overdraws (blow reeds opening in response to inhaled breath).

Look back at Figure 11-9 and check out the overblows and overdraws:

>> In Holes 1 through 6, the overblow in each hole is pitched one semitone above the draw note because it's produced by the draw reed opening.

>> In Holes 7 through 10, the overdraw in each hole is pitched one semitone above the blow note because it's produced by the blow reed opening.

Note that I said an opening reed produces a note almost a semitone higher than the same reed acting as a closing reed. When you play an overbend, it will sound out of tune unless you bend it up. The fact that you can bend an overblow or overdraw up in pitch is the other thing about these bends that seems to contradict the laws of the universe of bending down.

CHOOSING AND MODIFYING HARMONICAS FOR BENDING NOTES UP

Some models of harmonica overbend more readily than others, and you can modify any model to make it more responsive to the overblow and overdraw techniques. In general, a harmonica needs to be airtight, with reeds set fairly close to the reedplate and tight spaces between the edge of the reed and the edge of its slot in the reedplate.

Models least likely to overblow well include the less expensive models, most Chinese-made harmonicas, and, without modification, Lee Oskar models. Mid-priced to expensive models from Hering, Hohner, Seydel, and Suzuki tend to overblow reasonably well without modification.

For more extensive instruction in overbending, check out *Harmonica For Dummies,* written by yours truly and published by Wiley. For more extensive how-to information on setting up a harmonica to overbend well, check out both *Harmonica For Dummies* and www.overblow.com.

How to do it

If you exhale into Hole 6, shouldn't you hear the blow reed sounding? How do you get that reed to politely be silent while the draw reed opens instead?

Playing an overblow is a bit like standing in front of a class and asking a question (your exhaled breath) that stumps the overachiever who always raises his hand (the blow reed) but immediately catches the attention of the sullen kid in the back who never volunteers an answer (the draw reed going backward). Suddenly, the sullen kid lights up and is eager to respond because she knows the answer.

Simply put, you have to tune your mouth so precisely to the overblow note that the blow reed simply can't respond and the draw reed opens instead.

TIP

Playing overblows is a lot like playing high blow bends, so develop your high blow bending skills before you attempt overblows. Overbends are much easier to play with a pucker than with a tongue block.

The most useful overblow for playing blues is the overblow in Hole 6. To get the hang of playing it, you can try two different approaches. With each approach, you may get one of several results:

>> The blow note may bend down a tiny amount. Keep up the pressure and push your K-spot forward slightly.

>> You may get nothing but the sound of air rushing. You're on the right track and just need to locate the sweet spot.

>> You may get some awful combination of squeals and brays. That's good, but you need to focus your K-spot to isolate one of those noises, so keep up the pressure and slide your K-spot until you find the note.

PLAY THIS

Listen to Track 61 to hear the note you're going for so that you know when you find it.

To increase your chances of success in achieving a 6 Overblow, try surrounding the problem by using your existing skills in bending Blow 7 and Draw 6. I step you through both approaches in the next two short sections.

Approaching 6 Overblow from Blow 7

Try bending Blow 7 down. Notice where your K-spot is placed and the sensation of air pressing back against the front part of your tongue.

Now, try bending Blow 6. You should place your K-spot slightly farther back than for Blow 7 because you're aiming for a lower-pitched note.

Approaching 6 Overblow from Draw 6

Here's another approach:

1. **Play Draw 6.**

   This is the reed that actually sounds 6 Overblow, so you're getting it in motion before you play the overblow.

2. **Bend Draw 6 down and notice the location of your K-spot.**

3. **Holding the bent note, change breath direction and blow instead.**

   You'll feel air pressure against your tongue. To find the overblow, you may need to slide your K-spot forward slightly because you're aiming for a higher note.

After you get familiar with playing a clear overblow in Hole 6, try extending your abilities to playing overblows in Holes 5 and 4.

Playing overdraws

The easiest overdraw to access is 8 Overdraw. This produces the same note as Draw 9, making 8 Overdraw unnecessary. However, Draw 9 gives you a handy comparison note to remind you what you're going for as you attempt to isolate the overdraw.

Work on getting 8 Overdraw by approaching it from bent Blow 8, moving your K-spot a little closer to your front teeth for the overdraw.

For playing blues, the most useful overdraw is in Hole 7, as this overdraw provides a missing blue note.

Overblow tune: "Sass"

Tab 11-16 is a tune called "Sass" that focuses on 6 Overblow but also uses overblows in Holes 4 and 5. In the tab, the blow arrow with a circle through the shaft indicates an overblow.

PLAY THIS

You can hear and play along with Tab 11-16 on Track 62.

TAB 11-16:
"Sass."

4

Developing Your Style

Chapter **12**

Playing in Different Keys on a Single Harmonica

Harmonicas are designed so that you can use a C-harp to play a tune that's in the key of C, an A-harp to play in the key of A, and so on. Harmonicas exist for all 12 keys. Yet blues harmonica players choose to play harmonicas in keys they're not tuned to. For instance, when they play a C-harp, they often play it in the key of G, sometimes they play it in D, and every now and then — gasp — they play it in C. Likewise, they use an A-harp to play in E, in B, and every once in a while, in A.

You may wonder why blues players ignore the obvious and play harmonicas in keys they're not designed for. And you may puzzle over how players can keep track of the twisted relationships this weird behavior creates. Twelve keys of harmonica, each with the potential to play in 12 different keys, creates 144 possibilities! (No, we won't go into all of them, just the ones widely used in blues.)

In this chapter I explain a little about why harmonica players behave the way they do (I said a little — harp players do a lot of stuff that puzzles everyone else), and I also show how they use a system of positions to simplify all those possible relationships.

Introducing the Position Concept

When harmonica players talk about *positions*, they're talking about the relationship between the key of the harmonica and the key of the music they're playing.

For instance, every time you play a harmonica in the key it's tuned to, you're playing in first position. So if you play, for example, "Twinkle, Twinkle, Little Star" in C on a C-harp, you're playing in first position.

Try playing Tab 12-1 to hear the first phrase of "Twinkle, Twinkle" in first position.

TAB 12-1:
The first phrase of "Twinkle, Twinkle, Little Star" in first position.

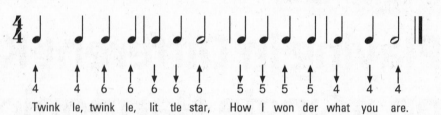

If you pick up a harp in a different key, such as an A-harp, and play the exact same sequences of holes and breaths, you still get "Twinkle, Twinkle, Little Star." From your point of view, you perform the same actions and achieve the same results. But in fact, several things are different about the second performance:

>> You're in a different key. (If you use an A-harp, you'll be in A, for instance.)

>> All the note names you play are different.

>> Anyone playing accompaniment would have to play a different set of chords.

So the idea of positions focuses on the things in common among different keys of harmonica.

Now let's say you pick up the C-harp again and play "Twinkle, Twinkle" again, only this time you start on Blow 6, as shown in Tab 12-2.

TAB 12-2:
The first phrase of "Twinkle, Twinkle, Little Star" in second position.

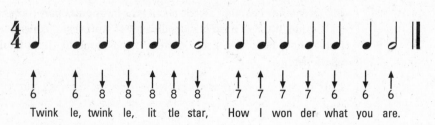

If you do this on a C-harp it comes out in the key of G. If you count up the scale from C to G, you find that G is a *fifth* above C — it's five notes up the scale.

If you transfer the same set of moves to an A-harp, you'll hear the same tune, but this time it will come out in the key of E, which is a fifth above A.

What I'm getting at is that identical relationships produce identical results.

You don't need an A-harp to play Tabs 12-1 and 12-2. Any key will do fine, but if all you have is a C-harp, don't worry.

PLAY THIS

You can hear Tabs 12-1 and 12-2 on Track 63.

Why is this relationship such a big deal? Focusing on relationships simplifies a large number of possibilities. You probably don't want to keep track of 144 different combinations of harmonica keys and song keys — or take the trouble to master them all!

Actually, only 12 relationships exist among those 144 combinations. Each relationship has its own set of musical structures and patterns that stay the same, no matter what keys are involved. Of those 12 relationships, only 3 are widely used in blues. I just reduced the complexity of all those possibilities from 144 down to 3 — that's 98 percent! Feeling any better?

Seeing the benefits of playing one harp in many keys

If harmonicas exist in all 12 keys, why bother to figure out how to play one harmonica in several keys? Blues players prefer the results they get by playing in a key different from the labeled key. So what do they find in those off-label keys that they like so much?

>> Blue notes (the notes outside the major scale that sound so bluesy)

>> Bendable notes that match the important notes in the key

>> Harmonies and chords that work well in that key

>> A range that's higher or lower than another key of harmonica

>> A unique overall character that adds variety to a player's sound

Later in the chapter, I give you an overview of first, second, and third position. And in Chapters 13 and 14, I show you the benefits of playing in these positions.

Simplifying the possibilities with the circle of fifths

Early on, harmonica players discovered that they could play a harmonica in at least two keys: the key it was tuned to and another key five steps higher. They called playing in the key of the harp *straight harp,* or *first position.* They called playing in a key five steps higher *cross harp, choking* (which implied the use of note bending), or *second position.* Some time later, players started using *third position,* which is in a key five steps higher than second position.

Over time, players stumbled on to more positions. Each player numbered the positions in the order in which he or she discovered them and sometimes gave them fanciful names as well. Older harmonica instructional books sometimes use these nonstandard position numbers and names.

Eventually, players decided to standardize a method of naming positions. They took their lead from the existing relationship among first, second, and third positions: Fourth position would be five notes above third, fifth position would be five notes above fourth, and so on. To make looking up these relationships easy, they adapted a well-known music diagram called the *circle of fifths.*

The circle of fifths is a series of note names that includes all 12 notes of the chromatic scale, arranged so that each note in the circle is a perfect fifth higher than the last (a perfect fifth is five letter names up the scale from the starting note and exactly seven semitones away). You can see the circle of fifths in Figure 12-1.

A BRIEF HISTORY OF POSITIONS

First position was born with the harmonica sometime in the early 19th century. Harmonicas were designed to be played in the key that they were tuned to. Harmonicas appeared in large numbers in the United States in the 1870s, and by the time rural harmonica players from the South started making recordings in the 1920s, they had used the intervening 50 years to develop sophisticated abilities and a repertoire that used second position. Every now and then, an artist would stumble on an odd position, such as twelfth, fourth, or fifth, but most players used first and second position exclusively. Third position didn't appear on the scene until the beginning of the 1950s in Chicago, with the playing of Little Walter and George Smith. It has since become an essential position to know and use.

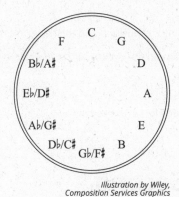

FIGURE 12-1:
The circle of
fifths.

*Illustration by Wiley,
Composition Services Graphics*

You can use the circle of fifths to figure out any relationship among the key of a harmonica, the key of music you may play on it, and the position that results.

Relating the key of the harmonica to the key of the tune and the position

When you approach playing a tune on the harmonica, you deal with three pieces of information:

>> The song's key

>> The harmonica's key

>> The position

Often, you may have only two of these pieces of information. How do you figure out the third one?

>> To find the key of the harmonica using the tune's key and the position

1. Find the key of the tune on the circle of fifths. Call this *1.*

2. Count clockwise around the circle until you come to the position number. The key of the harmonica corresponds to the position number.

>> To find the position using the key of the tune and the key of the harmonica

1. Find the tune's key on the circle of fifths. Call this *1.*

2. Count clockwise around the circle until you come to the key of the harmonica to get the position number.

>> To find the key of the song using the position and the harmonica's key

1. Find the key of the harmonica on the circle of fifths. Assign the position number to that key.

2. Count backward and counterclockwise around the circle until you arrive at *1*. The key that corresponds to *1* is the key of the song.

An Overview of First, Second, and Third Positions

Second position is by far the most frequently used position for playing blues, and up to this point, pretty much everything you've been doing has been in second position.

First position and third position, though, are essential to being a well-rounded harp player. In Chapters 13 and 14, I go into detail about first and third positions. I even cover third position on the chromatic harmonica in Chapter 15.

But before diving in, here I give you a brief overview of each of these popular positions, focusing on the home note and the home chord for each position, with reference to the bendable notes.

First position

The harmonica was designed to be played in first position. The home note and the home chord are blow notes. By placing your tongue on the harmonica, you can isolate single holes in the middle part of the harmonica to play melody, and you can lift your tongue off the harp to add accompanying chords.

Early harmonica players found that playing in the middle register didn't work well for playing blues because the blue notes were missing and the middle-register blow notes didn't bend down. To bend notes of the home chord, they had to play in the top register, so they developed a way of playing high, piercing melodies in the top register. Sometimes they'd skip over the middle register and jump down to the bottom register as well, using the deep draw bends in Holes 2 and 3.

In any key, blues uses the I chord, the IV chord, and the V chord (see Chapter 3 for more on chords). In first position, the blow notes form the I chord and the draw notes in Holes 1 through 4 form the V chord. However, the IV chord is missing. So early blues artists such as Will Shade and Noah Lewis tended to use first position to play non-blues songs, often derived from ragtime, that made heavy use of the V chord and minimal use of the IV chord.

Still, first position has a solid place in the world of blues harmonica, and some artists, such as Jimmy Reed, have made a specialty of using the high blow register to deliver some sizzling harp licks. Knowing how to play in first position is considered an essential part of the blues harmonica skill set, so go to Chapter 13 when you're ready to start working out in first.

TIP

You can apply everything you learn in first position to second position. The blow chord is the I chord in first position, but in second position it's the IV chord. So when you're playing in second position and the time comes to play the IV chord, you can use your expertise in first position to play some cool licks over that IV chord.

Second position

Second position takes advantage of some convenient facts:

>> The draw notes in Holes 1 through 5 form a dominant 7th chord — the kind of 7th chord that abounds in blues (for more on 7th chords, see Chapter 3).

>> While the draw chord gives you the I chord, the blow chord gives you the IV chord.

>> The scale in second position naturally includes a blue note, the flat 7th.

>> All the notes of the home chord in Holes 1 through 4 bend down. This chord full of bendable notes allows you to produce all the classic blues notes and is perfect for playing tons of bluesy licks in a register that won't tire your ears.

This combination of characteristics has made second position the most popular blues position.

However, second position has its own set of drawbacks (not that you'd notice them when you listen to the really great players):

>> The home note is a draw note in the lower register, but it's a blow note in the middle and upper registers.

>> You can't bend the notes of the home chord down in the upper register.

>> You don't have a true V chord, and you have to sort of fake your way around that fact. (You do have a sort-of-but-not-quite V chord in the draw notes from Hole 4 to Hole 10.)

Third position

Third position uses the draw notes from Hole 7 through 10 as its home chord. These notes form a minor 6th chord (see Chapter 3 for more on chords), which gives third position an eerie, minor-key sound. The draw notes in the bottom register, however, are the notes of the IV chord. You can bend down these notes to play the notes of the I chord in third position, but doing this requires good bending control. So you have the I minor chord and the IV major chord in third position. You don't have a true V chord, though the blow notes form a chord that you can use to fake the V chord.

TIP

You can apply everything you learn in third position to second position. The I chord in third position is also the V chord in second position. (Well, sort of. The true V chord would be a dominant 7th chord, and this chord is a minor 6th chord, but it works anyway.) So when you're playing in second position and the time comes to play the V chord, you can use your expertise in third position to play some cool licks over that V chord.

» Exploring the high, middle, and low registers

» Using pathways in first position

» Practicing your first-position skills with some tunes

Chapter **13**

Working Your Blues Chops in First Position

When you play in first position, you're being kind of subversive, like the guy who dresses in stiff, formal clothes but then breaks into a funky dance. The harmonica was designed to play cheerful German folk tunes in first position, not the slithery, growling blues style that works so well in second position. But when blues harmonica players invade the sunny land of first position, they bring all the bluesy possibilities that the good people of the Black Forest never dreamed of (though, nowadays, they hear it because blues harmonica has become so popular worldwide).

However, when you take a vacation from second position and start playing blues in first position, you have to kind of turn your head inside out for a few reasons:

>> You focus more on blow notes than on draw notes.

>> You spend a lot of time in the high register, some in the low register, but very little in the middle register.

>> When you play in first position instead of second position, every note has a different relationship with the background chords.

I cover these issues and more in this chapter.

Relating First Position to the Three Chords of the Blues

You can play blues with all sorts of sophisticated chords, but nearly all blues songs use the three most basic chords: I, IV, and V. (For more on chords, check out Chapter 3.) Musicians number the chords to indicate the chords' relationships to one another. For instance, in the key of C, C is the first note in the scale (the 1). When you add notes to C to build a C chord, that chord is the I chord in the key of C. On the fourth note of the scale you build the IV chord, and on the fifth note you build the V chord. The relationships among I, IV, and V are the same no matter what key you play in, even though the names of the notes and the chords are different in each key.

Before you try playing blues in first position, I show you how the notes and chords on the harmonica relate to the I, IV, and V chords.

Finding the home note and the home chord

When you play in first position, the I chord is easy to find; it's formed by all the harmonica's blow notes. Figure 13-1 shows the home chord, along with the blue notes you can get by bending those notes down.

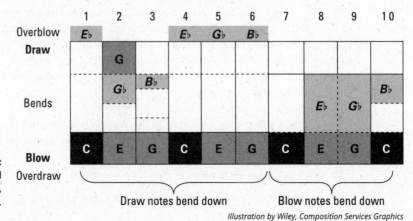

FIGURE 13-1: The home chord in first position, with blue notes.

Illustration by Wiley, Composition Services Graphics

The one downside to having blow notes form the home chord is that they don't bend down in the first six holes. Only the top four blow notes (Holes 7 through 10) bend down, giving you the blue notes. Those bent notes sound great, but they're awfully high, and you can't spend too long up there without tiring your ears. To spend some time away from the high notes, players jump down to the low register and find ways to use bendable draw notes. They often avoid the middle register, though you can find ways to make that register sound bluesy as well.

Playing over the IV chord

When you play in first position, you don't have a big, fat IV chord. In Figure 13-2 you can see that the IV chord includes some bent notes in the low register, some scattered blow notes, and two pairs of draw notes in the middle and high registers.

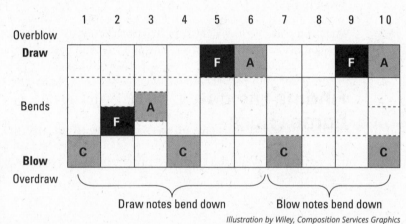

FIGURE 13-2:
Notes of the
IV chord in first
position.

Illustration by Wiley, Composition Services Graphics

However, you can inflect the high blow chord to fit with the IV chord by bending Blow 8. (For more on inflecting chords, see Chapter 7.)

Playing over the V chord

The V chord is five notes up the scale from the I chord, and in first position, the V chord is formed by the draw notes in Holes 1 through 4. Because these notes all bend down, this portion of the V chord is powerful sounding and easy to work. As you travel up the harp, though, the notes of the V chord break up into a collection that includes some draw notes that don't bend down and some blow notes, as you can see in Figure 13-3.

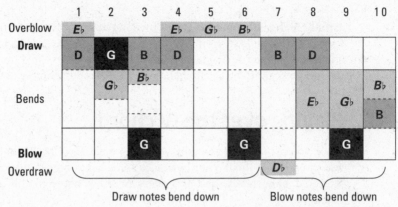

	1	2	3	4	5	6	7	8	9	10
Overblow	E♭			E♭	G♭	B♭				
Draw	D	G	B	D			B	D		
Bends		G♭	B♭					E♭	G♭	B♭
										B
Blow			G			G			G	
Overdraw							D♭			

Draw notes bend down   Blow notes bend down

Illustration by Wiley, Composition Services Graphics

FIGURE 13-3:
Notes of the V chord in first position, with second-position blue notes.

TIP

When you play over the V chord in first position, you can use a lot of the licks and riffs you may already know from playing in second position (hint: they're sprinkled throughout this book). Those second-position licks work because the chord they're based on is part of both positions — it's the I chord in second position and the V chord in first position.

Figure 13-3 shows the notes of the V chord, together with the blue notes that belong to second position. These borrowed blue notes happen to sound good in first position as well, and they're very convenient — you just bend a draw note down to get them.

Navigating the Three Registers in First Position

For each of the three basic chords, all three registers give you unique possibilities to either exploit, finesse, or avoid. In Tabs 13-2, 13-3, and 13-4 at the end of this chapter, I show you some of the cool things to explore in each register. Here I describe some of the things to look for.

Screaming in the high register

In the high register (Holes 7 through 10), all the blow notes bend down to give you expressive sounds and to create blue notes. Because these bendable blow notes are also the home chord's notes, you can

>> Get funky when you play over the I chord.

>> Inflect the I chord's notes when you play over the IV and V chords. (For info on inflecting the I chord, check out Chapter 7.)

>> Integrate blow notes and blow bends into licks that are based on draw notes.

The draw notes in the high register don't bend, but they supply important notes of the IV and V chords. You can often work some blow notes (and bends) into a sequence of draw notes, as well.

Cooking in the middle register

Blues harmonica players tend to view the middle register like the plain sister with thick glasses, which is kind of shallow. True, the middle register doesn't have deep bends, and you can only produce blue notes in the middle register by over-blowing when you play in first position. But you can still get the middle register to generate some steam if you work with what you have — and you have more than you may notice at first glance.

The draw notes in the middle register bend down, but they're not home chord notes. However, they're notes of the V chord and contain notes that belong to the IV chord, which many players overlook.

Growling in the low register

In the low register, the draw notes are all notes of the V chord. But by bending them, you can produce

>> Blue notes (Draw 2 or 3 bent down one semitone)

>> Notes of the IV chord (Draw 2 or 3 bent down two semitones)

You can also slide between bent notes for a sound that can be either slinky or aggressive.

Bearing Down on Blue Notes and Bendable Notes in First Position

Blue notes — the lowered third, fifth, and seventh degrees of the major scale — are available as blow bends in the high register and draw bends in the low register. However, in the middle register you can only get those notes by playing overblows. If you develop your overblowing skills (turn to Chapter 11 for more on overblowing), you'll have access to blue notes throughout the harmonica's range.

Tab 13-1 shows you some licks using blue notes in all three registers.

PLAY THIS

You can hear Tab 13-1 on Track 64.

TAB 13-1:
Blue notes in all
three registers.

Exploring Pathways to First-Position Licks and Riffs

A *pathway* is a long series of notes that you can follow for its entire length or for just a short segment. Between any two points along that pathway, you can focus on a group of notes and use them to fashion a lick or riff. (For more on pathways, flip to Chapter 6.)

Tabs 13-2, 13-3, and 13-4 show you a blizzard of notes, but don't be daunted. You can play through these notes as slowly as you like. The point is to get familiar with the sequence; you're cutting a new path through the undergrowth. After you blaze the trail, you'll be able to move rapidly through the woods and find all sorts of new places to go.

Tab 13-2 shows some pathways for the I chord in first position.

Tab 13-3 shows some pathways for the IV chord in first position.

Tab 13-4 shows some pathways for the V chord in first position.

PLAY THIS

You can hear Tabs 13-2, 13-3, and 13-4 on Tracks 65, 66, and 67.

TAB 13-2:
Pathways for the
I chord in first
position.

TAB 13-3:
Pathways for the
IV chord in first
position.

TAB 13-4:
Pathways for the
V chord in first
position.

Three First-Position Study Tunes

In this section I give you three tunes in order to work on the juiciest parts of first-position blues. The first focuses on the high register, the second on the often-overlooked middle register, and the third on the low register.

"Jimmy's Boogie"

"Jimmy's Boogie" (Tab 13-5) is named for Jimmy Reed, one of the great masters of playing the high register in first position. The relaxed shuffle tempo lets you take your time and make short statements that take full advantage of the high blow bends.

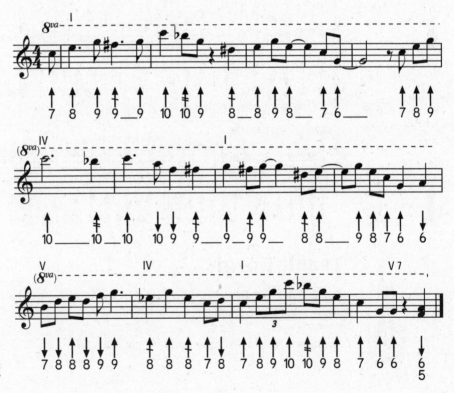

TAB 13-5:
"Jimmy's Boogie."

"Madge in the Middle"

If you look past the granny glasses, "Madge in the Middle" has a lot to offer. You just have to take the time to get acquainted with some of the fine home cookin' to be found in that middle register, as you can taste in Tab 13-6.

TAB 13-6:
"Madge in the
Middle."

"Tear It Down"

"Tear It Down" (Tab 13-7) lets you use the deep draw bends in the low register to express some fierce emotions.

PLAY THIS

You can hear Tabs 13-5, 13-6, and 13-7 on Track 68.

TAB 13-7:
"Tear It Down."

Chapter **14**

Accelerating the Blues with Third Position

Third position is the dark horse of blues harmonica, with its minor, mysterious-sounding home chord. Third position is an odd mix of qualities, and it can feel like the most flexible position because its home chord stretches over two octaves — going right to the top of the harp and plunging into the deep bends at the bottom of the harp. Though third position is a natural for deep, soulful blues, it's also a great way to crank into over-the-top, pedal-to-the-metal speed playing.

Third position reflects an urban approach to blues harmonica. It didn't really find its feet until the 1950s in Chicago, and since then, it has become a favorite of many players and a must for certain tunes in the blues repertoire. If you're intrigued by the possibilities I'm suggesting, read on.

Relating Third Position to the Three Chords of the Blues

All three of the popular harmonica positions offer two of the three main chords used in blues. A complete set of chords would be great, but two out of three ain't bad, eh? First position has the I (blow) and V (draw) chords. Second position has the I (draw) and IV (blow) chords. Third position has the I and IV chords too, but they're both draw chords. The IV chord is in Holes 1 through 4, and the I chord is in Holes 4 through 10 (Draw 1 and 4 are part of both chords). The blow chord is none of the above, but it can fake the V chord. Despite its odd collection of chords, though, third position offers a freedom and flexibility that's unique among the three main positions.

Finding the home note and the home chord

In third position you find the home note in Draw 1, Draw 4, and Draw 8 (the notes in the black cells in Figure 14-1). All the notes from Draw 4 through Draw 10 form the home chord or I (one) chord. In third position, the I chord is a minor chord with an exotic, mysterious sound. The note in Draw 7 isn't technically a part of the chord, but it's in the line of action and contributes a part of that mysterious sound. In the low register, you have to bend Draw 2 and 3 down to reach some of the home chord's notes, as you can see in Figure 14-1.

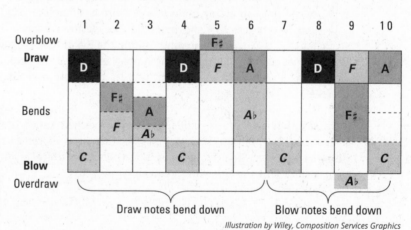

FIGURE 14-1:
The home chord in third position.

Illustration by Wiley, Composition Services Graphics

Playing over the IV chord

One nice thing about the IV chord in third position is that it's the same chord as the I chord in second position, so you can take everything you already know about second position and reuse it when the IV chord comes around in third position. You can see the notes of the IV chord laid out in Figure 14-2.

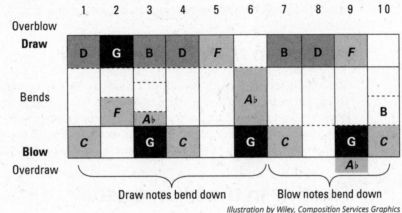

FIGURE 14-2:
Notes of the IV chord in third position.

Illustration by Wiley, Composition Services Graphics

Playing over the V chord

If you examine Figure 14-3, you can see that the notes of the V chord are a mixed bag of bends, draw notes, and blow notes that can't all be played together. However, the blow chord's notes form a sort of close-enough-for-the-blues substitute.

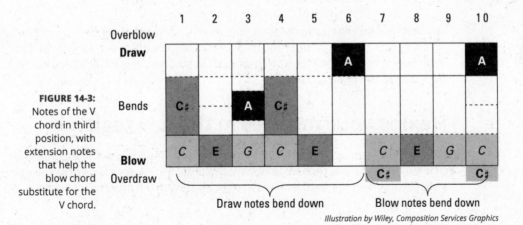

FIGURE 14-3:
Notes of the V chord in third position, with extension notes that help the blow chord substitute for the V chord.

Illustration by Wiley, Composition Services Graphics

The Three Registers in Third Position

In third position, each register has a unique character that you can exploit to good effect. In this section, I take you through the special qualities of each register.

Wailing in the middle register

The middle register offers you a full I chord as well as bendable notes in that chord. Those bendable home chord notes make this register the main territory where you can play wailing, searing licks. Players tend to use the middle register as the home area in third position, making excursions up to the high register and down to the deep bends of the low register but usually returning to the middle.

Floating in the high register

In the high register the home chord's notes don't bend down, but when you simply float up the draw notes from the middle register to the high register, you travel along an extension of the home chord, and it sounds great.

REMEMBER

The secret to getting the high notes to respond is not to force them. Gentle breathing is the way to get them to sound, but you also have to make sure that your throat is open, your tongue is relaxed, and your breathing comes from the abdominal area below your rib cage.

The bendable blow notes in the high register don't form notes of the home chord in third position, and perhaps for that reason, players often overlook them. But those notes can add some great sounds to third position, especially when you use them during the IV and V chords.

Flexing your muscles in the low register

If the middle register is searing and wailing and the high register is floating and ethereal, then the low register is brawny and deep. This register is where you get a big payoff on all the hard work you put in mastering the draw bends in Holes 2 and 3.

>> By bending Draw 2 and 3, you can transform them into notes of the I chord, extending the home chord's sweep through the harmonica's entire range.

>> By bending Draw 3 all the way to the bottom, you can access one of the low blue notes.

>> You can outline the notes of a major home chord by bending Draw 2 only a semitone. This major chord makes an interesting contrast with the minor chord that covers Holes 4 through 10.

TIP

For the IV chord in third position, you can use the licks and riffs you already know and use on the I chord in second position. It's the same chord but just playing a different role in each position.

Blue Notes and Bendable Notes in Third Position

In third position, two of the three blue notes are built into the scale, and you can bend them down (refer to Figure 14-1 for the I chord and the blue notes for third position).

But if you refer to Figure 14-2 (showing the IV chord) and Figure 14-3 (laying out the V chord), you can see that I include a set of blue notes for each chord. These supplementary blue notes are easier to play in third position than in the other two positions, adding to the sophistication and flexibility of third position.

Exploring Pathways to Third-Position Licks and Riffs

A *pathway* is a series of notes, along which you can travel and find licks, riffs, and even melodies by moving back and forth along short segments of the pathway or by ranging through a longer stretch. By getting familiar with a few pathways for each of the main chords in a tune, you can develop fluidity and confidence in your approach to each chord. You'll always know where you are and several possible places you can go.

Tabs 14-1 and 14-2 give you pathways for notes to play during the I chord and the V chord in third position. They're resources, not requirements. Play around with the note sequences in these tabs, listen for them in what you hear, and find ways to use them yourself. Also, you don't have to play them with the rhythms I use in these tabs. Those rhythms were just a matter of convenience. Let your creativity guide you in taking note sequences from these pathways and shaping them in whatever way strikes your fancy, including the rhythms you use.

Tab 14-1 gives you pathways for playing over the I chord in third position.

>> The pathway marked *a)* takes you through the home chord from Hole 4 to 10 and back and then takes you down into the low register, where you need to bend Draw 2 and 3 to reach two of the chord notes.

>> The pathway marked *b)* takes you through the scale, again from Hole 4 to 10 and back, and then down into the low register, where you need two bends.

>> The pathway marked *c)* lets you skip over the difficult bend in Hole 3. You often hear licks based on this pathway, for both the I chord in third position and the V chord in second position.

>> The pathway marked *d)* steps you through the blues scale, first going up to the top (though I omitted one blue note [the flat five] from the scale in the high register because it requires an overdraw) and then going down into the low register.

>> The pathway marked *e)* gives you a workout on all the available bends in the low register, which offers a lot of possibilities.

The IV chord in third position is the same chord, with the same pathways, as the I chord in second position, so for more on that, see Chapter 6.

Tab 14-2 focuses on pathways through the V chord in third position.

>> The pathway marked *a)* maps out the basic V chord that's built into the harp. Technically, this is a minor 7th chord, and the actual chord playing in the background is a dominant 7th. But in blues, this chord mismatch works okay and adds to the bluesy sound.

>> The pathway marked *b)* steps you through the scale, using no bent notes except the bends in Holes 2 and 3, when you get down into the low register.

>> The pathway marked *c)* adds the bendable notes in all three octaves. You can use these bends to add expressiveness when you play over the V chord, even though the bent notes may sound a little strange when you first try playing this pathway.

PLAY THIS

You can hear Tabs 14-1 and 14-2 on Tracks 69 and 70.

TAB 14-1: Pathways for playing over the I chord in third position.

TAB 14-2: Pathways through the V chord in third position.

Three Third-Position Study Tunes

The three third-position blues tunes in this section let you explore the different ranges and different approaches to playing blues in third position.

"Blue Cinnamon"

"Blue Cinnamon" (Tab 14-3) breezes down from the summit of the draw chord and then works its way back up through the IV and V chords. Remember to breathe lightly using all the air in your lungs to get those high notes to sound without struggling. Try using tongue techniques such as slaps on the IV chord (turn to Chapter 10 for info on tongue slaps).

PLAY THIS

You can hear Tab 14-3 on Track 71.

TAB 14-3:
"Blue Cinnamon."

"Sizzlin' Ice"

"Sizzlin' Ice" (Tab 14-4) is a slow blues that exploits the bends in Draw 6 and Blow 8. Try adding tongue slaps or other tongue techniques on this tune.

PLAY THIS

You can hear Tab 14-4 on Track 72.

TAB 14-4:
"Sizzlin' Ice."

232   PART 4 **Developing Your Style**

"Low Kicks"

"Low Kicks" (Tab 14-5) explores the low register. Though the basic scale in third position is a minor-sounding scale, the bends available in Holes 1 through 4 give you the flexibility to create a more major-sounding scale, and this tune gives you the opportunity to work out with those low-register bends.

PLAY THIS

You can hear Tab 14-5 on Track 73.

TAB 14-5:
"Low Kicks."

Chapter **15**

Playing Blues Chromatic Harmonica in Third and First Positions

The chromatic harmonica didn't start out as a blues instrument — but then, neither did the diatonic. Yet both are capable of magnificent blues sounds, each one distinctive, and both instruments have a firm place in every urban harmonica player's kit.

The chromatic harmonica is a relative latecomer to blues, though. For as long as anyone has been keeping track, the diatonic seems to have been present in blues and southern rural music in general, probably since the 1870s. But the chromatic entered the picture one day in the early 1950s when Little Walter saw a cucumber-sized harmonica in a Chicago music store and got curious. It turned out to be a 16-hole chromatic with a huge, four-octave range, and he quickly figured out how to get blues out of it with a magnificent sound that was strikingly different from the diatonic, making it valuable to him and desirable to his legion of emulators.

TIP

I recommend that you at least get familiar with the chromatic's sound. Chapter 18 has a list of essential blues harmonica recordings, including several great chromatic solos. If the sound of blues chromatic grabs you like it does so many of the best players, then come back to this chapter and I'll get you started on it.

Why Play Chromatic? Getting Accustomed to Its Face

The chromatic harmonica gives you something the diatonic doesn't — all the notes of all the scales in every key, without having to bend notes to get them. Blues musicians cheerfully ignore this universe of possibilities. Instead, they focus on the chromatic's majestic draw chord, and rather than spend arduous months studying scales, they hone their abilities to texture that chord's notes by using tongue techniques such as splits, hammers, slaps, and the other techniques that I describe in Chapter 10.

The chromatic from a blues perspective

Early on, Little Walter discovered that the chromatic is great for playing in third position. When he picked up the chromatic, he was probably experienced in playing third position on the diatonic (which I describe in Chapter 14), but when he tried it on the chromatic, he found some differences:

>> On the diatonic, the home chord for third position is the draw chord — but only from Hole 4 up. Below Hole 4, you get a different chord, which can sound strange if you play it at the wrong time. Consequently, you shouldn't include Draw 2 and 3 in your chords a good part of the time.

>> On the chromatic, the entire range of the instrument gives you the home chord for third position. It's an organ-like, dark, brooding chord, and on the chromatic, that chord sounds massive. Because of the way it's built, the chromatic harmonica sounds less like a high-pitched human voice than the diatonic and more like a thundering pipe organ — if you can imagine a pipe organ playing blues.

Chromatics come in several sizes, from 8 holes to 10, 12, 14, and even 16 holes. The 12-hole chromatic delivers the same three-octave range as a 10-hole diatonic, but Little Walter discovered that the 16-hole chromatic includes one additional octave below the range of a diatonic C-harp. That low register delivers some dark, gritty sounds that are perfect for Chicago-style electric blues. For more on how the chromatic harmonica is built, check out Chapter 2.

REMEMBER

In this chapter I focus on the 12-hole chromatic in C. Anything you can do on the 12-hole chromatic you can do over a wider range on the 16-hole chromatic.

The chromatic's uniqueness

The chromatic harmonica sort of looks like a really big diatonic. Though the two instruments are closely related, the differences are just strong enough to cause some consternation when you first try to play the chromatic. In the following sections I ease you through the differences and how to deal with them.

Tuning in to the note layout

The chromatic's note layout is called *solo tuning*. Solo tuning is based on the diatonic's middle register, its most logical part (though with the harmonica, you sometimes have to ask, "Logical compared to what?"). Figure 15-1 shows how the note layout from the diatonic's middle register was borrowed and cloned to create the high and low registers of the 12-hole chromatic. (A 16-hole chromatic would have four additional holes to the left of Hole 1, numbered 1 through 4, with dots under the numbers, and tuned to the same layout.)

Diatonic:

	1	2	3	4	5	6	7	8	9	10
Draw	D	G	B	D	F	A	B	D	F	A
Blow	C	E	G	C	E	G	C	E	G	C

Chromatic:

	1	2	3	4	5	6	7	8	9	10	11	12
Draw	D	F	A	B	D	F	A	B	D	F	A	B
Blow	C	E	G	C	C	E	G	C	C	E	G	C

Illustration by Wiley, Composition Services Graphics

Because every register on the chromatic has the same note layout, you can easily transfer a melody, lick, or riff from one register to another, and you never have to puzzle over how to supply a missing note, because every note is always available.

Getting it in your hands

The chromatic isn't heavy, but it's far bigger than the diatonic. Still, you hold both harps in a similar way. Figure 15-2 shows holding the chromatic from behind (the picture labeled *a*), while pictures *b* and *c* show holding the 12-hole and 16-hole chromatics from the player's viewpoint. Picture *d* shows holding the chromatic with your right index finger on the slide button, ready to press it in to access notes of the chromatic scale.

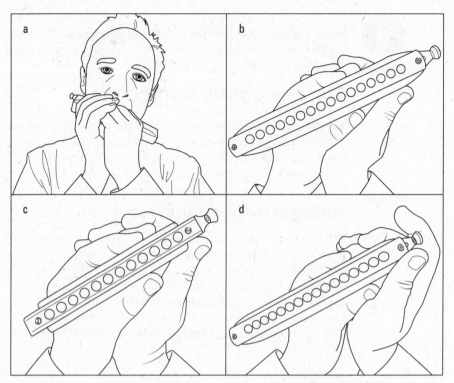

FIGURE 15-2:
Holding a chromatic harmonica.

Illustration by Wiley, Composition Services Graphics

Slipping it in your mouth and breathing through it

When you get the chromatic in your mouth, you'll really notice the size difference, simply because you have to open your mouth wider and drop your jaw deeper to accommodate the chromatic's size.

The chromatic doesn't tolerate strong breath attacks the way the diatonic does. When you breathe through the diatonic, air goes to the reed that you're not playing. Some of the exhaled air goes to the draw reed, and some of the inhaled air goes to the blow reed. The reed that doesn't sound acts as a sort of shock absorber, allowing you to attack the sounding reed more strongly.

But when you play the chromatic, all your breath goes to the reed you're playing, so that reed is much more sensitive to strong attacks and may clam up and refuse to sound if you come on too strong. You can still play the chromatic in a vigorous way, but you have to get accustomed to how it responds.

TIP

Chapter 4 walks you through holding and breathing through the diatonic. You can use the same series of steps to lay a good foundation for your relationship with the chromatic.

Third Position Blues Chromatic: Tongue Blocking Is King

The chromatic's draw chord has a huge sound, and you can shape that chord and make it sound even better by using your tongue to select different groups of holes to sound together or in alternation. The holes' large size helps to make some of these combinations easier to target and select.

In Chapter 5 I show you how to tongue block on the diatonic, and in Chapter 10 I cover how to use your tongue to create texture with slaps, pull-offs, hammers, rakes, and splits. I recommend that you review those chapters because those tongue-blocking techniques form the basis of the approach to blues chromatic that I describe in this chapter.

Adding body with splits

When you play a *split* you have several holes in your mouth, and normally, these would sound a chord. However, you use your tongue to block out the middle holes, splitting the chord into a high note in the right corner of your mouth and a low note in the left corner.

When you play blues chromatic, you use splits to beef up the sound of your licks, riffs, and melodies.

REMEMBER

Most of this chapter's tabs show single-note melodies. You can enhance any of them by playing splits and adding any of the tongue-blocked textures. Writing out all the possibilities would take a book of its own, so I encourage you to experiment.

On the chromatic, players mostly use three sizes of split:

> » **The three-hole split:** With this split you have three holes in your mouth and block out the hole in the middle. This split gives a hollow, ringing sound, and players use it sparingly.

> » **The four-hole split:** With this split you have four holes in your mouth and block out the two middle holes. This is the split favored by Little Walter. It produces mostly rich harmonies, though it does contain one discordant combination.

>> **The five-hole split:** With this split you have five holes in your mouth and block out the middle three. This split produces octaves, giving plenty of sizzle to whatever you choose to play. However, five holes on a chromatic is a wide spread for your mouth, and you may need to take some time to get comfortable playing octaves.

The five-hole octave split is a signature sound of the West Coast chromatic style. It was introduced by George "Harmonica" Smith and was adopted by other West Coast players such as Rod Piazza, William Clarke, Mark Hummel, and Dennis Gruenling (a New Jersey guy who plays like a West Coaster).

Working out with draw-chord splits

When you move from one draw note to another, you usually want to play a locked split — you lock the size of your split, usually either a four-hole split or a five-hole split. Then you just move the harmonica to the right or left in your mouth to change the combination of notes you sound with that split.

Tab 15-1 shows a simple line consisting of all draw notes played in a series of neighboring holes. Try playing this with a three-hole split, a four-hole split, and a five-hole split. Don't worry if you can't manage the five-hole split yet. That split uses a wide-open jaw position, and you'll probably need some time to get comfortable with it and then gain control of it. Start with the most comfortable split you can play and focus on getting it to stay at a consistent size while you slide the harmonica in your mouth.

TAB 15-1:
Locked splits on
the draw chord.

PLAY THIS

You can hear and play along with Tab 15-1 on Track 74.

When you play Tab 15-1 using a four-hole split, you may notice that one split sounds discordant — the one where you have Draw 7 in the right corner of your mouth. If you move around quickly, this discordant combination just sounds like a part of the chord. But if you linger on Draw 7 with a four-hole split, the dissonance can sound jarring. (You get the same result when you have Draw 11 in the right corner of your mouth, and, on 16-hole chromatics, with Draw 3 as well.)

To deal with this problem, you can switch to a three-hole split for Draw 7 and then switch back to a four-hole split when you move to Draw 6 or Draw 8. To master the basic action of switching to a three-hole split, follow these moves:

1. **Start by playing a four-hole split with Draw 7 in the right corner of your mouth.**

   Listen for this split's dissonant sound.

2. **Pucker your lips slightly, as if to pout, by pressing them forward slightly.**

   When you do this, you make your mouth opening smaller (you're aiming for one hole smaller). You also push the harmonica forward slightly.

3. **As you narrow your mouth opening, make sure to**

   - Keep Draw 7 sounding in the right corner of your mouth.

   - Keep a one-hole opening between the left corner of your mouth and the left edge of your tongue.

TIP

When you master this move, you'll hear Draw 7 combined with a note that makes a ringing sound instead of dissonance.

When you make this switch while also moving from one hole to another, you need to change the size of your split while you move from one hole to the next. Figure 15-3 illustrates the changes you need to make to your embouchure as you move.

1. You play a four-hole split.

2. As you move the harmonica to the left, you pucker slightly and draw the left corner of your mouth inward to the right as you also point your tongue into a narrower shape at the tip.

FIGURE 15-3:
Changing your
split as you move
to and from
Draw 7.

3. You maintain the location of the left corner of your mouth, and allow the right edge of your mouth and the tip of your tongue to widen to a four-hole spread.

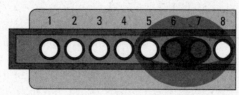

Illustration by Wiley, Composition Services Graphics

Playing melodic lines with splits

Tab 15-2 shows some melodic pathways for third position chromatic. Try playing these first as single notes and then with splits of three, four, and five holes. When you play four-hole splits, though, try using a three-hole split for Hole 7.

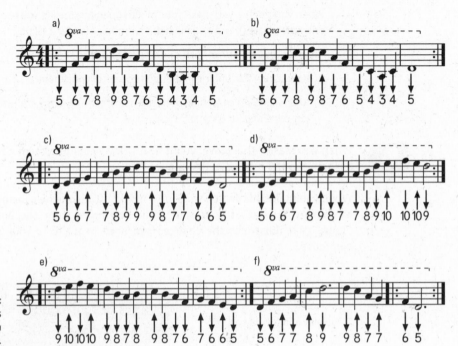

TAB 15-2: Melodic pathways for third position chromatic.

PLAY THIS

You can hear and play along with Tab 15-2 on Track 75.

Study tune: "Grits and Grease"

Tab 15-3 gives you your first blues chromatic tune, "Grits and Grease." The tab shows single-note melody lines, but after you learn the melody, try spicing it up with splits and other tongue techniques, as you can hear me doing on the track.

If you look at what the chromatic is doing during the I chord and the IV chord, you'll see that it's pretty much using the draw chord's notes in both cases. The draw chord notes work over both chords, so you can build your phrases freely, without paying much attention to what notes fit with which background chord. Over the V chord, however, the draw chord notes don't fit as well, so the blow notes, especially Blow 6, become the focal point of playing the V chord. (Blow 10 plays the same note of the scale in the high register; you can also find that note in Blow 2 in the low register.)

You can hear and play along with Tab 15-3 on Track 76.

TAB 15-3: "Grits and Grease."

Using the Slide

You can play blues chromatic without ever using the slide button that sticks out of the harmonica's right end. A famous photograph of Little Walter shows him holding a 16-hole chromatic with the slide button broken off. But even Walter used the slide occasionally, and over time, players have warmed to adding some slide touches to their playing, such as

>> Blue notes

>> Chromatic notes tucked between notes of the scale

>> Embellishments to melody notes using slide ornaments

>> Playing in a different key by holding the slide in

If you play a note with the slide out, you play a *slide-out* note. If you press the slide in and play a note that way, you play a *slide-in* note. Now I show you some of the slide delights on the menu.

Locking into tenth position with the slide

So far in this chapter I've showed you how to play third position without ever touching the slide — the slide remains in the out position. When you do this on a C chromatic, you play in the key of D. However, you can also play in the key of E♭ — one semitone higher than the key of D — just by pressing the slide in and locking it in place. Now you can play everything you already know in third position but have it come out in a different key — you get a double usage out of all that knowledge. This locked-slide method works for any key of chromatic harmonica, doubling your third-position potential.

When you lock the slide in place and play as if you're in third position, you're in tenth position. If you don't move the slide while you play, third and tenth play identically, and you can actually forget which position you're playing in. However, when you start moving the slide in and out as you play, third position and tenth position play very differently. If you learn to play with the slide either in (for third position) or out (for tenth position), you can later start to explore using the slide in each position.

Adding blue notes and slide ornaments

When you play in third position, two of the three blue notes — the flat 3 and the flat 7 — are built into the scale. You can use the slide to supply the one missing blue note, the flat 5. But you can also play the other two blue notes as slide-in notes. When you do this, you can move to and from the note in the scale that's just below the blue note, which often sounds cooler than playing the note without the slide, especially if you bend the note slightly as you start the note.

Tab 15-4 shows you some melodic lines that use the slide to play the blue notes and chromatic notes.

REMEMBER

The tab arrows with hollow heads are slide-in notes — notes you play with the slide held in.

PLAY THIS

You can hear and play along with Tab 15-4 on Track 77.

TAB 15-4:
Using the
slide for blue
notes and
chromatic notes.

Ornaments are like jewelry — you don't need it, but you may look nicer wearing it. You ornament a melody note by adding a quick flurry of neighboring notes. When you play the chromatic harmonica, you can move the slide in or out to create four kinds of slide ornaments:

>> **Slide bump:** When you play a slide bump, you play a slide-out note, but you bump the slide in momentarily and let it spring back right away.

>> **Slide dip:** When you play a slide-in note, you can let the slide out momentarily and then quickly press it back in. When you do this, the note dips down by a semitone and then returns to the note you were playing.

>> **Slide jab:** When you're about to play a slide-in note, you can start with the slide out and then quickly jab the slide in to arrive at your target note.

>> **Reverse jab:** When your next note is a slide-out note, you can start with the slide in and then quickly let it out to slide down a semitone to arrive at your target note.

Tab 15-5 demonstrates all four types of slide ornaments.

You can hear and play along with Tab 15-5 on Track 78.

PLAY THIS

Study tune: "Blue Bling"

Tab 15-6 is a tune called "Blue Bling" that adds the sound of slide ornaments, blue notes, and chromatic passing notes to third position chromatic.

You can hear and play along with Tab 15-6 on Track 79.

PLAY THIS

TAB 15-5:
Slide ornaments.

TAB 15-6:
"Blue Bling."

First Position Blues Chromatic

Third position gets the lion's share of action when you play blues on the chromatic, but a few players have figured out how to actually play the thing in the key that it's tuned to. This highly logical behavior may seem shockingly conventional and too straightforward for blues, but it actually works. We have George "Harmonica" Smith to thank for making this a credible choice for blues musicians, but you can sometimes hear Stevie Wonder's influence in the first-position chromatic playing of some blues musicians.

Adding the blue notes and slide ornaments

One cool thing about first position is that all the blue notes are available as slide-in draw notes, and slide jabs, bumps, dips, and reverse jabs all work to ornament these blue notes. Tab 15-7 shows a scale in first position that concentrates on the slide-in blue notes but also includes the slide-out note just beneath each blue note. The pairs of slide-in and slide-out notes have little brackets beneath them. When you play this scale, try creating slide ornaments using those pairs. Also try playing the scale in octaves as you develop your ability to play splits.

TAB 15-7:
First position scale with blue notes.

PLAY THIS

You can hear and play along with Tab 15-7 on Track 80.

Study tune: "Bumping the Slide"

To work out a bit more with the blues scale and slide ornaments in first position, try playing Tab 15-8, a tune called "Bumping the Slide."

PLAY THIS

You can hear and play along with Tab 15-8 on Track 81.

Playing splits in first position

Splits work great with first position, although you have to be choosy about how you combine them; you don't have that big, wet kiss of a draw home chord that you get in third position. The home chord in first position is the blow chord, and it doesn't have the automatic bluesiness of the third-position draw chord.

TAB 15-8: "Bumping the Slide."

Octave splits enhance anything you play without adding notes that may not fit. I recommend that you try playing all the first-position tunes in this section with octaves as you develop your octave embouchure.

WARNING

When you play splits that cover three or four holes, you can get combinations that sound weird, either on their own or against the background chords. You have to especially watch out for the two blow Cs that are placed side by side, each with a different draw note.

In Tab 15-9 and later in Tab 15-10, I break down each four-hole split precisely with a "stack" of tab:

>> On top are the breath arrow and note that you play in the right corner of your mouth.

>> In the middle are one or more tongue-blocked holes, represented by black lozenges, with none lozenge for each blocked hole.

>> On the bottom is the hole number that you play out of the right corner of your mouth.

In Tab 15-9 I walk you through all the four-hole splits with the range of slightly more than one octave. Remember, you can play the same splits exactly the same in any register, provided you don't run out of notes at the far ends of the harp. I include some splits that you might not use to play blues so that if you run into them accidentally, they won't sound strange. And who knows, you may find some clever way to use them.

TAB 15-9:
First position
splits.

PLAY THIS

You can hear and play along with Tab 15-9 on Track 82.

Study tune: "Splitsville"

"Splitsville" (Tab 15-10) is a first-position blues tune that exploits four-hole splits.

PLAY THIS

You can hear and play along with Tab 15-10 on Track 83.

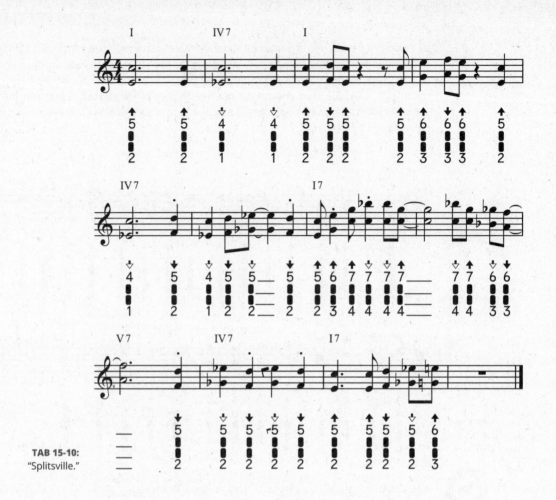

TAB 15-10: "Splitsville."

Chapter **16**

Playing Blues in Minor Keys

lues has its origins in the singing and playing of people with no formal education who developed their musical ideas in the middle of a collision of African and European cultures. As a result, blues doesn't fit neatly into the European musical categories of major and minor. Certain notes in the blues sound closer to minor than they do to major, but when blues musicians started playing chords, they chose major chords to accompany their melodies. The apparent clash between major background and minor foreground worked and became an important element in the sound of the blues. (Wondering what the differences are between major and minor? Check out Chapter 3.)

However, when you use minor chords to back the blues, major melody notes clash in a way that doesn't seem to please anybody. Blues in a minor key requires that you play minor scales. The diatonic harmonica was designed to play in major keys, so what do you do when you want to play a blues song in a minor key? Read on.

What Is a Minor Key?

When you play in a minor key, you use the notes of a minor scale to play melodies. The chords you use to accompany a minor melody are also minor chords (mostly). And those chords are usually made up of notes that belong to the same minor scale that you draw the melody from.

Okay, so what are minor scales and minor chords? I cover this topic more thoroughly in Chapter 3, but here's a brief recap:

» A *minor key* uses a scale whose third degree is lowered by one semitone, making that note a minor third.

» The home chord contains the scale's minor third, which makes the chord you build on the scale's home note, or *tonic,* a minor chord.

» In a *natural minor scale,* the scale's sixth and seventh degrees are also lowered by a semitone, and the IV and V chords are also minor chords.

- The IV chord contains the sixth degree of the scale as its third, so if the sixth degree is minor, the IV chord is a minor chord.

- The V chord contains the seventh degree of the scale as its third, so if the seventh degree is minor, the V chord is a minor chord.

Making Minor Keys Easy with Minor Keyed Harmonicas

As a blues harmonica player, you play mostly in second position (I describe positions in Chapter 12). So why not just get a harmonica that's tuned to play a minor scale and minor chords in second position? That way you can simply play the licks and riffs you already know, and they'll just come out in a minor key.

Natural minor tuned harmonicas do just that — convert what you already know to work in minor keys. This tuning gives you a minor blow chord for the IV chord and two minor draw chords for the I chord (Draw 1 through 4) and the V chord (Draw 4 through 6 and Draw 8 through 10).

Figure 16-1 shows the note layouts for a C-harmonica in standard tuning and a harmonica in natural minor tuning. In the natural minor harp, the notes E and B are lowered by one semitone, to E♭ and B♭ respectively.

C harmonica in standard tuning:

Hole	1	2	3	4	5	6	7	8	9	10
Draw	D	G	B	D	F	A	B	D	F	A
Blow	C	E	G	C	E	G	C	E	G	C

Natural minor tuning, with chords in second position:

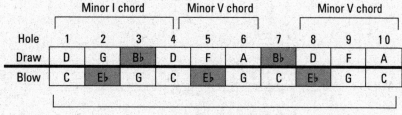

	Minor I chord				Minor V chord			Minor V chord		
Hole	1	2	3	4	5	6	7	8	9	10
Draw	D	G	Bb	D	F	A	Bb	D	F	A
Blow	C	Eb	G	C	Eb	G	C	Eb	G	C

Minor IV chord

Illustration by Wiley, Composition Services Graphics

FIGURE 16-1:
Note layouts in standard tuning and natural minor tuning.

Figuring out which key you need to play natural minor in second position can be confusing, though, because different manufacturers follow different conventions:

>> **Some manufacturers label minor key harps in first position.**

The natural minor harmonica in Figure 16-1 is an alteration of a regular C-harp, so Hohner labels this as a C natural minor, even though it produces a G natural minor scale and is intended to be played in second position (in the key of G minor in this case).

>> **Some manufacturers label minor key harps in second position.**

Lee Oskar designed natural minor tuning to be played in second position, so he labels it in second position. The natural minor harmonica in Figure 16-1 is labeled as G natural minor in the Lee Oskar catalog. Seydel also follows this convention.

WARNING

The *harmonic minor* tuning plays a different type of minor scale in first position. Harmonic minor sounds great in styles such as klezmer, gypsy, and Eastern European music, but it sounds rather weird in blues. So unless you're fairly daring and very knowledgeable in music theory, avoid the harmonic minor tuning.

Tab 16-1, "Fuzzy Dice," is a 12-bar blues in G minor. I wrote it to play on a harmonica in natural minor tuning (G natural minor using the Lee Oskar system or C natural minor using the Hohner system).

TAB 16-1:
"Fuzzy Dice."

You can hear and play along with Tab 16-1 on Track 84.

PLAY THIS On a natural minor harp, Draw 2 and Draw 5 bend down farther than they do on a standard harmonica. Especially on Draw 2, you can easily bend past the note you're aiming for, so you have to adjust your bending technique to hit that bend accurately.

If you're clever and really want the challenge, you may be able to figure out how to play the tune in Tab 16-1 using some of the methods in the next part of this chapter. Fourth position on a B♭ harmonica has notes that most closely match this tune's notes, but to try it you need a good command of bending Draw 3 down.

Using Familiar Positions to Play in Minor Keys

Maybe you don't relish the prospect of acquiring a whole set of harmonicas in natural minor tuning, lugging them around, and arraying them along with all your other harps at a playing session. Or maybe you're just thrifty and would rather get more use out of your existing harmonicas. So how do you adapt a standard harmonica to play in a minor key? Here are three strategies:

>> Play in a position that gives you a minor scale or a partially minor scale, such as third, fourth, or fifth positions. (I cover fourth and fifth positions later in this chapter.)

>> Bend notes to create any missing minor-scale notes. (I cover note bending in Chapter 11.)

>> Steer clear of notes that clash with the minor scale. These are the *avoid notes.*

In the following sections I show you five different positions and how you can use them to play in minor keys. For each position, I use a harmonica note layout to show you

>> Notes of the minor I chord, which are shaded in black.

>> Notes of the minor V chord, which are shaded in gray.

>> Notes of the minor IV chord, which have no shading.

>> The root note of the chord, which has tiny parentheses beside it. If that note also belongs to one of the other chords, the number of that chord is inside the parentheses.

>> Avoid notes, which are marked with an X.

>> Notes to avoid only on the IV chord, which are marked with an asterisk.

Adapting third position to minor keys

Third position gives you a minor I chord, an incomplete minor V chord, and a major IV chord that you can partially convert to a IV chord. Stated that way, third position doesn't sound terribly promising for minor blues, but in practice it works pretty well.

The only avoid notes when you play third position in a minor key are Draw 3 and Draw 7, and then only during the IV chord. When the IV chord is playing, though, you can bend Draw 3 down to fit with the chord.

Figure 16-2 maps out the notes of the I, IV, and V chords and the avoid notes in third position.

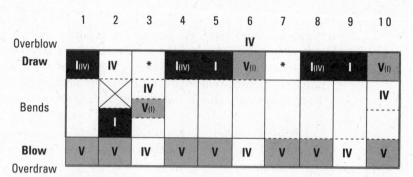

	1	2	3	4	5	6	7	8	9	10
Overblow						IV				
Draw	I(IV)	IV	*	I(IV)	I	V(I)	*	I(IV)	I	V(I)
Bends		X	IV							IV
			V(I)							
		I								
Blow	V	V	IV	V	V	IV	V	V	IV	V
Overdraw										

FIGURE 16-2: Notes of minor I, IV, and V in third position.

Illustration by Wiley, Composition Services Graphics

"Dark Stretch" (Tab 16-2) is a minor tune in third position. You can play minor keys in third position with very little adaptation. Just remember that when the IV chord comes around, avoid Draw 7 and bend Draw 3.

PLAY THIS

You can hear and play along with Tab 16-2 on Track 85.

TAB 16-2: "Dark Stretch."

Adapting second position to minor keys

"Help Me," by Sonny Boy Williamson II, is one of the most popular blues harp tunes of all time. It's a minor tune, and Sonny Boy played it in second position, deftly bending Draw 3 to fit with the I chord and avoiding Blow 2 and Blow 5, which would have clashed with the IV chord. Additional avoid notes are Draw 7 and Blow 8.

Figure 16-3 maps out the notes of the I, IV, and V chords and the avoid notes in second position.

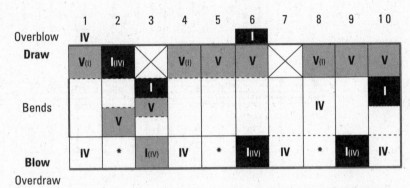

FIGURE 16-3:
Notes of minor I, IV, and V in second position.

Illustration by Wiley, Composition Services Graphics

"Junior's Jive," named for Junior Wells, is a second-position minor tune, tabbed out in Tab 16-3.

PLAY THIS

You can hear and play along with Tab 16-3 on Track 86.

Adapting first position to minor keys

First position is seldom used for minor keys. Blow 2 and Blow 5 clash and don't bend down, but you can bend Blow 8 down to create a minor note, making the high register the most welcoming place to play minor tunes in first position. Still, if you don't nail that bend exactly, you run the risk of sounding sour.

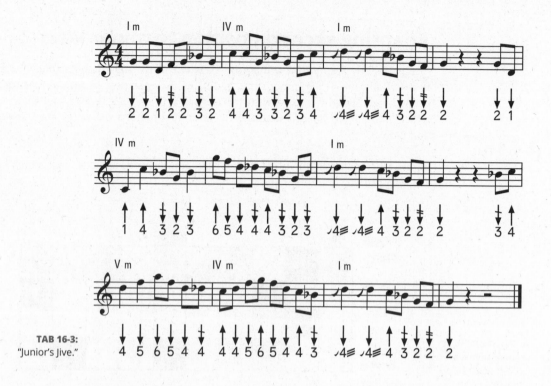

Figure 16-4 maps out the notes of the I, IV, and V chords and the avoid notes in first position.

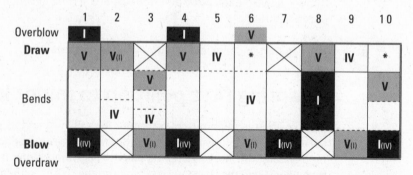

FIGURE 16-4:
Notes of minor I, IV, and V in first position.

Illustration by Wiley, Composition Services Graphics

Rhythm Willie's "Bedroom Stomp" is one of the very few known uses of first position to play in a minor key, along with Rod Piazza's "Murder in the First Degree." But Tab 16-4 shows a new first-position minor blues I came up with by taking inspiration from Bubber Miley, who played great minor-key blues trumpet in the early Duke Ellington band.

TAB 16-4:
"Bubber's Blues."

 You can hear and play along with Tab 16-4 on Track 87.

PLAY THIS

Getting Hip to Minor Positions

The positions that give you a minor scale without bending seem like the most logical positions to play minor key blues. But blues didn't develop on the planet Vulcan (Mr. Spock as a blues singer? Hmm . . .), and somehow, the logical appeal of minor positions has never caught on in a big way, probably because they don't offer a nice, cushy home chord with several safe-sounding notes in neighboring holes. Also, sometimes the avoid notes are notes you really do want to avoid. But if you're looking for some new possibilities, check out fourth and fifth positions.

Playing in fourth position

Fourth position blues is seldom heard (Rhythm Willie's 1940 recording of "Breath-takin' Blues" is a rare exception). Fourth position has a natural minor scale and the notes of minor I, IV, and V chords, but two features make it a little awkward:

>> The notes of the I chord are scattered between blow and draw notes.

>> The home note in the low register is a bent Draw 3, which can be hard to play in tune and to sustain.

Figure 16-5 maps out the notes of the I, IV, and V chords and the avoid notes in fourth position.

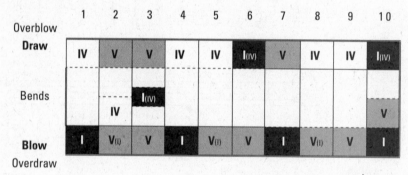

FIGURE 16-5:
Notes of minor I, IV, and V in fourth position.

Illustration by Wiley, Composition Services Graphics

Tab 16-5 is a minor blues in fourth position. You can play it as a slow and mournful dirge, but it perks up nicely, so I treat it more like the sort of dance tune you might have heard in the jazz clubs of 1930s Paris.

You can hear and play along with Tab 16-5 on Track 88.

PLAY THIS

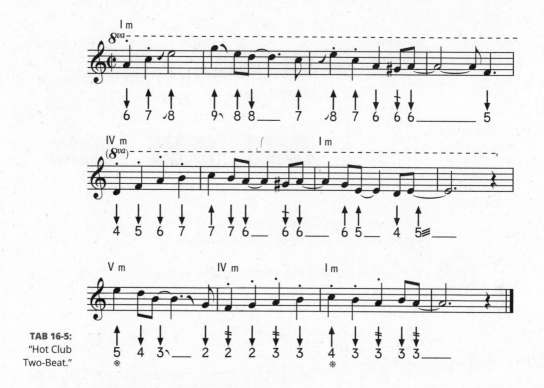

TAB 16-5:
"Hot Club Two-Beat."

Playing in fifth position

Perhaps the earliest use of fifth position in blues was on William McCoy's 1929 "Central Tracks Blues." You hear fifth position on pop and country records now and then, but blues players don't use it much, perhaps because it has two strong avoid notes (Draw 5 and 9) that can make chording and tongue-blocking effects sound rather sour. Aside from those avoid notes, though, fifth position has a great feel for minor blues. The draw bends in Holes 1 through 4 all fit with the home chord, and by alternating Blow 2 and 3 with Draw 2 and 3, you get a complete home chord.

Figure 16-6 maps out the notes of the minor I, IV, and V chords and the avoid notes in fifth position.

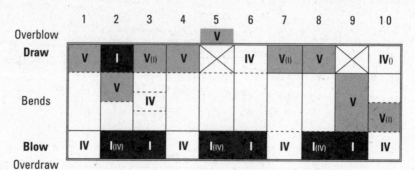

FIGURE 16-6:
Notes of minor I, IV, and V in fifth position.

Illustration by Wiley, Composition Services Graphics

Tab 16-6, "Tumbleweed Crawl," explores the vaguely slithery qualities of fifth position while staying away from the avoid notes.

PLAY THIS

You can hear and play along with Tab 16-6 on Track 89.

TAB 16-6:
"Tumbleweed Crawl."

Chapter **17**

Groovin' with Non-12-Bar Blues

The 12-bar blues, which I cover in Chapter 7, is by far the most popular form for blues songs, as well as the most popular chord progression for blues harmonica players to strut their stuff. But every now and then you need a little variety, so a few alternative forms show up here and there for some welcome relief.

Non-12-bar blues usually uses the same three basic chords as 12-bar blues, but those same chords show up at different places in the verse, and the phrases themselves are different lengths.

In this chapter, I show you how to adapt your 12-bar smarts to other blues song forms and how to find your way in two of the most enduring alternative blues forms, the 8-bar blues and Saints changes.

Strategies for Adapting to Different Song Forms

You've probably had the experience of visiting someone's house for the first time and looking for the bathroom. You know it's there somewhere; you just have to find it. The familiar patterns of moving around in your own house no longer apply, but at least you know what you're looking for. And if someone can tell you, "Go down the hall and turn right," you're in great shape. In this section I give you some strategies for finding what you're looking for in unfamiliar song forms and chord progressions.

Every song form has three main features:

>> An overall length that's measured in number of bars, which is usually a multiple of 4, such as 8, 12, or 16.

>> A series of shorter segments called *phrases* — usually either 2 bars or 4 bars in length.

>> A series of chords that occur during the song form, usually at the beginning or end of a phrase.

All these features taken together can be called a *song form* or a *chord progression*. Using the term *chord progression* simply puts focus on the chords — what order they come in and how long each one lasts.

Finding familiar chords in new places

When you play 12-bar blues, you know where the IV and V chords come along, and you know what they sound like when they arrive. You can identify these chords without knowing what key the band is playing in because you hear the relationships between the chords. (I explain the concept of chord relationships in Chapter 3, and I put them into action in Chapter 7.)

Most chord progressions start with the I chord. When you hear a new chord progression, the first thing you listen for is what happens after the I chord. Is the next chord a IV or a V? What happens after that? You're listening for the major events in the chord progression. You may find it helpful to jot down the sequence of chords as they come up.

Mapping out the beats and bars

After you note the chords as major landmarks along the journey, you measure the distance between the landmarks by counting beats and bars. When you do this, you can see how long the song form is, how long each chord lasts, how long each phrase lasts, and how the phrases fit together. (When you get really good at this, you'll be able to map out the chords while you count beats, but at first you'll probably find it easier to perform one step at a time.)

To map out the beats and bars, you can create a slash chart, similar to Figure 17-1, which appears a little later in this chapter. You jot down a little diagonal slash for each beat as it goes by, and you draw a vertical bar line after each bar, or group of beats. If the song is in 4 (and most blues songs are), then the beats are clustered in groups of 4, and you'd place a bar line at the end of each 4-beat bar.

After you count beats and bars, you listen again and write each chord above the beat where that chord begins. Now you have your basic map of the chord progression.

The length of most chord progressions is a multiple of 4 bars, such as 8, 12, or 16. Most musical phrases are either 2 or 4 measures in length, so writing your chord chart with 4 measures on a line can help you see the tune structure clearly on the page.

TIP

If the tune's length isn't a multiple of 4 bars, listen again to make sure you counted correctly. Chances are that most of the tune has clearly audible 4-bar phrases and that any phrase that's unusually long or short occurs during just one short segment of the tune, so try to identify that segment.

Listening to tunes in a new form

Chapter 18 contains a list of blues harmonica tunes that every harmonica player should hear and get to know. I include notes on each tune's form, and you can seek out tunes in non-12-bar form to sharpen your skills in listening for chord progressions, especially the two forms that come up most often, 8-bar blues and Saints changes.

The 8-Bar Blues Form

Eight-bar blues has been around since at least the 1910s, and a number of famous blues songs use this form. The granddaddy of all 8-bar blues tunes is "Stagger Lee." Other often-heard 8-bar blues include Leroy Carr's "How Long Blues," Big

Maceo's "Worried Life Blues," Elmore James's "It Hurts Me Too," and, from the country side of the blues, Willie Nelson's "Night Life."

Mapping the 8-bar form

Eight-bar blues is similar to 12-bar blues, but it's just different enough to trip you up if you don't know it. Eight-bar blues and 12-bar blues often share this sequence of major events:

1. Start with the I chord.

2. Go to the IV chord.

3. Go back to the I chord.

4. Go to the V chord (and then pass through the IV chord in 12-bar blues).

5. Go home to the I chord (and maybe have a quick series of turnaround chords to end the verse).

The main difference between 8-bar blues and 12-bar blues is in how long each chord lasts. Figure 17-1 shows a chord chart for the most basic form of 8-bar blues. (Ignore the chords in parentheses; those are variations that I deal with later.)

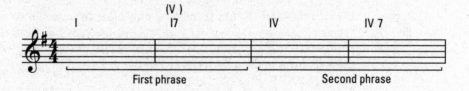

FIGURE 17-1: Chord chart for 8-bar blues.

The first thing you may notice about 8-bar blues is that it has four major phrases instead of the three phrases in 12-bar blues and that each phrase is 2 bars long instead of 4.

When you look at the chord progression, you find several distinct features:

» You go to the IV chord after only 2 bars instead of 4. So you don't get a pair of 2-bar phrases in question-and-answer form while you're still on the I chord.

» The IV chord lasts as long as the I chord that precedes it.

» The V chord comes halfway through the third phrase instead of at the beginning, and the IV chord doesn't follow it.

» The turnaround is equal in length to the other phrases, so it feels more prominent than it does in 12-bar blues.

Study tune: "Blue Eight"

To get familiar with 8-bar blues, listen to some of the 8-bar tunes listed in Chapter 18. Then try your hand at playing "Blue Eight," as shown in Tab 17-1.

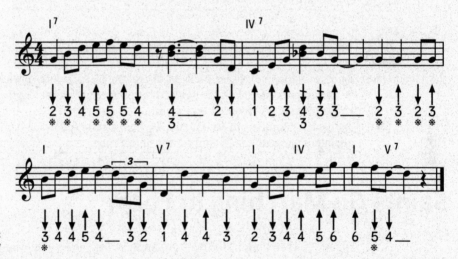

TAB 17-1: "Blue Eight."

PLAY THIS

You can listen and play along with Tab 17-1 on Track 90.

Noteworthy variants

Some 8-bar blues tunes go to the V in the second bar, including "Key to the Highway" as recorded by Little Walter and "Georgia on My Mind" as recorded by Ray Charles, although the latter has several additional complexities, mixing a sophisticated type of 8-bar blues with other elements.

"Five Roads Blues" (Tab 17-2) is a harmonica solo that uses the V chord in the second bar of an 8-bar blues.

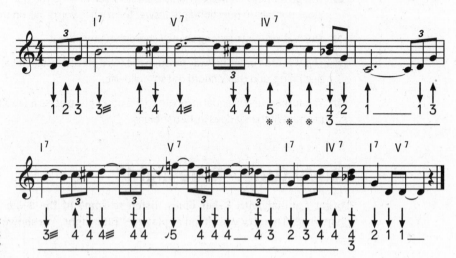

TAB 17-2: "Five Roads Blues."

You can listen and play along with Tab 17-2 on Track 91.

PLAY THIS Another variant of 8-bar blues is to add an instrumental phrase following the 8-bar progression that adds 1 or 2 bars to the verse's total length. "Sittin' on Top of the World" as recorded by Howlin' Wolf has this feature, and so does Robert Johnson's "Come on in My Kitchen," which clearly follows 8-bar blues form even though it stays on the I chord for the entire tune.

Saints Go Marching In Form

Saints Go Marching In form — or simply *Saints form* — follows the form of the New Orleans marching tune "When the Saints Go Marching In." (I hope that surprise isn't too much of a shock.) You can hear Saints form, or variants of it, in such songs as "Careless Love," "My Babe" (one of Little Walter's biggest hits), Ray Charles's "I Got a Woman," Little Walter's "One More Chance with You," and Paul deLay's "Ain't That Right." And harmonica player George "Papa" Lightfoot recorded a rockin' version of "The Saints" itself.

Mapping Saints form

Figure 17-2 shows a chord chart for Saints form. Note the early V chord in parentheses. Several of the tunes based on Saints changes feature this variant.

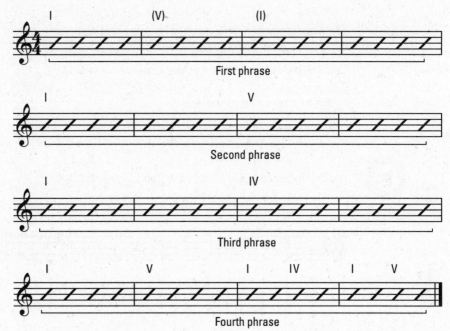

FIGURE 17-2:
Chord chart for
Saints form.

The form as shown here is 8 bars long (though Saints form also exists in a 16-bar version, where every chord lasts twice as long). Each phrase is 4 bars long and has the following notable features:

>> The first phrase stays on the I chord. (The V in parentheses is a variant that you hear in such tunes as "I Got a Woman" and "Careless Love.")

>> The second phrase ends with the V chord, and that V chord is the first major target to hit.

>> The third phrase steps from the I chord to the second major target, the IV chord, which comes halfway through the phrase instead of at the beginning.

>> The fourth phrase cycles from the I to the V and back to the I, with an optional turnaround.

Saints study tune: "High Water Strut"

Tab 17-3 is "High Water Strut," a tune in the 16-bar version of Saints form, consisting of four 4-bar phrases. All four phrases start the same way but end differently to deal with the different chords that arrive during the phrase:

>> The first phrase lands on Draw 2, the root note of the I chord, and then plays a little side comment.

>> The second phrase lands on Draw 4, the root note of the V chord, and also has a little follow-up comment.

>> The third phrase lands on Blow 4, the root note of the IV chord, but it jumps around a bit after it arrives. Heightened activity late in the verse helps keep the forward momentum going.

>> The fourth phrase is still in motion when the last V chord arrives, but it passes through its root note (Draw 4) to coincide with the chord's arrival.

PLAY THIS

You can listen and play along with Tab 17-3 on Track 92.

TAB 17-3:
"High Water Strut."

Second Saints tune: "All I Want"

What can I say? I'm feeling inspired. Tab 17-4 is a tune based on the Saints form with the early V chord, and it emulates some of Little Walter's playing. I've written in warbles and tongue slaps, which are optional. (See Chapter 10 for instructions on how to execute warbles and tongue slaps.) However, you do need to have command of your bends in Draw 2 and 3 to play this tune. (Flip to Chapter 11 for the lowdown on bending notes.)

PLAY THIS

You can listen and play along with Tab 17-4 on Track 93.

TAB 17-4:
"All I Want."

5

Taking It to the Streets: Sharing Your Music

IN THIS PART . . .

You learn about using amplification equipment, playing with other musicians, playing for audiences, and playing at jam sessions.

Chapter **18**

Developing Your Blues Repertoire

M ost of this book is about getting the harmonica in your mouth, ears, and brain and getting it moving to make bluesy sounds. Eventually, though, you'll want to play actual blues songs.

I recommend that you start checking out some of the all-time great harmonica solos and instrumental tunes, partly because they're fun to play, partly because you'll learn a lot from playing them, partly because you can impress people by playing them, and partly because, if you go to jam sessions or join a band, you'll be expected to know many of them — along with many blues standards that aren't harmonica songs.

At the end of this chapter, Tables 18-1 through 18-6 list essential harmonica songs, with each table covering a specific style or period in the blues. For each song, I list which type and key of harmonica was played, the harmonica position, the song's key, who played it, and what album it's on where relevant.

For many of the songs, the artist chose the songs that best represent his or her playing. For many of the others I had the assistance of such experts as Joe Filisko, Kim Field, Dennis Gruenling, and Peter Madcat Ruth.

Also in this chapter, I give you some pointers on how you can teach yourself to play the harmonica parts you hear on recordings. I also show you ways to fit harmonica into a song that doesn't have a harmonica part, and I give you some tips on assembling phrases over song form to assist you when you make up your own harmonica parts and solos.

Learning by Ear from Blues Records

Blues harmonica has always been an ear tradition; players learned by ear and never wrote anything down. Very few harmonica solos have been transcribed into harmonica tab or music notation, so if you want to learn them, the best way is to develop your ear by listening closely and then to pick up the harmonica and try to find what you hear. You can write things down if you want to, and I encourage you to do so if it helps you remember and learn.

Developing your ear

To train your ear, you could take an ear-training course at a music school, take a self-study course, or spend some time at an ear-training website. You don't need to be able to name the notes you hear (that ability is called *absolute pitch* or *perfect pitch*). What you need is to be able to identify the relationships among the notes you hear and relate them to the holes, breaths, and bends on the harmonica.

As a harmonica player, your experience in recognizing what another harmonica player is playing helps train your ear. Blues harmonica players may not identify note names, but they usually learn to identify much of what they hear, such as

>> Which hole a player is playing and whether it's a blow or draw note.

>> What position the player is playing.

>> Which chord the background musicians are playing in relation to the tune's key. (Musicians describe these relationships with numbers; see Chapters 3 and 7 for more on this.)

REMEMBER

Ear training and music theory help strengthen these abilities, but you develop them by listening and trying to figure out what you're hearing.

Figuring out harmonica parts from recordings

When you learn music by ear, you break it down into segments of short duration that you can remember easily, perhaps as few as two or three notes. You might try to hum the notes and then pick up a harmonica and try to find the notes. As you gain experience, you'll start to be able to predict what hole and breath on the harmonica gives the notes you're looking for.

You often need to listen to that same short segment of music several times to refresh your memory or to play along and check whether you've got it right. However, the standard controls on music playback devices and apps don't do a very good job of starting and stopping in precise locations. To make this job much easier, you can get apps that allow you to

>> Mark the beginning and end of a short segment of music and then play and repeat that exact segment.

>> Slow down the segment so that you can hear what's happening if the notes go by too quickly for you to figure them out.

TIP

Apps that work well for figuring out tunes include Audacity (www.audacity. sourceforge.net) and the Amazing Slow Downer (www.ronimusic.com/slowdown. htm).

However, before you get into the small details of a harmonica performance, you can benefit by mapping out the shape of the entire recorded performance and then noting what the harmonica player does in each part of the tune.

First, map out the tune itself:

>> What key is it in? Is it in a major or a minor key? And what key of harmonica might be good to play that tune in that key?

>> Does it have an intro before its main part begins?

>> How many bars long is the verse? Does it have a chorus or bridge?

>> Does the verse follow the standard pattern of 12-bar blues, or maybe 8-bar blues or Saints changes, or something else?

>> How many verses does the song have? Count and number them for easy reference.

>> Does it have solos in the middle (and maybe a harmonica solo)?

>> Does it have a *breakdown,* a nonstructured section where the song form goes away and the band just plays rhythm for awhile?

>> What do the musicians do to end the song?

Now listen to the harmonica player, who may be doing several things:

>> Where does she play and where does she *lay out* (not play)?

>> Does she play during the vocal or play fills in between the vocal phrases?

>> Does she add her own layer to the sound by playing long held notes, rhythmic chords, or bluesy lines?

>> Does she coordinate with the other musicians by playing the same rhythms and melody lines as other instruments, either in unison (the same notes) or in harmony?

>> Does she play a solo? If so, where does it come in the sequence of verses and how long does it last?

Now focus on the part of the tune you want to learn. Mark where that part begins and ends, and start listening to short segments, trying to figure them out.

Start by finding the first note of the harmonica part. Listen to just that first note and stop the playback. Now try finding that note on whatever harmonica you think is the same key as what the harmonica player on the recording is using. Then find the next note on your harmonica by listening, and so on.

At first this process of hearing notes, stopping the playback, and finding the notes on the harmonica goes very slowly. But when you successfully figure out even one harmonica lick, you'll gain a huge sense of satisfaction and accomplishment, and you'll have a new lick to play. And the more you do it, the easier it gets.

Sometimes, what the player does will seem elusive. If you study the techniques in this book and learn to both play them and identify them when you hear them, you'll have an advantage in being able to identify what you hear.

Improvising a Blues Solo with Licks and Riffs

The big moment for any blues harmonica player is when he gets to step forward and take a solo. Some players perfect a solo, memorize it, and then repeat it verbatim every time they play that song. Others toss off a new solo every time they play and couldn't remember what they played a moment ago if their lives depended on it.

Most players follow a middle path, building up a collection of memorized licks, riffs, and even complete solos by the greats and then drawing on that material to make up new combinations in the heat of the moment.

All through this book I give you licks and riffs, often as part of complete blues verses. As you develop your ear, you'll start to absorb and play riffs from hearing the players you admire and want to emulate. Though you can learn a lot from trying to copy those players exactly, eventually you'll want to come up with your own stock of phrases and start putting them together in a way that expresses your own personality as a player.

One method of coming up with an original solo is to take the licks you've learned from existing solos and recombine them in different ways. For instance, you could take two different solos from 12-bar blues songs and swap licks from corresponding parts of the verse, such as swapping the opening lick from one solo into the other. Or you can move licks around to different parts of a verse, perhaps by taking a lick that usually comes at the end of the verse and playing it in the middle instead. Not everything you try will work, but some combinations will please you, and you'll also discover a lot about why licks are placed at certain points in a verse.

Another thing you can do is to note how a lick or riff in one tune is similar — but not identical — to a lick or riff in another tune. As you start to notice how different licks are variations on a basic idea, you'll start to think of new ways to vary some basic riffs.

Adding a New Harmonica Part to a Song

You may want to add a harmonica part to a song that has no connection to the harmonica. How do you come up with something that fits in with the tune? Doing this is sort of like the reverse of mapping out a tune that already has a harmonica part.

Start by listening to the tune and what all the instruments are doing and then ask these questions:

>> Does the tune use a repeating riff played by other instruments, such as guitar, bass, saxophone, or keyboards, that you can play on harmonica?

>> Can you play fills between the vocal phrases?

>> Can you add a rhythmic part that adds texture to the overall sound without being too busy?

>> Can you add to the fullness of the overall sound by playing long notes that fit the backing chords?

>> Can you just kind of wail in the background to add to the general bluesy feeling of the song?

>> Would a harmonica solo really make this song come alive?

By answering these questions and listening to songs that already have harmonica parts, you may get some good ideas. For more on filling an instrumental role in a band, check out Chapter 20.

Blues Harmonica Songs to Get in Your Ears

When you're ready to listen to harp players who are firmly rooted in the blues and have made major contributions to the art, check out Tables 18-1 through 18-6. Each table covers a different style or historical period. For each song, I list what key it's in, what harmonica was used, the harmonica position, and the harmonica player's name. If the harmonica player played with someone else on that artist's record, I list that artist. Early recordings came out as singles on 78 rpm or 45 rpm singles, but for more recent recordings, I also list the album the song appears on.

TIP

On older recordings, the speed of a turntable or tape deck can be inaccurate and result in the key of a song changing by more than a semitone and sometimes the key being put in the cracks between standard pitches. As a result, take the key on older recordings with a grain of salt, and if the key is in the tracks, use pitch-shifting software to put it in tune with your harmonicas.

TABLE 18-1 **Prewar, Jug Band, and Early Chicago**

Song	Song Key	Harmonica Key	Position	Harmonica Player
Fox Chase	E	A-harp	2nd	DeFord Bailey
Ice Water Blues	A	A-harp	1st	DeFord Bailey
Pan American Blues	E	A-harp	2nd	DeFord Bailey
Mean Low Blues	G	G-harp	1st	Blues Birdhead
Mama Blues	G	C-harp	2nd	William McCoy
Train Imitations and the Fox Chase	G	G-harp	1st	William McCoy

Song	Song Key	Harmonica Key	Position	Harmonica Player
Stovepipe Blues	D, G	D-harp	1st, 12th	Daddy Stovepipe
Railroad Blues	B♭, F	B♭-harp	1st, 2nd	Freeman Stowers
Locomotive Blues	A	A-harp	1st	Sonny Terry
Lost John	E	A-harp	2nd	Sonny Terry
Walk On	F	B♭-harp	2nd	Sonny Terry & Brownie McGhee
Frisco Leaving Birmingham	E	A-harp	2nd	George "Bullet" Williams
Beale Street Breakdown	C	F-harp	2nd	Jed Davenport with Beale Street Jug Band
How Long How Long Blues	C	F-harp	2nd	Jed Davenport
Save Me Some	C	F-harp	2nd	Jed Davenport with Beale Street Jug Band
Bring It with You When You Come	C	C-harp	1st	Noah Lewis with Cannon's Jug Stompers
Going to Germany	G	C-harp	2nd	Noah Lewis with Cannon's Jug Stompers
Madison Street Rag	F	F-harp	1st	Noah Lewis with Cannon's Jug Stompers
Cocaine Habit	C	C-harp	1st	Will Shade with Memphis Jug Band
Viola Lee Blues	G	C-harp	2nd	Will Shade with Memphis Jug Band
You May Leave but This Will Bring You Back	C	C-harp	1st	Will Shade with Memphis Jug Band
Boarding House Blues	G	G-harp	1st	Rhythm Willie Hood
Breathtakin' Blues	G minor	B♭-harp	4th	Rhythm Willie Hood
New Block and Tackle Blues	C	C-harp	1st	Rhythm Willie Hood
Early in the Morning	A	D-harp	2nd	Sonny Boy Williamson I
Good Morning Little Schoolgirl	C	F-harp	2nd	Sonny Boy Williamson I
Shake the Boogie	G	C-harp	2nd	Sonny Boy Williamson I
Sloppy Drunk	C	F-harp	2nd	Sonny Boy Williamson I
Sugar Gal	G	C-harp	2nd	Sonny Boy Williamson I

TABLE 18-2　Chicago Blues from the Classic Period

Song	Song Key	Harmonica Key	Position	Harmonica Player
I Ain't Got You	E	A-harp	2nd	Billy Boy Arnold
I Wish You Would	G	C-harp	2nd	Billy Boy Arnold
I'm a Man	G	C-harp	2nd	Billy Boy Arnold with Bo Diddley
Easy	F	B♭-harp	2nd	Walter Horton
Evening Sun	E	A-harp	2nd	Walter Horton with Johnny Shines
Hard Hearted Woman	A	A-harp	1st	Walter Horton
Walkin' By Myself	A	D-harp	2nd	Walter Horton with Jimmy Rogers
Walter's Boogie	E	A-harp	2nd	Walter Horton
Blue Lights	D	C chromatic, G-harp	3rd, 2nd/3rd	Little Walter
Blues with a Feeling	A	D-harp	2nd	Little Walter
Hoochie Coochie Man	A	A-harp	1st	Little Walter with Muddy Waters
I Want You To Love Me	G	C-harp	2nd	Little Walter with Muddy Waters
Juke	E	A-harp	2nd	Little Walter
Long Distance Call	F	B♭-harp	2nd	Little Walter with Muddy Waters
My Babe	F	B♭-harp	2nd	Little Walter
Off the Wall	G	C-harp	2nd	Little Walter
Roller Coaster	E	A-harp	2nd	Little Walter
Rollin' and Tumblin'	G	C-harp	2nd	Little Walter with Baby Face Leroy
Sad Hours	F	B♭-harp	2nd	Little Walter
Thunderbird	D	G-harp, C chromatic	2nd, 3rd	Little Walter
Boogie Twist	C	F-harp	2nd	Snooky Pryor
Boogy Fool	F	B♭-harp	2nd	Snooky Pryor

Song	Song Key	Harmonica Key	Position	Harmonica Player
Bright Lights, Big City	A	A-harp	1st	Jimmy Reed
Honest I Do	A	A-harp	1st	Jimmy Reed
You Don't Have to Go	F	B♭-harp	2nd	Jimmy Reed
Chicken (aka Chuck-a-Luck)	C	F-harp	2nd	Sonny Boy Williamson II with Baby Boy Warren
Bring It on Home	E	A-harp	2nd	Sonny Boy Williamson II
Bye Bye Bird	G	Low C-harp, C-harp	2nd	Sonny Boy Williamson II
Help Me	F minor	B♭-harp	2nd	Sonny Boy Williamson II
In My Younger Days	C	F-harp	2nd	Sonny Boy Williamson II
Mighty Long Time	G	C-harp	2nd	Sonny Boy Williamson II
Nine Below Zero	C	F-harp	2nd	Sonny Boy Williamson II
All Night Long	G	C-harp	2nd	Howlin' Wolf
Moanin' at Midnight	E	A-harp	2nd	Howlin' Wolf
Smokestack Lightnin'	E	A-harp	2nd	Howlin' Wolf

TABLE 18-3 ## Southern Postwar

Song	Song Key	Harmonica Key	Position	Harmonica Player
Sugar Coated Love	E	A-harp	2nd	Lazy Lester
Jump the Boogie	D	G-harp	2nd	George "Papa" Lightfoot
When the Saints Go Marching In	D	G-harp	2nd	George "Papa" Lightfoot
She's Tough (1961 version)	F	B♭-harp	2nd	Jerry McCain
Steady	F	B♭-harp	2nd	Jerry McCain
Baby Scratch My Back	F	B♭-harp	2nd	Slim Harpo
Got Love if You Want It	F	B♭-harp	2nd	Slim Harpo
Rainin' in My Heart	G	C-harp	2nd	Slim Harpo

TABLE 18-4 **Continuing the Chicago Tradition**

Song	Song Key	Harmonica Key	Position	Harmonica Player
Blues in My Sleep	D	G-harp, C-harp, C chromatic	2nd, 3rd, 3rd	James Cotton on *Best of the Vanguard Years*
Creeper Creeps Again	E	A-harp	2nd	James Cotton on *100 Cotton*
Love Me or Leave Me	A	D-harp	2nd	James Cotton *on Best of the Vanguard Years*
Cha Cha in Blues	E	A-harp	2nd	Junior Wells
Hoodoo Man	A	D-harp	2nd	Junior Wells
Messin' with the Kid	C	F-harp	2nd	Junior Wells on *Best of the Vanguard Years*
School Is Over	F	B♭-harp	2nd	Steve Guyger
Snake Oil	E	E-harp	2nd	on *Past Life Blues*
Sugar Mama	G	C-harp	2nd	Steve Guyger with Paul Oscher on *Living Legends Deep in the Blues*
Clarksdale Getaway	A	A-harp	1st	Charlie Musselwhite on *The Well*
Cristo Redentor	B♭ minor	A♭-harp	3rd	Charlie Musselwhite on *Rough Dried*
If I Should Have Bad Luck	A	D-harp, A-harp	2nd, 1st	Charlie Musselwhite on *Rough Dried*
Blues in a Dream	E	A-harp	2nd	Jerry Portnoy on *Home Run Hitter*
Snakeskin Strut	E	A-harp	2nd	Jerry Portnoy with Legendary Blues Band on *Life of Ease*
Down at Antone's	E	A-harp	2nd	Kim Wilson with Fabulous Thunderbirds on *Tuff Enuff*
Floyd's Blues	E	A-harp	2nd	Kim Wilson with Barrelhouse Chuck on *Got My Eyes on You*
Reel Eleven, Take One	D	C chromatic	3rd	Kim Wilson on *Tigerman*

TABLE 18-5 **West Coast**

Song	Song Key	Harmonica Key	Position	Harmonica Player
Blowin' Like Hell	C	B♭ chromatic	3rd	William Clarke on *Blowin' Like Hell*
Blowing the Family Jewels	A	G-harp	3rd	William Clarke on *Tip of the Top*
Lollipop Mama	G	C-harp	2nd	William Clarke on *Blowin' Like Hell*
Coastin' Hank	C♯	B chromatic	3rd	Rick Estrin with Little Charlie & the Nightcats on *That's Big*
Headin' Out	E	A-harp	2nd	Rick Estrin on *On the Harp Side*
Old News	G	Low C-harp	2nd	Rick Estrin on *Twisted*
Hot Shot	D	C chromatic	3rd	Dennis Gruenling on *I Just Keep Lovin' Him*
House Party	C	Low F-harp	2nd	Dennis Gruenling on *History of the Blues Harmonica*
Twelve O'Clock Jump	B♭	Low F-harp	12th	Dennis Gruenling on *Dennis Gruenling & Jump Time*
Humblebug	C	C chromatic	1st	Mark Hummel on *Blues Harp Meltdown*
Jungle Scotch Plaid	C	B♭-harp	3rd	Mark Hummel on *Married to the Blues*
Summertime	D minor	C chromatic	3rd	Mark Hummel on *Mark Hummel's Blues Harmonica Blowouts*
4811 Wadsworth	D	C chromatic	3rd	Rod Piazza on *California Blues*
Chicken Shack Boogie	G	C-harp	2nd	Rod Piazza on *California Blues*
Harpburn	D	C chromatic	3rd	Rod Piazza on *Harpburn*
Blues in the Dark	D	C chromatic	3rd	George Smith
Got to Get to My Baby	A	D-harp		George Smith with Sunnyland Slim
Sharp Harp	F	B♭-harp	2nd	George Smith

TABLE 18-6 **Modern Stylists**

Song	Song Key	Harmonica Key	Position	Harmonica Player
Everything Gonna Be Alright (live)	G	C-harp	2nd	Paul Butterfield on *Live @ The Troubadour, Los Angeles*
Too Many Drivers	G	C-harp	2nd	Paul Butterfield with Better Days on *It All Comes Back*
Work Song	F	B♭-harp	2nd	Paul Butterfield on *East West*
Big Road Blues	D	G-harp	2nd	Carlos del Junco with Thom "Champagne" Robert on *Big Road Blues*
B-Thing Intro	B	E-harp retuned	2nd	Carlos del Junco on *Just Your Fool*
Skatoon	G	C-harp	2nd	Carlos del Junco on *Blues Mongrel*
Can't Quit You No	B	A-harp	3rd	Paul deLay on *Take It from the Turnaround*
Hopefully	F	B♭-harp	2nd	Paul deLay on *Ocean of Tears*
Nice & Strong	D, B minor	C chromatic	3rd, 6th	Paul deLay on *Nice & Strong*
Second Hand Smoke	C	C chromatic	2nd	Paul deLay on *Take It from the Turnaround*
The Other One	E♭	C chromatic	10th	Paul deLay on *Take It from the Turnaround*
Why Can't You Love Me	G	C chromatic	2nd	Paul deLay on *Take It from the Turnaround*
Crossroads Blues	A	D-harp	2nd	Adam Gussow on *Kick and Stomp*
I Want You	E	A-harp	2nd	Adam Gussow with Satan & Adam on *Harlem Blues*
Thunky Fing Rides Again	E	D-harp	3rd	Adam Gussow with Satan & Adam on *Back in the Game*
Whammer Jammer	E	A-harp	2nd	Magic Dick with J.Geils Band on *The Morning After*
Broken Toy	D	C chromatic, C-harp	3rd, 3rd	Jason Ricci on *Done with the Devil*
Loving Eyes	A	Low F-harp, D-harp	5th, 2nd	Jason Ricci on *Rocket Number 9*
Walter's World	F	B♭-harp	2nd	Jason Ricci on *Blood on the Road*

Song	Song Key	Harmonica Key	Position	Harmonica Player
Another Man Done Gone	G	Low C-harp		Sugar Blue on *From Paris to Chicago*
Help Me	G	C-harp	2nd	Sugar Blue on *Blue Blazes*
Miss You (extended disco mix)	D	D-harp	1st	Sugar Blue with the Rolling Stones on *Some Girls*
Going Down Slow	A	D-harp	2nd	Al "Blind Owl" Wilson with Canned Heat on *Canned Heat*
I'm Her Man	D	C solo tuned	3rd	Al "Blind Owl" Wilson with Canned Heat on *Hallelujah*
My Crime	E	A-harp	2nd	Al "Blind Owl" Wilson with Canned Heat on *Boogie with Canned Heat*
On the Road Again	A	A-harp	2nd	Al "Blind Owl" Wilson with Canned Heat on *Boogie with Canned Heat*

Chapter **19**

Blues Harmonica Amplification: Making a Big Noise with a Tiny Little Thang

To be heard in this world, you gotta make some noise. The more air you can move and the more vigorously you can shake it, the bigger the noise and the more attention you command. Harmonica reeds don't move much air — each one is smaller than the tine of a fork — though your breath can make them move vigorously for their size. The harmonica can hold its own with acoustic guitars and singing voices in a medium-sized room.

But when you need to fill a bigger space with sound, harmonicas, guitars, and voices can all use some help, especially when they have to contend with louder instruments such as drums and with the background noise of conversation, clanking dishes, and roaring traffic. That's where amplification comes in. Amplification equipment

1. Captures *input* by turning sound into electrical signals with *microphones* or by accepting input signals from electric guitars, keyboards, synthesizers, turntables, computers, and other devices with something to contribute to the sound of a performance.

2. Optionally enhances the signals in subtle and not-so-subtle ways with *signal processing* and *effects*.

3. *Amplifies* the signals to make them louder, using an *amplifier* or *amp*.

4. Sends the amplified signals as *output* to *speakers* that turn the amplified signals back into a louder sound.

So to be heard when you perform, you should just buy the biggest, loudest amplification equipment you can afford, right? Well, the terrain of amplification is bumpy and filled with both delightful gardens and explosive land mines, so in this chapter I guide you through some of the highlights so you can smell the flowers while preserving your major appendages.

Two Major Approaches to Amplification

When you play music with amplification, you encounter two different approaches that often coexist and collaborate to deliver the sound of a performance: *sound systems* and *individual amps*.

Sound systems and individual amplification often combine, with the sound system used in one of two ways:

>> **Minimally,** to amplify vocals and acoustic instruments such as acoustic guitars and saxophones. Some instruments use their own amplifiers, and drums go unamplified because they may be loud enough to be heard acoustically.

>> **Comprehensively,** for complete control of the performance's entire sound, with all amplifiers routed through the sound system, along with vocals, acoustic instruments, and even drums.

Using sound reinforcement for central control

Sound reinforcement transmits performers' sounds to an audience with clarity and minimal alteration, so that a whispering voice can magically fill a large theater and still seem perfectly natural. Though the goal of sound reinforcement is simple, its workings are complex and are embodied in a centralized *sound system* (also called a *PA* or *public-address system*). Here's how a sound system works:

1. **All the inputs from multiple performers go to a command center called a *mixing console* where an operator called a *sound tech* creates a *house mix* by adjusting the inputs' levels so that everything can be heard clearly in balance.**

2. **The house mix goes to a power amplifier (or *power amp*) that boosts the signal so that it's powerful enough to drive the speakers that will convert it back into sound.**

3. **The amplified house mix goes to the *mains,* which are arrays of speakers placed in multiple locations in the *house,* the space where the audience experiences the performance.**

4. **A second mix, called the *monitor mix,* goes to the stage and is fed to *monitors,* small speakers that rest on the floor and are angled upward, toward musicians' ears.**

   Monitors let you hear yourself and certain other players amid the din.

Many performance venues, such as theaters, nightclubs, and auditoriums, have permanently installed sound systems and in-house sound techs to run them. However, many smaller venues such as coffeehouses and gymnasiums may not have sound systems. As a result, some bands and even individual performers own and operate their own small sound systems, carrying them to gigs as needed.

Competing and cooperating with individual amplifiers

Instead of using a complex, centralized system, each performer can play through his or her own stand-alone amplifier. Each competitor — er, player — can either crank up the volume to drown out their opponents or cooperate to achieve a pleasing balance. On any given day, the collection of personalities and moods involved will determine the outcome.

REMEMBER

Playing through your own amplifier gives you another kind of independence, though. Both blues harmonica players and electric guitarists use amplification to alter the character of their instruments in ways that sound cool and actually change the instruments' potential — your amp becomes an extension of your instrument and alters the way you play it. An electric guitar isn't just a louder acoustic guitar; it sounds different, and you play it in a different way. Likewise, the sound of amplified blues harmonica is so unique that listeners may not even realize that they're hearing a harmonica.

When you play through your own amp, you also have your choice of microphone, any effects that change your sound, and the amplifier and speakers that you run them through. This chain of equipment is your *rig*, and you can configure your rig to suit your individual preferences and needs. Harmonica players love to talk about their rigs and all the parts that go into creating their amplified sound. I discuss how to choose and adapt amplification equipment in the later section "Piecing Together the Amplification Chain."

Using Distortion and Avoiding Feedback

Whether you play through a sound system or your own amp, you always have to deal with two realities, distortion and feedback. Though sound reinforcement avoids them both, blues harmonica players (and guitarists) cultivate and use distortion.

Distortion

A key element in amplified blues harmonica is *distortion*. Think of distortion as any change that amplification makes to natural sound, just as a weed is any plant you don't want in your garden. The goal of sound reinforcement is to minimize those changes in order to deliver clean sound. The kind of distortion that guitarists and harmonica players seek out and cultivate comes from driving amplification equipment beyond the limits of its ability to deliver clean sound.

This type of distortion is often referred to by such terms as *overdrive, saturation,* and *breakup*. Subtle distortion adds color to your sound, while more pronounced distortion is often described as *fat, dirty, gritty,* or *crunchy*.

Both clean sound and distorted sound are important elements in playing blues harmonica, and I discuss them in the context of each component in your rig.

Feedback

Feedback is a loud, squealing sound that's painful to human ears and tends to overpower the sound you're trying to amplify. It occurs when a microphone picks up the sound from the speakers and feeds it back through the amplification system. The sound then gets amplified, fed back into the microphone, and so on, in a *feedback loop*.

Electric guitars are less sensitive to feedback than microphones, and some electric guitarists, such as Jimi Hendrix, can harness feedback and incorporate it into their playing. However, most harmonica players avoid feedback. To avoid feedback, make sure you

>> Aim your microphone away from the speakers that amplify your microphone's signal (or place speakers so that they're not aimed at your mic).

>> Keep your amplified volume level low enough that the speaker signal can't get into your mic.

>> Use equalization to reduce specific frequencies in the sound spectrum that may cause feedback.

>> Use an anti-feedback device made for amplified harmonica, such as a Kinder Anti-Feedback unit.

I discuss how to avoid feedback in specific situations throughout the chapter.

Piecing Together the Amplification Chain

Whether you play through a sound system or your own rig, your sound travels through several stages. At each stage you can choose equipment that serves your purpose and adjust or manage it to give you the sound you want.

Each piece of equipment in the chain has to work with the other pieces. If you have a mic you really like, for instance, you won't know whether it sounds good with a particular amp unless you try the two together. Fortunately, if you shop near where you live, you can often try before you buy. Getting together with other players can also give you opportunities to try out unfamiliar equipment. You can use amplification equipment for three different approaches to playing the harmonica:

>> **Acoustic:** You use amplification to capture the sound you'd produce naturally if no amplification were present and you weren't competing with other loud sounds.

>> **Clean:** You embrace and incorporate amplification into your playing and let the amplification change both your sound and your approach to playing in subtle ways that a casual listener may not notice.

>> **Amplified:** You significantly alter your sound and approach to playing by using your own *rig* (your combination of microphone, special effects, and individual amplifier).

Understanding microphones

A microphone detects nearby sound and converts it to an electrical signal that it feeds to the next stage in the amplification process. The type of microphone you use and how you handle it influence the sound you produce. A mic has the following components:

» **An outer housing or shell:** The part you see and hold.

» **An element:** The internal part that captures sound and converts it to electrical signals.

» **A connector:** A socket that you connect to a cable that carries the signal to the next stage.

» Optional features such as an **on-off switch** or **volume control knob.**

The following sections describe some of the more important characteristics of microphones.

Directionality

An *omnidirectional* microphone picks up sound from every direction, no matter which way you aim it. For harmonica, you want to pick up just the sound of the harmonica. Omnidirectional mics pick up more sound than you want, including the audience, other instruments and amplifiers, and speaker sounds that can cause feedback.

A *directional* mic picks up sound only from the direction in which you aim it. Directional mics have a *cardioid* or a *hypercardioid* (extremely directional) response pattern. A directional mic is great for harmonica because it targets only the sounds you want to amplify and helps avoid feedback.

Frequency response

An ideal high-fidelity microphone would reproduce all sound across the audible spectrum in equal proportions. However, most mics enhance some parts of the audible spectrum and de-emphasize others. When you plot a mic's frequency response on a graph, the resulting line is called a *response curve*. You can view the response curves for most mics.

The harmonica emits a lot of high-frequency energy that can tire the listener's ear. A good mic for harmonica *rolls off* — de-emphasizes — high frequencies. *Bullet mics* roll off high frequency sound severely, contributing to the dark sound favored by amplified blues players.

Proximity effect

When you get close to a mic, you change how it delivers sound. This is known as the *proximity effect*. When you cup a mic in your hands, you get an extreme version of the proximity effect that changes sound in two ways:

>> The sound gets more compressed — the difference between loud and soft sounds is reduced.

>> The sound gets bassier — the low and midrange frequencies get stronger and the high frequencies roll off.

Impedance

Impedance is an electrical value that's measured in ohms, often expressed with the symbol Ω. A microphone's impedance must match the impedance of whatever you plug it into. If impedances don't match, volume and sound quality are reduced. Microphones and the equipment they connect with come in three types of impedance:

>> **Extreme high impedance (or extreme hi-z):** This range of impedance values — around 5 *megohms* (5 million ohms) — is used for bullet mics and mics designed for use with radio communications. To plug a bullet mic into a guitar amp, you may need to have internal modifications made to the mic or route it through an *impedance matching transformer*.

TIP

To plug a bullet mic into a sound system, you need a matching device called a *direct box* (or *DI*). Larger sound systems usually have these available, but you can't count on it in smaller venues.

>> **High impedance (or hi-z):** This impedance range (around 1 megohm) is used by electric guitars, guitar effects, and guitar amplifiers. Very few microphones operate in this impedance range. Bullet mics are often labeled as being high impedance while actually having extreme high impedance. Most microphones designed for high-quality audio output are low impedance, though a few, such as the Shure 545SD, are equipped for easy conversion to high impedance.

>> **Low impedance (or lo-z):** Sound system equipment and most vocal mics use low impedances of less than 600 ohms. Lo-z mics can plug directly into sound system equipment and acoustic instrument amplifiers that have microphone inputs, but you need impedance matching transformers to plug them into high-impedance guitar amplifiers and guitar effects.

Length and weight

If you're going to hold a mic in your hands for clean or amplified playing, you need to be able to hold it for extended periods. The mic's length and weight shouldn't cause muscle fatigue; short and light are best.

Cuppable shape

A mic should be small enough to cup comfortably in your hands but not so small that you cramp your hands trying to hold it. Bullet mics such as the Astatic JT-30 and the Shure Green Bullet have good diameters for cupping. Some stick-shaped mics, such as the Shure SM-57, make great harp mics but have a small diameter that may be uncomfortable to hold for long periods. BlowsMeAway Productions makes the Bulletizer, a funnel-shaped attachment that you mount around the end of a stick mic to direct the sound toward your hands and give you a diameter that's large enough to hold comfortably.

Ability to distort

Some microphones deliver a clean signal no matter how tightly you cup them or how loud you play. Such mics are good for acoustic playing and ideal for clean playing. However, for amplified blues, a mic that can deliver some distortion is a good thing. It gives you unique opportunities to control and shape distortion by cupping the mic tightly in your hands.

TIP

Vintage bullet mics deliver classic distortion (the new ones don't). However, some dynamic mics, such as the Shure SM-57 and the Shure 545, also deliver a good distorted sound when you cup them, especially when fitted with a sound-concentrating funnel such as a Bulletizer (see Figure 19-1 for a mic fitted with a Bulletizer).

Choosing the right mic for you

Microphones come in several different types that are named for the kind of element they use to convert sound into electric signals. The types you find onstage are usually dynamic and condenser mics. For singers and wind instruments, most players and sound techs prefer to use dynamic mics over condensers, often favoring such workhorse mics as the Shure SM-57 for instruments and the SM-58 for vocals. You can see several types of microphones in Figure 19-1.

Photo courtesy of Greg Heumann, BlowsMeAway Productions

FIGURE 19-1:
Top from left to right: BlowsMe-Away Ultimate 57 with Bulletizer, Audix FireBall, Astatic JT-30. Bottom left to right: Shure 545S, Shure SM-58.

For the classic sound of amplified blues, many harmonica players favor obsolete, low-tech bullet mics (named for their shape). Bullet mics were originally cheap and widely used in public address systems and radio dispatch systems where high sound quality wasn't an issue, and for years you could easily find them secondhand for low prices. The two enduring classics are the Astatic JT-30 with either a crystal MC-151 element or a ceramic MC-127 element and the Shure 520 series Green Bullet with either a controlled reluctance (CR) or controlled magnetic (CM) element. Each type of element has a different sound, and each has its devotees among pro players.

Unfortunately, none of the original bullet mic elements is made anymore, and the originals are getting rare, especially the crystal elements, which absorb moisture and stop working over time (while ceramic elements are easily damaged by impact). As a result, the remaining vintage mics are getting hard to find and are either in poor condition or ridiculously expensive. If you really want a good bullet mic, be prepared to go to a harmonica mic specialist with a good reputation and to shell out several hundred dollars.

In today's marketplace you can find modern versions of bullet mics, some still called JT-30 and 520DX. They look cool and deliver an approximation of the classic sound, but they pale in comparison with the real thing because the elements either aren't as good (in the case of crystals) or, in the case of the newer CM elements, are a little too good and don't deliver the distortion and compression that players want.

TIP

Fortunately, you can get good amplified blues sound from some modern dynamic mics such as the Shure SM-57 and 545 models. Or you can use a clean-sounding mic and then use effects to deliver a bluesier tone.

Developing your microphone technique

You can get the best sound from a microphone in any playing situation by effective use of microphone technique.

Acoustic mic technique

When you play harmonica, you use both hands. One hand holds the harmonica and the other one folds around the holding hand and the back of the harp. You may move the free, nonholding hand, closing and opening the cup around the harmonica and even swinging your hand away from the harmonica and back again.

When you amplify your harmonica's acoustic sound, the microphone is on a stand in front of you. The mic captures the harmonica's sound and also picks up another key element in acoustic sound — *air*, which is the sound of a voice or instrument diffusing in the air around it. To capture this sound, you position yourself several inches away from the mic.

You need to stand close enough to the mic to capture your sound but far enough from it so that the mic captures sound in the air around the harp. You also need to be far enough away from the mic so you can move your free hand without hitting the mic, which will make a loud noise and could even knock the mic stand over.

If you sing and play through the same mic, make sure that your harmonica volume matches your singing volume. If you sing louder than you play (or vice versa), you may need to move closer or farther from the mic when you switch from one to the other. Ideally, you can match your playing and singing volume so that you can just make music without constantly leaning forward and pulling back. Work with the sound tech to make sure you have a good balance between vocal sound and harmonica sound.

TIP

You can avoid causing feedback when you play acoustic by playing loud enough (or close enough to the mic) that the sound tech doesn't have to turn up the mic's volume too far. Sometimes the opening in your hands — or even your open mouth — can act like an antenna that collects and concentrates all the sound in your environment and feeds it back into the mic. If this causes a problem, try changing the shape of your hand cup or pointing it slightly away from the mic's center.

WARNING

Never cup a vocal mic in your hands without warning the sound tech. If you cup a mic adjusted for singing or acoustic harmonica playing, the resulting sound will be extremely loud and may feed back, could damage the hearing of anyone who hears it, and could potentially even damage sound equipment.

Driven acoustic technique

You can play through a vocal mic without cupping it in your hands and get a nearly amplified sound. You do this by cupping the harmonica tightly in your hands but leaving a small opening along the edges of your palms, just below your little fingers. Then you position the opening in your hands so that it almost touches the microphone. This configuration gives you a bassy, compressed sound but still allows some acoustic-style, hand-cupping effects. Gary Primich used this technique to great effect, and Phil Wiggins uses something like it to lend a slightly amplified sound to his otherwise acoustic, Piedmont-style playing.

Clean amplified technique

When you cup a mic and a harmonica together with your hands, you keep out the sounds of other instruments and amplifiers, and you can move around the stage instead of being stuck in one spot in front of a mic on a stand. However, you don't have the ability to use hand effects much, and your sound will be bassier and more compressed. If you plan to spend significant stage time holding a mic, practice playing this way.

TIP

For clean amplified playing, you might choose a vocal mic that doesn't distort easily, doesn't create feedback when cupped, and is easy to hold. The Shure SM-58 is a widely used choice, along with the Audix FireBall, which is marketed as a clean harmonica mic. Some pros — notably Lee Oskar — choose a high-end ribbon mic such as the Beyerdynamic M160.

Distorted amplified technique

To get a distorted sound from a microphone, you cup it in your hands with the harmonica so that no air can escape. This ensures that all the sound goes to the mic and drives the mic element beyond its normal clean response into distortion. To grip a microphone for distortion, follow these steps (and see Figure 19-2):

1. Hold the harmonica between your left forefinger and thumb.

2. Rest the tip of the mic on your left palm, close to the back of the harmonica, and wrap your ring and pinky finger around the mic.

3. Press the heels of your hands together.

4. Touch your thumbs together along their length.

5. Drape the fingertips of your right hand over the fingertips of your left hand.

6. Wrap the edges of your little fingers and your palms around the mic.

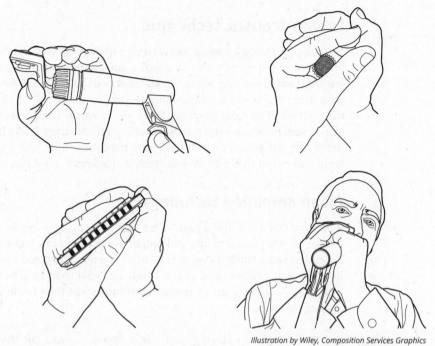

FIGURE 19-2:
Gripping a
microphone for
distortion.

Illustration by Wiley, Composition Services Graphics

Avoid using pressure to create a good seal, as your hands will cramp. Instead, try to fit your hands, the harmonica, and the mic together so that their placement creates a seal by not creating any air gaps.

TIP

To test your seal, cup your mic, take away the harmonica, wrap your grip around your lips, and then inhale and exhale. You'll quickly discover where air leaks through your grip. When you can seal the air leaks, your breath will exert pressure and suction on your cup with minimal air leakage.

Some players curl the middle finger of their left hand down to create a barrier between the harmonica and the mic. This helps you avoid bumping the harmonica and mic together and creating unwanted noise. It also creates a small tone chamber that you can vary slightly for tonal effects by moving your middle finger and by flexing your knuckles and fingers to vary the cup's shape.

To really fatten your cupped sound, you can also press the harmonica's upper holes (the ones on the right side) against your right cheek, as shown in Figure 19-3. When you do this, you seal off those holes so that no air or sound can escape from your cup. If you need to play the holes to the right, slide the harmonica off your cheek and into your mouth, and then slide it back against your cheek when you move back to the left side of the harmonica.

FIGURE 19-3:
Sealing the
harmonica
against your
cheek.

Illustration by Wiley, Composition Services Graphics

TIP

When you cup a mic, your hands collect sound and funnel it to the mic. This is exactly what you want when you play, but if you take the harmonica out of your mouth, the mic may start picking up sound from speakers in the room and causing feedback. To avoid this, either uncup the mic, turn it down or off (if it has a volume control or an on/off switch), or press your cup against your chest or shoulder to block room sounds from getting into your mic.

Passing the microphone signal on to the next stage

Microphones and cables use various types of connectors, depending on their impedance and what they're connecting to. Each type of connector consists of a plug, or *male connector*, that plugs into a socket, or *female connector*.

>> Low impedance mics and sound systems use *3-pin XLR connectors*.

>> High impedance equipment, including electric guitars, uses ¼-inch *phone plugs* that plug into *phone jacks* on amplifiers and stomp boxes.

>> Vintage bullet mics use a *screw-on Amphenol* or *Switchcraft connector* on the mic housing. The connecting cable usually has a ¼-inch plug on the other end.

REMEMBER

Always match the impedances of any two devices that you connect to each other. If you don't match impedances, the sound will lack volume and tonal fullness. Impedance matching is just as important as matching dissimilar connectors. For instance, if you need to plug a vocal mic into a guitar amp and you have a cable with a female XLR socket on one end and a phone plug on the other, your quest isn't over. Instead, use an XLR cable to connect to the mic and plug it into a low-to-high impedance matcher that has an XLR socket on one end and a phone plug on the other. Then plug the phone plug into the guitar amp.

Processing your sound

Before you pass your signal to the amplifier or mixing console, you may want to either enhance your natural sound or create an altered sound by using effects.

Effects come in many physical forms. Sound systems and acoustic instrument amplifiers may incorporate effects that enhance natural sound. Guitar amplifiers may include reverb or an overdrive channel to create distortion. In addition, *multi-effects units* bundle several types of effects into a single unit that you can route to a sound system or an individual amp.

Amp modelers include not only effects but also the ability to emulate the sound of specific amplifiers and the speakers they connect to. Korg, Line 6, and DigiTech all make devices that combine amp modelers with multi-effects units.

Stomp boxes are small, single-purpose effects built into a small box, with foot-operated switches that you can activate with a tap of your toe. Most stomp boxes are built for electric guitar and need hi-z input, either from a high impedance mic or by plugging a lo-z mic through an impedance matching transformer.

When you play acoustic or clean, you may want to enhance your natural sound with the following effects, which may be built into the sound system or amp or may be part of your individual rig:

» **Equalization, or eq:** An *equalizer* divides the spectrum of sound vibrations into as many as 30 segments, or *bands,* from low to midrange to high frequencies. It allows you to raise or lower the level of each band to make the sound brighter or darker and to *notch out,* or eliminate, certain bands that may cause problems such as feedback.

» **Reverberation, or reverb:** Reverb mimics the subtle, echo-like reflections of sound that occur in a room. Reverb can make a sound more exciting and distinct by simulating the size of the room, the hardness of its reflecting surfaces, and the way that sound behaves in that space.

>> **Compression:** Compression can reduce the difference between the volume level of your softest and loudest sounds so that your soft sounds aren't inaudible and your loudest sounds aren't overpowering. Compression can make your overall sound seem louder without the need to turn up the volume, so it can be useful in avoiding feedback.

>> **Exciters:** These devices can make your sound more warm and present through a combination of processing techniques that include synthesis of high *harmonics* (multiples of the frequencies of sound waves).

When you play amplified, you may want to include natural-sounding effects and supplement them with more noticeable alterations to your acoustic sound, such as

>> **Echo, slapback, and delay:** These effects send some of your mic signal forward normally while delaying part of the signal for a few *milliseconds* (thousandths of a second) to create an echo-like effect.

>> **Octave effects, pitch shifters, and harmonizers:** These effects divide or multiply the frequency of a note you play in order to change the note to sound an octave higher or lower, play the original note and the octave note simultaneously, or play a harmony note along with the note you play. The resulting sound can be huge and very different from the harmonica's natural sound.

>> **Anti-feedback units:** Feedback is a significant problem when playing amplified with electric guitars, which can always get louder than amplified harmonica simply because electric guitars are less susceptible to feedback than microphones. An anti-feedback unit gives you the ability to play at higher volumes without feedback.

>> **Distortion units:** Amplifiers can create distortion when turned up loud, and this kind of distortion is the traditional way of getting amplified blues sound. However, to avoid the weight and expense of a traditional amp, as well as the various modifications required to adapt guitar amps for harmonica, some players simply use a distortion unit to create the distorted, compressed sound of an overdriven amp and then feed that sound into a sound system or clean amplifier.

Using amplifiers and speakers

When you choose an amplifier to use as part of your personal rig, you have several choices to make. If you want the classic amplified blues harmonica delivered in the classic way, then choose a *tube amp* made for guitar and modified for harmonica, such as a Fender Bassman, or an amp made especially for harmonica from a small company such as Kendrick, Kinder, MegaTone, Meteor, Sonny, Jr., or Victoria.

If you want a clean amplified sound, a clean amp that you can color with effects, or an amp modeler to emulate the classic blues sound, then choose an amp made for keyboards, bass, or acoustic instruments. You may choose to have no amp at all and to plug your mic and effects units (including an amp modeler) into the sound system wherever you play.

The more power an amp can deliver, measured in *watts,* and the larger the area of the speakers delivering the sound, the louder your amp will be. As you turn an amp up toward its maximum volume, it will begin to distort at a certain point. If you want clean sound, stay below that volume level. If you want distortion, push past that level. Select an amp that delivers the kind of sound you want at the volume level you want. A low-powered amp, rated at up to 15 watts, delivers distortion at low volume, while a 50 or 100 watt amp delivers clean or distorted sound at higher volume levels. For loud, clean sound, you may want an amp with as much as 300 watts of power.

Optimizing guitar amps for harmonica-friendly distortion

Harmonica players look for amplifiers that have the right combination of stages to deliver good harmonica sound and often alter their amplifiers to improve that sound even further. The *rectifier* takes electrical current from a wall socket and converts it into power that the amplifier uses to function. Older amps used tube rectifiers, but newer tube amps often use solid-state rectifiers. Tube rectifiers play a part in creating amplified sound because they tend to *sag,* or fail to deliver enough power at high volumes. Sag compresses the sound output, reducing the difference between soft and loud sounds. Harmonica players and guitarists often cultivate sag by replacing solid-state rectifiers with tube rectifiers.

The *preamp* boosts your mic signal to prepare it for the power amp stage. The amount by which the preamp boosts the signal is called *gain*. Gain can create desirable distortion, but too much gain in the preamp stage will cause feedback at low volumes.

To minimize feedback, harmonica players seek amplifiers with only one preamp stage. They also reduce gain in a tube preamp by *tube swapping* — replacing high-gain preamp tubes with lower-gain tubes. For instance, you can replace the high-gain 12AX7 tube with (in descending order of power) the 12AT7, 12AY7, 12AV7, or 12AU7. Using lower gain preamp tubes lets you turn the amp up higher into its distortion range without feeding back. High powered amps can benefit from the greatest gain reduction simply because they put out more sound.

Making amplification work onstage

When you take your rig onstage, you face the need to hear yourself, be heard by the audience, and not get feedback. If your amp isn't powerful enough to cut through other amplifiers onstage, you can get more sound by running it through the sound system, either by placing a mic in front of the speakers and running the mic to the sound system or by feeding the line out signal from your amp to the sound system.

TIP

To hear yourself, you can raise your amp by placing it on a chair or box. Some players use their amps just to hear themselves onstage and let the sound system handle sending their sound to the audience.

6

The Part of Tens

All *For Dummies* books end with a few top-ten lists, and this book is no exception. I give you ten things to know about sharing your music with others and ten important tidbits about blues harmonica history.

Chapter **20**

Ten Things to Know about Sharing Your Music with Others

I f you're like most harmonica players, you dream big but play for your own enjoyment. You may even hesitate to play in front of others for fear that you'll annoy them or that you won't be very good. But after you've been playing for a while, the dog may stop whimpering and your significant other may stop wincing and start smiling when you pull out a harmonica.

Emboldened by positive signs, you may feel the urge to take a giant step and start sharing your harmonica passion with listeners and with other musicians. When you get to that point, this chapter can help you with ten pointers that can make your new quest less of a white-knuckle plunge into terror and more of a voyage of discovery and growing empowerment. I start with five tips on collaborating with other musicians and follow with five tips on delivering a great performance.

Five Ways to Collaborate with Other Musicians

Harmonica players sometimes get up onstage alone and perform as true soloists, and unaccompanied virtuosity has a long tradition in blues harmonica. But playing with accompaniment and accompanying others can be very rewarding experiences.

Finding compatible players

Where do you look to find other musicians to play with? After you're connected with the local music scene, you'll have candidates to choose from, but first you have to find the scene. Here are some ways to start out:

>> Check local bulletin boards for musicians looking for collaborators, whether physical corkboards in music stores or online listing services such as Craigslist. You can also place your own ad seeking players.

>> Scan the entertainment listings in your daily or weekly newspaper for local bars, restaurants, and nightclubs to see whether they feature blues artists or host a weekly blues jam. (Clubs often schedule jams at slow business times, such as Sunday afternoons or Monday evenings.) You can probably meet other musicians in the audience.

>> Find out whether your area has a club or association devoted to blues or harmonica and whether it has meetings where you can go and meet other players.

After you find potential collaborators, you have to figure out whether they're a good fit for you. Whether you want to play in a duo or with a full orchestra, here are some things to consider when you start a new musical group or join an existing one:

>> **Complementary instruments:** Harmonica plays in the middle-to-upper range of the sound spectrum, and instruments that can play in the spectrum's lower-to-middle part, such as guitar and piano, can really fill out the harmonica's sound. On the other hand, a trio of two flutes and a harmonica (all treble instruments) wouldn't have any bottom end. It may sound rather ethereal in a blues context, and you and the flute players would likely have a limited repertoire in common.

>> **Similar musical styles:** If you want to play acoustic, down-home blues and you hook up with a death-metal guitarist who wants to shred at stadium-level sound volumes, you have either fertile ground for a new stylistic hybrid or

grounds for a quick musical divorce. Look for people who want to play the same kind of music that you do.

WARNING

» **Appropriate skill levels:** It's often said that you should always play with musicians who are better than you are because they'll sound good and you'll learn from them. But if the difference in skill level is too great, you'll end up being the weak link; you'll sound bad by comparison and may feel inferior. On the other hand, if you're by far the best player in a band, you may get bored or frustrated. Overall, try to find players whose skill level is near your own.

» **Compatible goals:** If you want to just jam in your living room or play at nursing homes while holding down a steady job but your prospective band mates want to go on an extended tour of punk clubs hundreds of miles apart and crash in the van between gigs, you may want to look for partners whose goals more closely match your own.

» **Positive personalities:** You don't have to be best friends with your musical partners (though it's nice if you can be). But even when you have great musical rapport, if someone you play with drives you nuts because of a personality conflict or irresponsible behavior, either the music had better be really, really good or you may want to part ways with that person.

» **Matching schedules:** Even if you find cool people who play complementary instruments in your desired style and share all your musical goals, you need to be able to get together in the same place at the same time on a regular basis. Compare schedules to make sure you actually have enough opportunities to do the things you want to do together.

Filling an instrumental role in a band

Anytime two or more musicians play together, they assume roles that are partly musical and partly organizational. This section covers some of the roles that are directly related to making music.

Taking charge as leader

The bandleader is like a traffic cop who tells everyone when to start and end a song, sets the tempo (the speed of the beat), and indicates through gestures when to get louder or softer, who should take the next solo, and when the solo should end. In a band, one person might always lead or the role may sometimes pass to another band member during some tunes.

When you lead, you need to know how to communicate clearly when you begin and end tunes, how to direct soloists, and how to convey any special actions the band may take, such as stopping and starting again during the tune.

When you follow the leader, you need to be attentive and ready to act on the leader's signals.

Fronting the band

The front person is the band member who sings most of the tunes and is the personality who relates directly to the audience. The front person may or may not also be the bandleader.

Blues and rock musicians often expect the harmonica player to sing and front the band. Depending on your talents and personal inclinations, you may want to either develop your singing and fronting skills or find other ways to add value to a band, such as playing percussion and singing harmony.

Sharing the foreground

You may inhabit an area where you share the front of the stage with a collaborator or co-soloist. You may sing a duet with another singer, entwine your harmonica closely with a singer, or join forces with another instrument such as guitar or saxophone.

REMEMBER

To collaborate successfully with a fronting partner, make sure that you both agree on who leads, who takes the upper or lower harmony, who plays fills and solos, and any other details where you may conflict or collide.

Weaving yourself into the fabric of the band

Every instrument or voice adds something to a band's sound, and harmonica can work effectively in the background by joining with other instruments in their roles. Listen for opportunities to fit into the overall sound of the band by augmenting the roles of other instruments:

>> Drums, bass, and rhythm guitar keep the rhythm going and fill out the bottom end. Harmonica can join in by matching their rhythms.

>> Horn sections and lead guitar play kicking riffs that help create a signature sound for the backing group. If you can play those riffs in tune and in time with the others, you might join in.

>> Harmony singers don't need help from the harmonica (though you may also sing harmony when you're not playing harp). But harmonica plays in the same range as voices, so you may want to stay away from the notes the singers are singing.

You can also simply play long, sustained notes drawn from the backing chord to thicken the sound.

Backing a singer

If you're accompanying a singer, your role is to make the singer sound even better.

WARNING

To do this well, you need to avoid

>> **Stepping on the singer;** that is, interfering with the vocal by

- Playing while the singer is singing.

- Overlapping the beginning or ending of the singer's phrase when you play fills (you play *fills* whenever you play licks to fill up the time between the melody's phrases).

>> **Overshadowing the singer** by playing loudly, playing a lot of fast notes, or drawing too much attention to yourself.

Actually, you can play while the singer is singing, but only if the singer clearly indicates that he or she is okay with it. But when you do play behind a singer, listen actively and stay in the background by playing

>> Long notes that belong to the backing chords and don't stick out or clash with the singer's notes.

>> The same backing riff as the other instruments, which often repeats multiple times.

>> An unobtrusive rhythm part that's simple and repetitive, similar to what a rhythm guitar would play.

When you play songs that use the 12-bar blues form, the vocal often takes up the first 2-bar phrase, leaving the last 2 bars for you to play a fill. When you play fills, you can avoid stepping on the vocal by listening for the beginnings and endings of the vocal phrases and tailoring your fills accordingly. A vocal phrase can overlap the artificial boundaries of 2 bars, so listen to the singer's phrasing. His phrases may

>> Start with a pickup consisting of a few notes that lead up to the *downbeat* (the strong first beat of a bar), though it may also start on or just slightly after the downbeat.

>> End on the downbeat of the third bar.

REMEMBER When you accompany a singer, tailor your playing to the song's mood. Even when you take a solo, you're still accompanying the singer. True, the solo is your moment to shine, and during that moment, you're the center of attention. But when you finish soloing, hand the spotlight back to the singer at a level of intensity that fits the song's mood and the singer's style. Always try to end your solo in a way that makes the singer seem welcome when he resumes the song.

Taking a solo

Taking a solo is your big moment to grab the spotlight and strut your stuff. Does this mean that you should play everything you know in every hole of the harmonica as fast and loud as you can? Uh, not really.

The time to explore every nook and cranny of the harmonica is at home, playing solo or with recorded backing tracks, or maybe with a patient and forgiving friend backing you on guitar. When you do that, you can go everywhere on the harp and try every weird possibility.

When you solo while playing in a jam or performance, though, you want to put your best foot forward. Pace yourself, edit your ideas, and craft a dynamic solo that tells a story that holds the listener's interest. I go into more detail about crafting a solo in Chapter 18, but here are a couple of quick observations on delivering a solo when you play with others:

» **Play within your abilities.** If you go out on a limb with techniques you haven't yet mastered or haven't even tried, you stand a good chance of crashing, especially when you're under performance pressure. Stick with what you've already mastered and you'll play with confidence and strength.

» **Be bold.** Being timid when your big moment arrives misses the point. You can be sly and tease the audience and then come on strong, but be sure to deliver an authoritative statement. This is your moment to leave the background, step forward into the limelight, and really shine.

Playing in a jam session

Jam sessions are for players to interact with other players and make music in a freewheeling environment, without having to be concerned about pleasing an audience. Some jams are impromptu, one-time occurrences, while others are weekly events that may happen in a private setting or in a public venue. Jams may focus on a particular style of music or even a particular instrument, and every jam has its own culture and etiquette.

Though you can jam with live participants in virtual space, jamming live is always preferable. No matter how fast your Internet connection is, physical distance introduces a delay that prevents you from synchronizing your rhythm with your jam mates, and you can't read the body language cues that help you collaborate and coordinate with other musicians on the fly.

So where do you look for jam sessions where you live? You find jams the same way you find other players — by checking ads, entertainment listings, and local music associations that may hold jams.

After you find a jam, don't expect to show up and get playing time immediately. You could benefit from treating your first visit as a reconnaissance mission. Find out whether the jam excludes outsiders or snubs anyone who doesn't play guitar, bass, or drums. And if you show up once or twice before you try to play, you'll become a familiar face, and familiarity can help you gain acceptance.

On your first visit, find out who runs the jam, introduce yourself to the jam boss, and ask how the sign-up process works. Expect to be viewed skeptically, because the jam boss doesn't know you yet and because he often gets attitude from players who think they're the world's gift to music and have the right to dominate his session. The jam boss may even ask you to briefly audition to show that you can play. One unfortunate reality is that some folks believe that just owning a harmonica means that you can automatically play it, and the jam boss has probably run across a few such characters in his time.

After you do sign up, as a newcomer you'll likely be at the end of a long line of regulars, all eager to play. But if you exhibit patience and respect for the regulars, you'll feel more welcomed when you do get up to play. And if you're courteous and considerate to others, you don't hog the stage, and you can start playing without a lot of fussing with your harps or the sound system, you just may make a few friends.

Five Tips for Delivering a Polished Performance

Performing for an audience can be a major thrill; you just might get hooked on it. But it can also be nerve-wracking, and it can be humiliating if it goes badly. To ensure that your performance goes well, spend a little time with this section to figure out how to get ready, have a good time playing, and enjoy the results.

Preparing to play

To get your music, instruments, equipment, and yourself ready to play, follow the advice in the following sections.

Make a set list

Follow these steps to put together a set list:

1. **List your songs on a sheet of paper in letters big enough to read if you lay the sheet on the floor.**

2. **Put the songs in set order — the order in which you'll play the songs during your set or time onstage.**

3. **Next to each song, list its key and which harmonicas you need for that tune.**

4. **If you're going to sing, you might also write in the first line of the lyrics, just in case you forget them.**

Rehearse your parts

Practice singing each song from beginning to end, at the same volume level and with the same expression that you'll use when you perform. Don't just hum through bits of the tune.

Memorize the lyrics to each tune, and also have an unobtrusive cheat sheet with reminders.

Practice your harmonica solo spots, and memorize the first few notes of each solo. Play the solo over and over until it's automatic. That way, if stage fright hits you along with the spotlight, you can go on autopilot until the deer-in-the-headlights syndrome subsides.

Model your onstage setup

When you rehearse singing or playing, stand the same way you will onstage, and if you'll be holding a harmonica and/or a microphone while you sing, do that while you practice singing.

If you're using your own harmonica microphone and amplifier, practice playing harmonica using the same combination that you'll be using onstage.

Prepare your instruments and equipment

Make sure you have all the keys and types of harmonicas that you'll need, and ensure that they all work properly and play in tune. Replace or repair any harps that aren't performance-ready.

Don't forget to bring your instruments or equipment to the gig. Make a list, and check it before you leave home.

Prepare a way to lay out your harps onstage so that you can quickly reach them, pick up the harp you need, and put down the one you're done with. For example, you could use a small table, the seat of a chair, or the top of an amplifier. As long as you can get at your harps easily and they're not in danger of being knocked on the floor, crushed, or inundated with beer, you should be in good shape.

TIP

Plan for an alternative in case your equipment fails, such as playing through a vocal microphone (see Chapter 19 for more on amplification).

Looking good onstage

Some performers maintain that you should always dress better than your audience. The audience members have made the effort to come out and listen to you, so you can reward that effort by looking good; they'll feel like they're experiencing something special when they see well-dressed performers onstage. Of course, that doesn't mean that showing up to play a beach party wearing a tuxedo or evening gown is a good idea. Dress well, but dress appropriately for the occasion.

Clothing isn't the only part of looking good, though. If you stand with confidence, move gently to groove with the music, and have a pleasant expression, you'll feel good, and you'll help your band mates and audience to feel good, too.

Conquering anxiety

Performing brings out the fight-or-flight syndrome in everyone. Professionals know how to harness the energy that comes with a massive infusion of adrenaline. Watching them get ready to go onstage can be like watching a mild-mannered scientist turn into a hulking, muscle-bound superhero ready to do battle with monsters. But if you're not used to the rush you get from it, all that adrenaline can paralyze you with fear, in addition to dropping your IQ by 40 points. So how do you handle this condition?

>> Envision yourself as that powerful superhero — or think of bunnies in a field of daisies if that works for you.

>> Remember that the audience isn't the monster. They want you to do well. Try to feel all that goodwill as you walk onstage.

>> Think about how you can use that huge jolt of nervous energy to deliver an energetic, passionate performance.

>> Take deep breaths, calmly and slowly. Envision your first moves as you walk onstage, and then remember the first few notes you'll sing or play.

After you finish your first song, you may feel as if you gave the worst performance in human history, and that it's time to go home, close the curtains, take the phone off the hook, and crawl under the blankets with a chocolate cheesecake (or booze; pick your consoling poison). But that's just how you feel, and not how you played. Look around at your band mates — are they staring at you in horror and disbelief? Is the audience trying not to snicker openly? I doubt it very much. They'll probably tell you later how well you played. When they do, listen to them and let their words sink in. And whatever you do, remember to say, "Thanks."

Relating to an audience

Audiences are out to have a good time and are looking to the musicians to help provide it. They want you to succeed and will cheer you on. You can return the favor by acknowledging them, feeling their goodwill, and letting it radiate back from you to them. These folks are your new best friends, and they're looking for you to make them feel good. What's more, they're confident you can do it, even if it takes a little encouragement.

To put yourself and your audience at ease, say a few words. Just a few, something as simple as, "How's everybody doing tonight?" You don't need to make a speech or tell jokes; a simple greeting will do. You might mention the name of the tune you're about to play and then get down to business.

TIP

When you talk to your audience, try to look just over their heads. They will see you looking sort of into their eyes, as if you're talking to them personally.

Sitting in as a guest

You may be honored with an invitation to sit in for one or two songs at someone else's gig. If you're new to performing, a guest appearance gives you an opportunity to get a small dose of the spotlight without overwhelming your still-developing abilities. To make your cameo role a good experience for all, you need to both prepare and then deliver.

Prepare

A little preparation goes a long way. Make sure to do the following:

>> Find out in advance what song you'll be playing and what key it's in, and then figure out what harp you need to use.

>> Solicit information about the song, starting with the chord progression (12-bar blues, 8-bar blues, Saints changes, or something else — see Chapters 7 and 12 for more on this).

>> Find out what you can about the arrangement, such as whether it has an intro, when the vocal verses and instrumental solos occur, whether it has any changes of key, and how the song ends.

>> Ask what you're expected to do, such as accompany a singer, play an ensemble role in the band, or take a solo.

>> Be ready to take direction from the leader and play as a sideman, but also have a song ready to sing or play in case you're asked to front the band.

Deliver

Before you step onstage, have the harmonica you need already in your hand and be ready to start. These tips can help:

>> Try to get onstage quickly and with a minimum of fuss, and stand where the leader indicates.

>> During the song, pay close attention to the leader and be prepared to play or to stop playing when the leader gestures you to do so.

>> If you come to places in the song where you don't understand what's going on or don't know what to play, lay out. You run the risk of ruining the sound of the song if you play something that doesn't fit. Knowing when not to play is just as important as playing, and knowing when to be quiet makes you sound better when you do play.

>> When the song ends, take a bow; acknowledge the audience, the leader, and the band members; and get offstage quickly.

Chapter **21**

Ten Important Periods and Styles in Blues Harmonica History

As instruments go, the harmonica is a youngster. Nobody has yet unearthed bone harmonicas carved by Neanderthals, and medieval tapestries fail to depict bards blowing bluesy riffs in between lines of poetry that celebrates the brave deeds of armor-clad heroes.

Along with its cousins, the accordion and the concertina, the harmonica got its start around 1820 in the German-speaking parts of Europe. No one knows for certain who invented the harmonica. A tale that's often told — though doubted by historians — points to a teenager named Friedrich Buschmann, who strung together a circular series of pitch pipes to play a scale by rotating the assemblage while blowing into each tube. (A *pitch pipe* is a little metal tube that contains one harmonica-like reed. You blow into it to hear a reference note so you can tune a guitar or give singers in a choir their starting note when they aren't being accompanied by instruments.) Right from the beginning, harmonicas were called *mouth harps* (or *mundharfe* in German).

This chapter presents the highlights in the history of blues harmonica over the past 150 years or so.

Early Harmonica History in the United States

At first, harmonicas were made by hand by part-time workers in semirural areas of Germany, and production was low. For example, the Hohner company, which later grew to dominate the world harmonica market, made only 650 instruments in 1857, its first year of production. The small output of harmonica manufacturers during this early period suggests that even if all the harmonica companies in Germany had shipped their entire output exclusively to American soldiers, perhaps 1 in every 70 Civil War combatants would have possessed a harmonica. As it was, manufacturers could barely keep up with local demand in central Europe and had to allocate output among eager retailers, with little or nothing left over for export.

Initially, domestic markets in Germany and Austria easily absorbed the production of harmonica manufacturers. By the mid-1870s, though, mechanization allowed Hohner alone to produce more than 50,000 instruments a year. Meanwhile, the company was already planning for the future and setting up its own overseas distribution networks, the first harmonica company to do so. By 1900 Hohner was pumping out more than 3 million harmonicas a year, with the lion's share going to the United States.

Meanwhile, mail-order catalogs helped distribute harmonicas to even the loneliest outposts. Mail order was the great marketing innovation of the 1880s, much as Amazon was in the 1990s. Companies such as Montgomery Ward enabled anyone within reach of the U.S. postal system to order anything from a mousetrap to a prefabricated house, and harmonicas were part of the cornucopia of inexpensive merchandise that delighted consumers could choose from.

By the mid-1880s, Midwestern music publishers were producing harmonica instruction books, attesting to the harmonica's growing popularity. The instruments depicted were very similar to modern diatonic harmonicas in both construction and note layout. However, the books made no mention of such blues techniques as bending notes or playing the harmonica in a key different from its labeled key.

Early recordings from the turn of the century include a few harmonica performances from such artists as Professor Dickens, Arthur Turelly, and Pete Hampton, the first African-American harmonica player (and possibly the first harmonica player) to record, who included some wordless vocalizations and crude pitch alterations that resemble the use of whoops and bending later heard on blues records.

Prewar Rural Blues Harmonica

During the early 1920s, the still-young commercial recording industry began to focus on recording and marketing regional and ethnic music, including the music of the rural South. Performers of all types flocked to cities such as Atlanta, Memphis, and Camden, New Jersey, in hopes of making records, and soon the markets for both blues (performed by and marketed to African Americans) and so-called "hillbilly music" (played by and aimed at Caucasian southerners) were established. In 1923, Henry Whitter was the first to record a second-position harmonica performance, a solo piece titled "Rain Crow Bill." On the same date, he also recorded "The Old-Time Fox Chase" and "Lost Train Blues," covering the three main types of solo harmonica pieces played during this period.

During the 1920s, several harmonica players made records that give a picture of the earliest blues harmonica styles. Those recordings reveal some interesting facts:

» During the 50 or so years since harmonicas had become widely available around 1870, southern rural players, both black and white, had evolved highly sophisticated abilities on the harmonica and developed styles that, though individual, shared many characteristics of technique, style, and repertoire.

» Rural harmonica players often recorded without accompaniment while playing imitations of trains and *fox chases,* sonic depictions of hunting expeditions with driving, rhythmic chords that propel the chase, punctuated by vocal cries that imitate the hunters' calls and yelping dogs.

» Both black and white players played bent notes as a matter of course and used first and second positions about equally, but a few players also explored fourth, fifth, sometimes sixth, and even twelfth positions.

Some of the notable early blues harmonica performers of the period include Daddy Stovepipe, George "Bullet" Williams, Kyle Wooten, William McCoy, Gwen Foster, Jaybird Coleman, and DeFord Bailey, who was the earliest star of the pioneering country music radio show *The Grand Ole Opry*, despite being a black harmonica player on an otherwise all-white show.

Traveling Life and the Migration North

One of the most striking aspects of the lives of southern musicians of the early 20th century is that so many of them roved from place to place. Legendary blues singer Robert Johnson is the best known of the legion of restless sufferers of the

"Walking Blues" (to quote one of his song titles), but harmonica players such as Sonny Boy Williamson II (then known as Willie Miller or Rice Miller), Big Walter Horton, and Little Walter Jacobs all took to the open road as well.

In the South, black musicians gravitated to towns that offered relaxed racial attitudes, nightclubs for gigging, and radio exposure. All these advantages attracted blues musicians to Helena, Arkansas, where the *King Biscuit Flour Hour* radio program helped the careers of future blues stars such as Sonny Boy Williamson II and B. B. King, among others. Big Walter Horton found his way to Helena from Memphis, and so did Little Walter Jacobs, wending his way up from Louisiana.

The next step for the itinerant performer was one of the larger southern population centers, especially the so-called *wide open* towns where illegal Prohibition-era whiskey and Depression-era money both flowed freely under corrupt civic governments headed by infamous mayors such as "Boss" E. H. Crump in Memphis and "Boss Tom" Pendergast in Kansas City. Blues songs of the period sometimes celebrated these patrons of the arts.

The biggest population magnets, though, were the northern and western cities that offered steady industrial jobs at wages much higher than could be found doing seasonal farm labor in the South. Detroit and Chicago were two of the biggest destinations. Chicago, however, had an additional lure: a strong and vibrant African-American community with black-owned businesses, theaters, and newspapers; good schools; and a social and cultural life that included artists, intellectuals, and, of course, musicians.

Later on, during the 1940s, the wartime shipbuilding industries in Los Angeles and the San Francisco area attracted a large influx of southern black folks, leading eventually to the West Coast blues styles that found expression on the harmonica with George "Harmonica" Smith and his disciples such as Rod Piazza, William Clarke, and Mark Hummel.

Memphis and Early Urban Blues

While rural musicians were singing and playing music influenced by their surroundings, urban recording artists mixed ragtime, early jazz, and *hokum blues*, derived from the stereotypes of old-time medicine shows. Hokum featured humorous and often saucy lyrics with thinly veiled sexual references. Sometimes, the music clearly emulated the jazz of the times, such as "Mean Low Blues," a harmonica tune recorded in 1929 by Blues Birdhead. Clearly an emulation of Louis Armstrong's trumpet style, this instrumental showcase also features the first known overblow on a recording.

In Memphis, Beale Street was the center of musical activity, and blues musicians there developed a ragtime-influenced style called *jug band*, named for the large whiskey jugs that players blew into to create trombone-like bass lines. Banjo, guitar, harmonica, and hokum lyrics with a jaunty air were typical of jug band music, and prominent harmonica players in this style included Will Shade of the Memphis Jug Band, Jed Davenport of the Beale Street Jug Band, and Noah Lewis of Cannon's Jug Stompers. Jug band music and repertoire later influenced 1960s rock bands such as the Grateful Dead and the Lovin' Spoonful (and its harmonica player, John B. Sebastian).

The Prewar Chicago Style

Blues in Chicago after World War II quickly coalesced into a new, consistent style that even today is a major influence on how blues is played. But prior to about 1947, two very different approaches to blues were heard:

>> Sophisticated, jazz-influenced blues using saxophones, trumpets, and other urban instruments reflected Chicago's role as a magnet for jazz musicians beginning in the early 1920s, especially such seminal New Orleans figures as Joe "King" Oliver and Louis Armstrong.

>> At the same time, rural southerners brought country blues with them, but when transplanted to the city, it began to change. Guitars, harmonicas, and mandolins might still be the featured instruments, but lyrics began to reflect such urban concerns as bill collectors and the indignities of collecting welfare. The feel of the music changed, too, with the relaxed, stately country blues speeding up and becoming more rhythmically active. This citified country music would evolve into what we now know as Chicago blues.

The giant figure in the nascent Chicago blues movement was John Lee "Sonny Boy" Williamson (usually referred to as Sonny Boy I, to distinguish him from Sonny Boy II, who was also a major figure, both as a blues singer and harmonica player). Williamson was popular personally in his community and as a performer and was a major harmonica influence on subsequent harmonica players in Chicago and beyond.

From 1937 until his death in 1948, Sonny Boy made more than 100 recordings as a featured artist and almost as many as a sideman. Most were made with acoustic instruments, and the driving, unified force of what we now think of as a blues band doesn't show up until some of his last recordings, when the use of drums and amplification begins to transform the more relaxed, countrified sound heard on earlier recordings.

The Rise of Amplified Blues Harmonica

Until the end of the 1940s, harmonica players either depended on their acoustic sound to be heard, played into megaphones to project their sound, or used microphones the way singers do, standing in front of the mic at a distance of several inches. But beginning sometime in the late 1940s, harmonica players started using amplification in a new way. With a small, portable amplifier and a cheap microphone, they would cup the mic in their hands, together with the harmonica, to create a highly concentrated sound that was loud enough to project over the din on street corners and in small nightclubs. This kind of amplification did more than make the harmonica louder; it changed the sound of the harmonica itself, just as the development of the electric guitar in the previous decade had started to change both the sound of the guitar and what players did with it. Players often mentioned as early adopters of the amplified harmonica style include George "Harmonica" Smith, Little Walter Jacobs, and Snooky Pryor. However, photos show Sonny Boy I cupping his hands around a bullet mic prior to his death in 1948, and Eddie Burns may have been the first to record amplified, on John Lee Hooker's "Burning Hell" in 1948.

By the beginning of the 1950s, electric guitars and amplified harmonicas were the rule in Chicago blues bands, backed by drums, bass, and piano. Most of the great blues harmonica players of the 1950s adopted and exploited amplification to forge a new style, with Little Walter leading the way, both as a solo act and as an accompanist to Muddy Waters and Jimmy Rogers.

The Postwar Chicago Style

Beginning in the late 1940s, small record companies started recording artists such as Little Walter, Snooky Pryor, Muddy Waters, John Lee Hooker, Howlin' Wolf, Junior Wells, James Cotton, Johnny Shines, Big Walter Horton, and many others. Some developed their careers in Chicago, while others, such as Sonny Boy Williamson II, Howlin' Wolf, and Walter Horton, transferred existing performing and recording careers to Chicago during the 1950s.

Early postwar attempts at recording these transplanted rural artists reveal an uncomfortable grafting of country blues onto an urbane, jazz-influenced backing that doesn't serve the direct, earthy character of the featured artists. However, the citified country boys started getting together on their own and developing a fully integrated style of their own, following in the footsteps of John Lee Williamson, whose last recordings show the direction they would all soon follow. Here are some hallmarks of this style:

>> Electrified rhythm and lead guitar, including delta-style slide guitar, begins to buoy up the rhythm, while bass lines borrowed from boogie-woogie piano but played on the bass strings of the guitar start to give the music its own up-tempo character.

>> Amplified harmonica starts to take on a new role, as Little Walter adapts jazz and rhythm-and-blues saxophone stylings to blues harmonica and integrates swing seamlessly into down-home blues.

>> Simple, to-the-point drumming propels the beat more aggressively than either jazz or older rural blues.

>> Down-home piano that could be at home in a gospel setting embellishes the overall sound while staying within the flavor of blues harmony.

The one blues band that exemplified this new style to the world was the Muddy Waters band, with Muddy on slide guitar and vocals, Jimmy Rogers on rhythm guitar, and Little Walter on harmonica. At the same time, Chicago was home to its own rock-and-roll movement, starting with the partnership of singer/guitarist Bo Diddley and harmonica player Billy Boy Arnold.

Regional Harmonica Styles

Small, independent record companies have long been important vehicles for blues artists to get their music to consumers, as the large companies either weren't interested in the small audiences for blues or were reluctant to promote music that was seen as socially disreputable. The independents didn't have the marketing or distribution capabilities of the major companies, and therefore, they often focused on their local markets, helping to foster and develop regional styles by serving both local preferences and the local artists who shaped and satisfied those preferences.

Some of the better-known regional companies highlighted blues harmonica and promoted early rock-and-roll. This combination later influenced the adoption of the harmonica by rock artists in the 1960s, who heard blues harmonica alongside the latest hits. Regional companies that recorded blues harmonica include Trumpet Records in Jackson, Mississippi, which recorded Sonny Boy Williamson II in the early 1950s; Excello Records in Nashville, which recorded such Louisiana artists as Slim Harpo and Lazy Lester; Sun Records in Memphis, which recorded both Walter Horton and Howlin' Wolf; RPM Records in Los Angeles, which recorded George "Harmonica" Smith; and Vee-Jay Records in Gary, Indiana, and Chicago, which recorded Jimmy Reed.

However, Chess Records in Chicago, together with its Checker and Argo imprints, did more to promote blues artists and harmonica players than any other independent label. Sonny Boy Williamson II, Howlin' Wolf, Little Walter, and Muddy Waters — who featured a series of excellent harmonica players, including Little Walter, Big Walter Horton, Junior Wells, James Cotton, Mojo Buford, George Smith, Paul Oscher, and Jerry Portnoy — all recorded for Chess. In addition, Chess launched the rock-and-roll careers of both Chuck Berry and Bo Diddley (who featured both Billy Boy Arnold and Little Walter on harmonica).

Rock, Blues, and the 1960s

By the late 1950s, white teenagers were obsessed with rock-and-roll, while black audiences had largely moved on from the blues. Blues artists began to face shrinking audiences and incomes, but two new audiences saved their careers and transformed the music, not only bringing in new fans but also stimulating the development of a new generation of blues musicians who had never ploughed a field or experienced institutionalized racism.

This transformation came about largely thanks to the folk music movement of the 1950s, which presented Americans with an alternative to current popular music. Folk fans saw this music as enlightened, not concerned with making money, and sensitive to the plight of the downtrodden. Folk fans began to see blues musicians as a part of the folk movement, with several effects:

>> College students hired blues artists and bands to play concerts and dances on their campuses, and a whole circuit of campus touring began.

>> Young Caucasian males started taking up blues harmonica, giving us such artists as Paul Butterfield, Charlie Musselwhite, Rod Piazza, Paul Oscher, Jerry Portnoy, Kim Wilson, Gary Smith, and Mark Hummel.

>> European and British music fans, who had been fascinated for several years with American music, especially jazz and blues, began promoting blues concerts in the UK and on the European continent.

>> Young British musicians started emulating the blues records they heard, resulting in such British rock bands as the Rolling Stones, with Brian Jones and Mick Jagger on harp; the Yardbirds, with Keith Relf on harp and also backing Sonny Boy Williamson II; John Mayall & the Bluesbreakers; Fleetwood Mac, with Peter Green and Walter Horton on harp; Cream, with Jack Bruce on harp; and Led Zeppelin, with harp by Robert Plant.

Modern Blues

Musicians worldwide have been bitten by the blues harp bug, and the virus often mutates and starts to interact with its new host. Here are a few artists and the stylistic crossbreeding they've been working between blues and other styles:

>> Early rock: Billy Boy Arnold (with Bo Diddley)

>> Funk, Latin: Junior Wells

>> Jazz-tinged blues: Carlos del Junco, Peter Madcat Ruth

>> Beatboxing: Son of Dave (Ben Darvill)

>> Psychedelic: Paul Butterfield (circa 1966)

>> Modern rock: Sugar Blue, John Popper (of Blues Traveler), Jason Ricci

>> Jump and swing: Dennis Gruenling

>> Soul: Paul deLay, Bobby Rush, Little Sonny

>> Brazilian: Flavio Guimaraes

7

Appendixes

Appendix A gives you the note layouts for all the keys of the harmonica. And Appendix B gives you a rundown of the music tracks that accompany this book.

Appendix A

Tuning Layouts for All Keys

The following figures show the note layouts for all keys of diatonic harmonica. For more on how these layouts work, see Chapter 11.

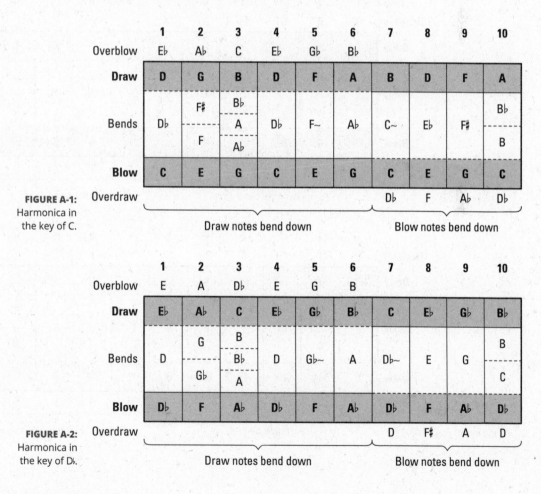

	1	2	3	4	5	6	7	8	9	10
Overblow	E♭	A♭	C	E♭	G♭	B♭				
Draw	D	G	B	D	F	A	B	D	F	A
Bends	D♭	F♯ / F	B♭ / A / A♭	D♭	F~	A♭	C~	E♭	F♯	B♭ / B
Blow	C	E	G	C	E	G	C	E	G	C
Overdraw							D♭	F	A♭	D♭

FIGURE A-1: Harmonica in the key of C.

Draw notes bend down — Blow notes bend down

	1	2	3	4	5	6	7	8	9	10
Overblow	E	A	D♭	E	G	B				
Draw	E♭	A♭	C	E♭	G♭	B♭	C	E♭	G♭	B♭
Bends	D	G / G♭	B / B♭ / A	D	G♭~	A	D♭~	E	G	B / C
Blow	D♭	F	A♭	D♭	F	A♭	D♭	F	A♭	D♭
Overdraw							D	F♯	A	D

FIGURE A-2: Harmonica in the key of D♭.

Draw notes bend down — Blow notes bend down

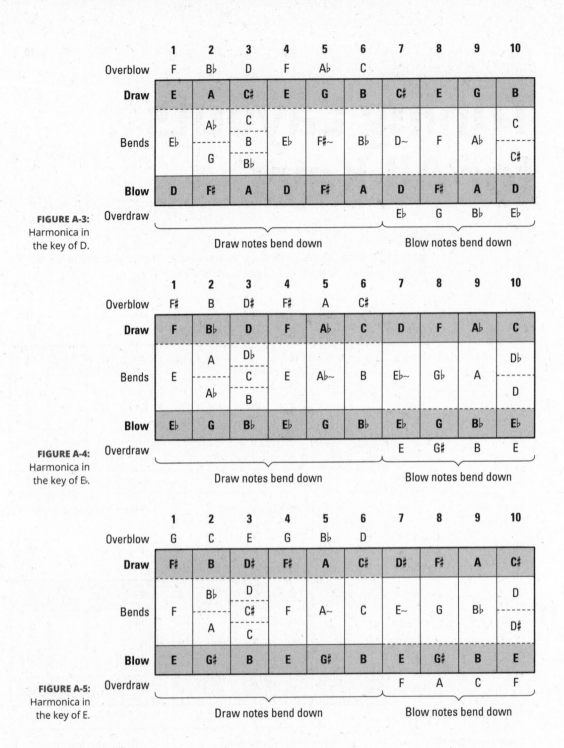

	1	2	3	4	5	6	7	8	9	10
Overblow	F	B♭	D	F	A♭	C				
Draw	E	A	C#	E	G	B	C#	E	G	B
Bends	E♭	A♭ / G	C / B / B♭	E♭	F#~	B♭	D~	F	A♭	C / C#
Blow	D	F#	A	D	F#	A	D	F#	A	D
Overdraw							E♭	G	B♭	E♭

FIGURE A-3: Harmonica in the key of D.

Draw notes bend down — Blow notes bend down

	1	2	3	4	5	6	7	8	9	10
Overblow	F#	B	D#	F#	A	C#				
Draw	F	B♭	D	F	A♭	C	D	F	A♭	C
Bends	E	A / A♭	D♭ / C / B	E	A♭~	B	E♭~	G♭	A	D♭ / D
Blow	E♭	G	B♭	E♭	G	B♭	E♭	G	B♭	E♭
Overdraw							E	G#	B	E

FIGURE A-4: Harmonica in the key of E♭.

Draw notes bend down — Blow notes bend down

	1	2	3	4	5	6	7	8	9	10
Overblow	G	C	E	G	B♭	D				
Draw	F#	B	D#	F#	A	C#	D#	F#	A	C#
Bends	F	B♭ / A	D / C# / C	F	A~	C	E~	G	B♭	D / D#
Blow	E	G#	B	E	G#	B	E	G#	B	E
Overdraw							F	A	C	F

FIGURE A-5: Harmonica in the key of E.

Draw notes bend down — Blow notes bend down

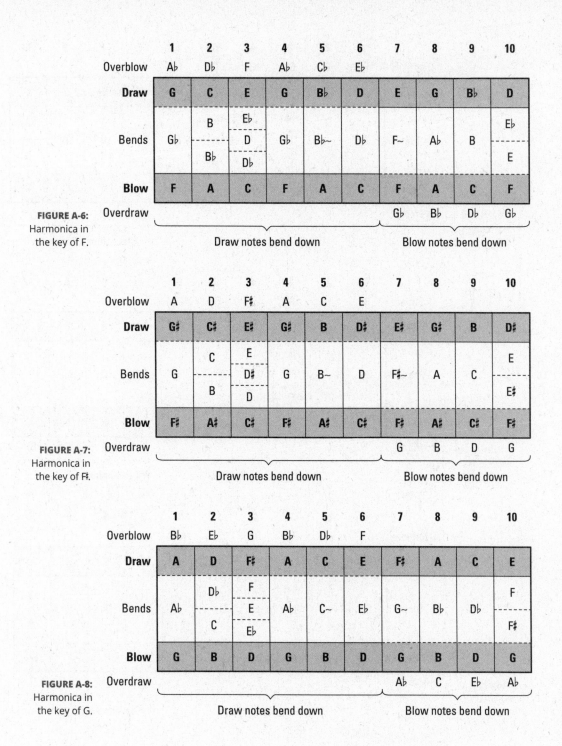

FIGURE A-6: Harmonica in the key of F.

	1	2	3	4	5	6	7	8	9	10
Overblow	Ab	Db	F	Ab	Cb	Eb				
Draw	G	C	E	G	Bb	D	E	G	Bb	D
Bends	Gb	B / Bb	Eb / D / Db	Gb	Bb~	Db	F~	Ab	B	Eb / E
Blow	F	A	C	F	A	C	F	A	C	F
Overdraw							Gb	Bb	Db	Gb

Draw notes bend down (holes 1–6) — Blow notes bend down (holes 7–10)

FIGURE A-7: Harmonica in the key of F#.

	1	2	3	4	5	6	7	8	9	10
Overblow	A	D	F#	A	C	E				
Draw	G#	C#	E#	G#	B	D#	E#	G#	B	D#
Bends	G	C / B	E / D# / D	G	B~	D	F#~	A	C	E / E#
Blow	F#	A#	C#	F#	A#	C#	F#	A#	C#	F#
Overdraw							G	B	D	G

Draw notes bend down (holes 1–6) — Blow notes bend down (holes 7–10)

FIGURE A-8: Harmonica in the key of G.

	1	2	3	4	5	6	7	8	9	10
Overblow	Bb	Eb	G	Bb	Db	F				
Draw	A	D	F#	A	C	E	F#	A	C	E
Bends	Ab	Db / C	F / E / Eb	Ab	C~	Eb	G~	Bb	Db	F / F#
Blow	G	B	D	G	B	D	G	B	D	G
Overdraw							Ab	C	Eb	Ab

Draw notes bend down (holes 1–6) — Blow notes bend down (holes 7–10)

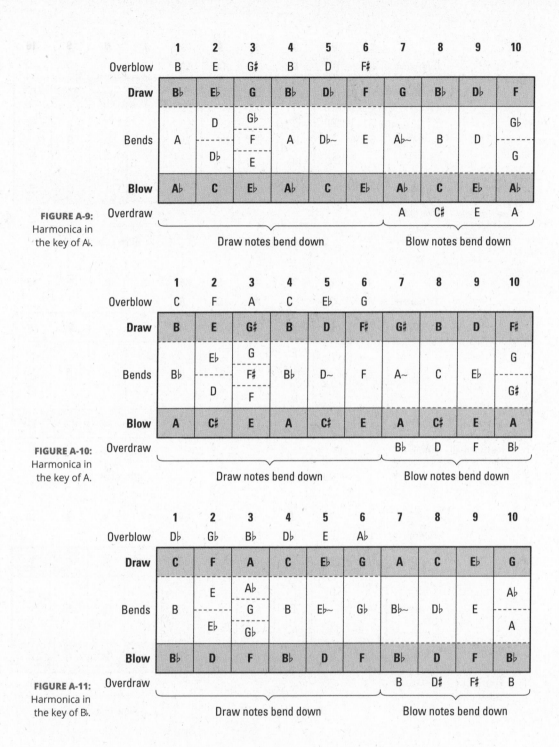

FIGURE A-9: Harmonica in the key of A♭.

FIGURE A-10: Harmonica in the key of A.

FIGURE A-11: Harmonica in the key of B♭.

	1	2	3	4	5	6	7	8	9	10
Overblow	D	G	B	D	F	A				
Draw	C#	F#	A#	C#	E	G#	A#	C#	E	G#
Bends	C	F	A	C	E~	G	B~	D	F	A
			G#							
		E	G							A#
Blow	B	D#	F#	B	D#	F#	B	D#	F#	B
Overdraw							C	E	G	C

FIGURE A-12:
Harmonica in
the key of B.

Draw notes bend down   Blow notes bend down

Appendix B

About the Website

The website that accompanies this book contains 93 tracks. Each of these tracks presents musical examples that you can listen to and practice as much as you need to in order to improve your harmonica playing.

TIP

A fun way to use *Blues Harmonica For Dummies* is to scan the chapters for the Play This icon. In every instance, the text flagged by this icon refers to a musical example that not only appears as written music but also is presented as an audio track on the book's website. When you see an example that seems interesting, skip to the corresponding track on the website and give it a listen.

Note: If you're using a digital version of this book, go to `www.dummies.com/go/bluesharmonicafd` for access to the music tracks.

Relating the Text to the Website Files

Throughout the book, the text contains musical examples in the form of figures that you can play and practice over and over again. If a piece of music appears on the website, the track number is listed in the text. Just use the cue button of the cue/review function (also known as the *fast forward/rewind* control) of the media player to go to the specific time, indicated in minutes and seconds, within that track. When you get on or near the start time, release the cue button and the example plays.

System Requirements

Make sure your computer meets the minimum system requirements shown in the following list. If your computer doesn't match up to most of these requirements, you may have problems using the software and files on the website.

>> A PC running Microsoft Windows or Linux with kernel 2.4 or later or a Macintosh running Apple OS X or later

- ❯❯ An Internet connection

- ❯❯ A web browser

The Tracks on the Web page

The following table lists all 93 tracks on the Web page along with the corresponding tab or figure numbers from the chapters in the book.

Track Number	Tab or Figure Number	Description
1	Figure 3-5	Example of 2/4, 3/4, and 4/4
2	Tab 4-1	Alternating draw and blow breaths for two beats each
2	Tab 4-2	Alternating draw and blow for four beats each
2	Tab 4-3	Alternating draw and blow breaths for one beat each
2	Tab 4-4	Articulating repeated notes with a "k"
2	Tab 4-5	Dividing the beat in two
3	Tab 4-6	Sneaking a breath with the jaw-drop move
3	Tab 4-7	Venting air by exhaling through your nose
4	Tab 4-8	Train rhythms
4	Tab 4-9	Whooping
5	Chapter 5 non-tab	Isolating Hole 4
5	Chapter 5 non-tab	Tongue-blocked single notes in Hole 4
6	Tab 5-1	"I Wanna Get Close To You," Versions 1 and 2
7	Tab 5-2	Two-bar phrases with hole changes
8	Tab 5-3	A 12-bar blues verse with question-and-answer phrases
9	Tab 6-1	Combining a breath change and a hole change

Track Number	Tab or Figure Number	Description
10	Tab 6-2	Extending the hole change–breath change pattern ("Pent-Up Demand")
11	Tab 6-3	"Easy Strides"
12	Tab 6-4	Five common blues riffs
13	Tab 6-5	Pathway No. 1
14	Tab 6-6	Pathway No. 2
15	Tab 7-1	Licks and riffs using the major pentatonic scale
16	Tab 7-2	Licks and riffs focusing on the blue notes over the I chord
17	Tab 7-3	Inflecting licks over the IV chord
18	Tab 7-4	Playing the notes of the IV chord
19	Tab 7-5	Playing blue notes over the IV chord
20	Tab 7-6	Inflecting the home chord over the V chord
21	Tab 7-7	Blue notes against the V chord
22	Tab 7-8	Exploring the notes of the V chord
23	Tab 7-9	Shooting the rapids on the home stretch
24	Tab 7-10	Staying on the home chord through a 12-bar blues ("The Denver Coast")
25	Tab 7-11	Following the chords through a 12-bar blues
26	Tab 7-12	Inflecting the home chord through a 12-bar blues
27	Tab 7-13	Leaning on the blue notes throught a 12-bar blues
28	Tab 7-14	Using a pickup to the first beat
29	Tab 7-15	Starting after the first beat
30	Tab 7-16	Riff-and-vocal phrasing
31	Tab 8-1	Licks that use Blow 3
32	Tab 8-2	Five-note scale in the high register

(continued)

(continued)

Track Number	Tab or Figure Number	Description
33	Tab 8-3	The complete scale in the high register
34	Tab 8-4	Hard-edged five-note scale from low to high and back
35	Tab 8-5	"Piping Blues, Parts 1 and 2"
36	Tab 9-1	Using tongued P
37	Tab 9-2	T and T-L articulations
38	Chapter 9 non-tab	Combined articulations (k, t, p)
39	Chapter 9 non-tab	Throat articulation
39	Chapter 9 non-tab	Diaphragm thrusts
40	Chapter 9 non-tab	Tongue and hand vowels
41	Chapter 9 non-tab	Tongue vibrato, throat vibrato, hand vibrato, combined hand and throat vibrato
42	Chapter 10 non-tab	A basic warble between Draw 4 and 5, with bends and with variations in speed, wetness, and brightness
43	Tab 10-1	"Walkin' and Warblin'"
44	Tab 10-2	Tongue vamping
45	Tab 10-3	"Pull-Off Blues"
46	Tab 10-4	"Tongue Slap Blues (White on Rice)"
47	Tab 10-5	"Hammer Blues"
48	Tab 10-6	"Rake Blues"
49	Tab 10-7	Blues with a locked split
49	Tab 10-7	Blues with hammered splits
49	Tab 10-7	Blues with shimmers
50	Tab 10-8	"Corner Switching Blues"
51	Chapter 11 non-tab	The sound of draw bends in Holes 4, 5, and 6
52	Tab 11-1	"Fishing Line Blues"
53	Tab 11-2	Stopping a bent note and starting it again

Track Number	Tab or Figure Number	Description
53	Tab 11-3	Stopping a bend and moving on (intros in bar count)
54	Tab 11-4	"All Choked Up"
55	Tab 11-5	Draw bends in Hole 2
55	Tab 11-6	Draw bends in Hole 1
56	Tab 11-7	One-semitone draw bend in Hole 3
56	Tab 11-8	Three-semitone draw bend in Hole 3
56	Tab 11-9	Two-semitone draw bend in Hole 3
57	Tab 11-10	"Tearing and Swearing"
58	Tab 11-11	Hole 7 blow bends
58	Tab 11-12	Hole 8 and 9 blow bends
58	Tab 11-13	Blow bends in Hole 10
59	Tab 11-14	"Wailin' High"
60	Tab 11-15	"Blue Blossoms"
61	Chapter 11 non-tab	Overblow in Hole 6
62	Tab 11-16	"Sass"
63	Tab 12-1	The first phrase of "Twinkle, Twinkle" in first position
63	Tab 12-2	The first phrase of "Twinkle, Twinkle" in second position
64	Tab 13-1	Blue notes in all three registers
65	Tab 13-2	Pathways for the I chord in first position
66	Tab 13-3	Pathways for the IV chord in first position
67	Tab 13-4	Pathways for the V chord in first position
68	Tab 13-5	"Jimmy's Boogie"
68	Tab 13-6	"Madge in the Middle"
68	Tab 13-7	"Tear It Down"
69	Tab 14-1	Pathways for playing over the I chord in third position

(continued)

(continued)

Track Number	Tab or Figure Number	Description
70	Tab 14-2	Pathways through the V chord in third position
71	Tab 14-3	"Blue Cinnamon"
72	Tab 14-4	"Sizzlin' Ice"
73	Tab 14-5	"Low Kicks"
74	Tab 15-1	Locked splits on the draw chord
75	Tab 15-2	Melodic pathways for third position chromatic
76	Tab 15-3	"Grits and Grease"
77	Tab 15-4	Using the slide for blue notes and chromatic notes
78	Tab 15-5	Slide ornaments
79	Tab 15-6	"Blue Bling"
80	Tab 15-7	First position blues scale
81	Tab 15-8	"Bumping the Slide"
82	Tab 15-9	First position splits
83	Tab 15-10	"Splitsville"
84	Tab 16-1	"Fuzzy Dice"
85	Tab 16-2	"Dark Stretch"
86	Tab 16-3	"Junior's Jive"
87	Tab 16-4	"Bubber's Blues"
88	Tab 16-5	"Hot Club Two-Beat"
89	Tab 16-6	"Tumbleweed Crawl"
90	Tab 17-1	"Blue Eight"
91	Tab 17-2	"Five Roads Blues"
92	Tab 17-3	"High Water Strut"
93	Tab 17-4	"All I Want

Troubleshooting

We tried our best to compile programs that work on most computers with the minimum system requirements. Alas, your computer may differ, and some programs may not work properly for some reason.

The two likeliest problems are that you don't have enough memory (RAM) for the programs you want to use, or you have other programs running that are affecting installation or the running of a program. If you get an error message such as Not enough memory or Setup cannot continue, try one or more of the following suggestions and then try using the software again:

>> **Turn off any antivirus software running on your computer.** Installation programs sometimes mimic virus activity and may make your computer incorrectly believe that it's being infected by a virus.

>> **Close all running programs.** The more programs you have running, the less memory is available to other programs. Installation programs typically update files and programs; so if you keep other programs running, installation may not work properly.

>> **Have your local computer store add more RAM to your computer.** This is, admittedly, a drastic and somewhat expensive step. However, adding more memory can really help the speed of your computer and allow more programs to run at the same time.

If you have trouble with the Web page, please call the Wiley Product Technical Support phone number at 800-762-2974. Outside the United States, call 1-317-572-3994. You can also contact Wiley Product Technical Support at http://support.wiley.com. John Wiley & Sons, Inc., will provide technical support only for installation and other general quality control items. For technical support on the applications themselves, consult the program's vendor or author.

To place additional orders or to request information about other Wiley products, please call 877-762-2974.

Index

Symbols and Numerics

A

blues harmonica. *See also* chromatic harmonica; diatonic harmonica; harmonica history and lore; harmonica/harmonicas
  about models and types, 3–4, 17–19
  commonly used positions, 204–205
  features to look for, 19–20
blues harp. *See* blues harmonica
blues keys, basic, 21
blues licks and riffs, 38
blues music. *See also* 12-bar blues; musicians; study tunes
  about the origins and history, 9, 13, 205
  association of the harmonica with, 11–12
  components of an arrangement, 52–54
  defining aspects of, 10–11
  minor key harmonics, 252–254
  musician's code of communication, 51–53
  phrases, 50
  Saints form, 268–271
  stylistic crossbreeding, 329
  verses and tune forms, 50–51
blues phrases
  breath-hole changes, 82–83
  "bring it on home," 84
  question-and-answer, 83, 84
  12-bar blues, 97–101
blues scale, 45, 103
"Blues with a Feeling" (CD example), 87
"Boogie" (Pryor), 90
Brazilian music, 329
breakdown, song arrangement, 54, 278
breath/breathing
  about harmonica playing and, 60
  achieving a balance point in, 69–70
  chromatic harmonica, 237–238
  classic train imitation, 70–71
  creating licks and riffs, 85–88
  holding harmonica to your mouth, 60–62
  learning to play by ear, 276–278
  playing blues phrases, 82–83
  playing single notes, 79
  puckering to play single notes, 74–75

  tongue blocking for single notes, 76–78
  whooping technique, 72
"Breathtaking Blues" (blues tune), 260
"bring it on home" phrases, 84
"Bubber's Blues" (blues tune), 259
bullet mics. *See* microphones
"Bumping the Slide" (blues tune), 247
"Burning Hell" (blues song), 326
Buschmann, Friedrich (harmonica inventor), 321

C

cables and connectors, sound system, 301–302
care and storage, harmonica
  airflow obstructions, removing, 123–124
  carrying cases and pouches, 24–25
  circle of fifths, 25
  cleaning and servicing, 30
  damage, preventing, 29
  identifying harmonica parts, 26–29
"Careless Love" (song), 269
CD
  e-book formats, 6
  installation, 340
  system requirements, 339
  technical support, 346
  troubleshooting, 345–346
CD players, 339
CD tracks. *See also* study tunes
  about locating and listening to, 1, 6, 339, 341–345
  approach to first beat with a pickup, 115–116
  beats per measure (timing), 37
  blow-draw shift, 128–132
  combining articulations, 137
  combining breath and hole changes, 86–88
  creating vibrato, 142–144
  creating warble, 148
  diaphragm thrusts, 139
  glottal stops (throat articulations), 137
  hammer sounds, 55
  licks and riffs, 92–93, 95
  licks and riffs on the I chord, 103–104
  licks on the IV chord, 106

N

About the Author

Winslow Yerxa was bitten by the harmonica bug as a teenage musician, contracting blues virus in the process. Since then, he's become a harmonica player, performer, composer, teacher, author, journalist, and even inventor in his quest to better understand this mysterious instrument and the intuitive yet hard to explain music called the blues.

His subsequent musical journey took him to composition, music theory, and jazz arranging studies at Vancouver Community College and McGill University, and later, to writing musical arrangements for Afro-Caribbean bands in San Francisco. Meanwhile, he explored a wide variety of musical styles, including jazz, French hot-club music and musette, and Celtic fiddle tunes. Through it all, the blues has remained an old and trusted friend.

From 1992 to 1997, Winslow wrote, edited, and published the magazine *HIP – the Harmonica Information Publication,* the most widely read harmonica periodical of its time. During that period, he transcribed John Popper's harmonica solos to musical notation and tab for the songbook to the Blues Traveler CD, *four.* He also authored the book and CD combination *Learn Blues Harp Effects in 60 minutes* and invented and marketed the Discrete Comb, a harmonica upgrade that unlocks all the note-bending capabilities of a diatonic harmonica. He also has worked with jazz harmonica virtuoso Howard Levy on his *Out of the Box* series of instructional DVDs and his teaching website, the Howard Levy Harmonica School.

Winslow is active in the harmonica community, helping to organize and run the annual harmonica festival staged by SPAH, the Society for the Preservation and Advancement of the Harmonica. He's also a member of the UK's NHL (National Harmonica League) and participates in the online harmonica world through Facebook and such forums as Harp-l.org, slidemeister.com, and ModernBluesHarmonica.com.

In addition to teaching privately, Winslow is a faculty member at the Jazzschool in Berkeley, California, and has taught at the Kerrville Folk Festival in Kerrville, Texas; Jon Gindick's Harmonica Jam Camp; and David Barrett's Harmonica Masterclass. He's an online expert advisor for David Barrett's Bluesharmonica.com, was a regular columnist for Mel Bay's HarmonicaSessions.com, and has contributed articles to *Harmonica World, Harmonica Happenings, American Harmonica Newsletter,* and *Echos France Harmonica.*

Dedication

To the memory of blues harmonica players we've lost in recent years, including Snooky Pryor, Carey Bell, Norton Buffalo, Gary Primich, Willie "Big Eyes" Smith, and Jerry McCain.

To Lorne, who knew how to keep things simple.

To Big Bear, for never giving up despite the odds.

To the memory of my spirit guide, Alberto Duque. I miss him and his mother very much.

Author's Acknowledgments

I'd like to thank Carole Jelen and Zach Romano, my agents at Waterside Productions, for bringing me this project; Acquisitions Editor David Lutton at Wiley for shepherding it through the acquisition and early shaping processes and keeping the whole thing on track; Project Editor Tim Gallan for his tact and wisdom in producing the manuscript; and Copy Editor Todd Lothery for his eagle eye and fine sense of language. Special mention goes to Joe Filisko for bringing his deep knowledge of blues harmonica to bear as technical editor.

I'd like to thank Joe Filisko (again), Clay Edwards at Hohner, Waichiro Tachikawa at Suzuki, and Rupert Oysler at Seydel USA for the harmonicas used to record the audio tracks.

I'd like to thank Greg Heumann of BlowsMeAway Productions for the great microphone and connector photos and for the Bulletizer that I used for some of the amplified recordings on the audio tracks.

I thoroughly enjoyed working with Rusty Zinn, the harmonica player's blues guitarist, to craft guitar accompaniments for the audio tracks, and with James Ward and Priscilla Rice at Live Oak Studio, who captured Rusty's sound so well and within my budget and time frame. Big thanks to Tom Stryker for mastering the audio tracks on a tight schedule.

Equipment used in recording the harmonicas includes a Neumann TLM 193 microphone with EA 1 elastic suspension mount and Stedman pop filter for acoustic sound and vocals, and a Shure 545S Series 2 high impedance mic with Bulletizer for amplified sound, all fed through an E-MU 1820 interface into Adobe Audition 6.0.

Publisher's Acknowledgments

Senior Project Editor: Tim Gallan
Acquisitions Editor: Michael Lewis
Copy Editor: Todd Lothery
Technical Reviewer: Joe Filisko

Editorial Manager: Michelle Hacker
Project Coordinator: Patrick Redmond
Cover Image: © Marino Darés/Getty Images

Take dummies with you everywhere you go!

Whether you are excited about e-books, want more from the web, must have your mobile apps, or are swept up in social media, dummies makes everything easier.

Find us online!

Leverage the power

Dummies is the global leader in the reference category and one of the most trusted and highly regarded brands in the world. No longer just focused on books, customers now have access to the dummies content they need in the format they want. Together we'll craft a solution that engages your customers, stands out from the competition, and helps you meet your goals.

Advertising & Sponsorships

Connect with an engaged audience on a powerful multimedia site, and position your message alongside expert how-to content. Dummies.com is a one-stop shop for free, online information and know-how curated by a team of experts.

- Targeted ads
- Video
- Email Marketing
- Microsites
- Sweepstakes sponsorship

20 MILLION PAGE VIEWS EVERY SINGLE MONTH

15 MILLION UNIQUE VISITORS PER MONTH

43% OF ALL VISITORS ACCESS THE SITE VIA THEIR MOBILE DEVICES

700,000 NEWSLETTER SUBSCRIPTIONS TO THE INBOXES OF *300,000* UNIQUE INDIVIDUALS EVERY WEEK

# of dummies

Custom Publishing

Reach a global audience in any language by creating a solution that will differentiate you from competitors, amplify your message, and encourage customers to make a buying decision.

- Apps
- Books
- eBooks
- Video
- Audio
- Webinars

Brand Licensing & Content

Leverage the strength of the world's most popular reference brand to reach new audiences and channels of distribution.

For more information, visit dummies.com/biz

PERSONAL ENRICHMENT

Staying Sharp

9781119187790
USA $26.00
CAN $31.99
UK £19.99

Facebook

Carolyn Abram

9781119179030
USA $21.99
CAN $25.99
UK £16.99

Guitar

Mark Phillips
Jon Chappell

9781119293354
USA $24.99
CAN $29.99
UK £17.99

Investing

Eric Tyson, MBA

9781119293347
USA $22.99
CAN $27.99
UK £16.99

Beekeeping

Howland Blackiston

9781119310068
USA $22.99
CAN $27.99
UK £16.99

Digital Photography

Julie Adair King

9781119235606
USA $24.99
CAN $29.99
UK £17.99

Meditation

Stephan Bodian

9781119251163
USA $24.99
CAN $29.99
UK £17.99

Pregnancy
ALL-IN-ONE

9781119235491
USA $26.99
CAN $31.99
UK £19.99

Samsung Galaxy S7

Bill Hughes

9781119279952
USA $24.99
CAN $29.99
UK £17.99

iPhone

Edward C. Baig
Bob "Dr. Mac" LeVitus

9781119283133
USA $24.99
CAN $29.99
UK £17.99

Crocheting

Karen Manthey
Susan Brittain

9781119287117
USA $24.99
CAN $29.99
UK £16.99

Nutrition

Carol Ann Rinzler

9781119130246
USA $22.99
CAN $27.99
UK £16.99

PROFESSIONAL DEVELOPMENT

Windows 10

Andy Rathbone

9781119311041
USA $24.99
CAN $29.99
UK £17.99

AutoCAD

Bill Fane

9781119255796
USA $39.99
CAN $47.99
UK £27.99

Excel 2016

Greg Harvey, PhD

9781119293439
USA $26.99
CAN $31.99
UK £19.99

QuickBooks 2017

Stephen L. Nelson, MBA, CPA, MS in Taxation

9781119281467
USA $26.99
CAN $31.99
UK £19.99

macOS Sierra

Bob "Dr. Mac" LeVitus

9781119280651
USA $29.99
CAN $35.99
UK £21.99

LinkedIn

Joel Elad, MBAs

9781119251132
USA $24.99
CAN $29.99
UK £17.99

Windows 10
ALL-IN-ONE

Woody Leonhard

9781119310563
USA $34.00
CAN $41.99
UK £24.99

SharePoint 2016

Rosemarie Withee
Ken Withee

9781119181705
USA $29.99
CAN $35.99
UK £21.99

Fundamental Analysis

Matt Krantz

9781119263593
USA $26.99
CAN $31.99
UK £19.99

Networking

Doug Lowe

9781119257769
USA $29.99
CAN $35.99
UK £21.99

Office 2016

Wallace Wang

9781119293477
USA $26.99
CAN $31.99
UK £19.99

Office 365

Rosemarie Withee
Ken Withee
Jennifer Reed

9781119265313
USA $24.99
CAN $29.99
UK £17.99

Salesforce.com

Liz Kao
Jon Paz

9781119239314
USA $29.99
CAN $35.99
UK £21.99

Coding

Nikhil Abraham

9781119293323
USA $29.99
CAN $35.99
UK £21.99

dummies.com

dummies
A Wiley Brand